More
PSYCHIC
ROOTS

Further Adventures in
Serendipity & Intuition
in Genealogy

Henry Z Jones, Jr.

Fellow of the American
Society of Genealogists

Published by Genealogical Publishing Co., Inc.
1001 N. Calvert St., Baltimore, Md. 21202
Second printing, 1998
Third printing, 1999
Fourth printing, 2001
Fifth printing, 2003
Library of Congress Catalogue Card Number 96-78239
International Standard Book Number 0-8063-1524-5
Made in the United States of America

Extracts from the following works have been used with the
permission of the authors or publishers:

Excerpt from *Women Who Run With the Wolves* by Clarissa
Pinkola Estes, Ph.D., Copyright © 1992, 1995. All
performance, derivative, adaptation, musical, audio and
recording, illustrative, theatrical, film, pictorial, electronic
and all other rights reserved. Reprinted by kind permission
of the author, Dr. Estes, and Ballantine Books, a division of
Random House, Inc.

Excerpt from *The Seat of the Soul* by Gary Zukav, Copyright
© 1989 by Gary Zukav, reprinted with the permission of
Simon & Schuster.

Excerpt from Sherry Suib Cohen's article "Miracle Alert" in
New Woman Magazine, March 1996, reprinted with the kind
permission of the author, Ms. Cohen.

"Nature Boy," by Eden Ahbez, is published by
Golden World Music (ASCAP).

Special thanks also go to:

Betty Williamson Chan for sharing "The Blessing of
St. Serendipity" on p. 224.

Marian Hoffman, Eileen Perkins, and Dr. Michael Tepper of
Genealogical Publishing Co. for their invaluable assistance in
the editing of this book.

WITH APPRECIATION

TO MY FRIENDS

AND COLLEAGUES -

WHO

"TOOK THE RISK"

AND TOLD THEIR

STORIES

More
PSYCHIC ROOTS

Further Adventures in
Serendipity & Intuition
in Genealogy

To Joan —
Good hunting!
Hank Jones
7 Feb 2013

CONTENTS

ILLUSTRATIONS

FOREWORD
by Jane Fletcher Fiske, F.A.S.G.
Editor of *The New England Historical and Genealogical Register*

For years, genealogists have been pursuing elusive ancestors - and then, not long ago, Hank Jones suggested that perhaps, at least in some cases, those ancestors have actually been chasing us! From the experiences he and others have had, it certainly does seem as though long-dead forebears have sometimes had a hand in the discovery of their names and details of their lives. Many people, including me, have been keenly aware of other realities which kick in occasionally, with no particular warning, to offer help in various forms. Other people scoff, on the basis that such occasions cannot be produced on demand, and that therefore the whole experience is not valid.

The response to Hank's first book, *Psychic Roots*, certainly proved that those of us who are believers in "the other side," whatever that may mean, have lots of company, and with good credentials, too. Moreover, it suggests that whatever is involved here goes far beyond the table-rapping and seances of the 19th century which discredited the spiritualism that intrigued some of our ancestors not so long ago. As a society, we love to play with the idea of the supernatural. Who, sometime in his or her life, has not shivered at ghost stories told late at night in front of a campfire? Or responded to the thought of angels, which currently seem to be on everyone's mind, popping up in gift shops and book stores and on magazine stands wherever you look?

Death as a reality was fairly immediate until the emergence of antibiotics and advanced medical techniques, and our ancestors tended to face their mortality pretty squarely. Modern medicine changed that situation; the past few generations have lived not only in fear of but in denial of death, either terrified of its being a total annihilation of consciousness, or afraid of being considered naive if admitting to a belief that there *was* another side. The whole subject of survival after death has become so bound up with religious beliefs that, on the one hand, many people hide their heads in the sand of fundamentalism of whatever faith they were reared in, while others, unable to accept religious doctrines which seem irrelevant or assault one's intellect, deny that there can be anything at all out there. (I've noticed, however, that my friends and acquaintances who fall into the doubting category are those who most enjoy science fiction.) One way or another, admit it or not, most of us have a curiosity about the idea that just maybe there's more to this world than we currently perceive.

Perhaps now, in this time when horrors like AIDS and the Ebola virus, or suicidal terrorism, are striking fear into hearts everywhere and reminding us once again of our mortality - to say nothing of the Millennium Consciousness preaching Doom and Gloom - it is a good moment to consider that we need to enter the 21st century spiritually as well as technically. Enlightened as we consider ourselves to be, we ought to be able to look back at history and understand how and why our ancestors, both ancient and recent, developed the religious beliefs they held, and just how the split between science and religion occurred that destroyed the intellectual credibility of our spiritual nature. Somewhere, growing up in the last few centuries, modern man (and woman) managed to throw the baby out with the bath water.

It's an exciting time to be alive. New things are being discovered at an exponential rate. Each of us can make his or her own decision to go hide, one way or another, or participate.

Hank's work suggests that our dead ancestors are trying to participate too! I don't doubt that some of them are, but I think that what's really happening here is more profound. It suggests that there is a world - worlds - of reality beyond what we know, and that there are consciousnesses out there that actually keep tabs on us, offering help, guidance, or playful nudges to remind us to look beyond, expand our own awareness, realize more of our own potential, become more than we are. Call it whatever you will: angels, gods, God, guides, higher selves, God/Goddess/All That Is, or dead ancestors - or all of the above. Primitive people believe in many spirits; the ancient Greeks believed in many deities; our Christian ancestors narrowed the playing field. My own experience suggests that the universe is teeming with lively consciousness, and we on earth are the ones who are limited. William Blake wrote, about 1793,

How do you know but ev'ry Bird that cuts the airy way,
Is an immense world of delight, clos'd by your senses
five?
and followed that with a thought we would do well to ponder:
What is now proved, was once only imagin'd.

As genealogists, we concentrate on the past, and on dead people. In our scrambling to make and publish new discoveries, we often walk right over the living people who make up our immediate world. We all know cases where book reviewers have sliced up authors needlessly while commenting on their books, or of amateur genealogists who so alienated their families with their preoccupation that their records were deliberately thrown out after their deaths. Hardly one of us can honestly claim never to have made a derogatory comment more or less publicly about somebody else.

And yet, that something out there, whatever it is, seems to be telling the genealogists in Hank's books that what we're doing in tracing the past is fine. The messages that come through as intuition are non-judgmental, and perhaps there's a suggestion in that, that we too might be better off suspending our own tendencies to judge both others and ourselves.

There's a new spirit stirring in the world as we approach the year 2000. Dare I suggest that we are becoming more conscious, more aware, even perhaps more responsible or at least aware of our responsibility? The experiences recounted here in a genealogical context can surely be found in the rest of the population to at least the same degree, relating to other kinds of situations and problems. When one of us starts to tell a story, others speak up ... but someone has to start, because we are all so afraid of appearing ridiculous, ready for that butterfly net.

Working with ancestors is all well and good, but let's recognize it as one of many possible pastimes. Let's realize, too, that our ancestors lived in times and surroundings much different than ours, even though perhaps in the same geographical location. If we profit from their experience, let's recognize also that we need to learn from their mistakes. They lived then, and we live now; they were themselves, and we are us, with new challenges and new ways to meet old ones.

One of the challenges, to my way of thinking, is to pull ourselves and our world back together again. Much that was once thought to be supernatural has now been proven to have "rational" explanation; people who never look in a microscope or telescope are willing to accept the existence of both galaxies and quarks they cannot themselves perceive, and we communicate with each other worldwide using a computer web that was inconceivable not many years ago. We understand now that attitudes affect states of mind, and that states of mind affect physical health. We know that everything is energy, and quantum physics is telling us that observation can affect results. More and more people are willing to report their own extraordinary experiences, from having a significant book fall off a shelf at their feet, to near-death encounters with light. We've come a long way since the 1692 Salem witch trials. Why, then, do we balk so at admitting that human beings are also spiritual beings?

Spirituality is not synonymous with religious belief; it does not involve submitting to a creed imposed by someone else. It does involve a search for one's own self, requiring a recognition of our true beliefs and attitudes and how these have affected our reality. With that recognition, change becomes possible, and brings with it a resulting sense of self-empowerment and confidence that there is real meaning and significance in life. To a greater degree than ever before, each of us needs to look within ourself for explanations of the world without. In ourselves, we find uniqueness that can lead back to a sense of the world as one whole, of which each one of us is an integral part. Amazingly, it does appear that something out there cares about us as individuals and is willing to help, if only we are willing to let it happen.

A few years ago, feeling in a really low mood on a summer Sunday, I resorted to the therapy of weeding our brick front walk. An abundance of weeds spring up every year between the old bricks, including clover, which I was digging out literally by the handful as I moved around on hands and knees. All of a sudden, there, resting on top of a brick in front of me was not a handful of clover, but just one, detached and single, perfectly formed *four-leafed* clover. Whatever presence arranged that appearance conveyed to me both a sense of humor and of caring.

Hank is doing the genealogical world a service in bringing our stories to light, and for some time I have both admired and envied his courage in being willing to get so close to that butterfly net. Our particular world involves working with the past, and it's through interaction with others in the field of genealogy that most of us are in a position to act, to show others that although we may be ancestor-collectors, we are not ourselves stuck in history.

But we are also members of a larger reality whether we admit it or not. Since we're here, why not explore? Let's consign to the past the prejudices and judgments, the guilt and the fears, that have hampered humanity for far too long, and open our minds joyfully to the thought that, really, *anything's possible*. We need to sharpen our intellects to evaluate - not to deny - whatever happens. Time's awasting - we've got a lot to learn and a lot to do.

Jane Fletcher Fiske
17 March 1996

1

HOW PSYCHIC ROOTS **BECAME** *AN "UNSOLVED MYSTERY"*

AMAZING!

Who'd-a-thunk-it?

After what seemed like a zillion years away from show-business, I found myself back on prime-time television - just because I wrote a *genealogy* book of all things!

I had thought that that part of my life was behind me. I never really meant to return to the tube. I had left it a decade before by choice after a twenty-year career as a character actor. I'd had a pretty good run, playing mostly wimps and nerds in situation comedies and Disney movies. But, after all, how many times can you "lose the girl" and not let it bother you? In my heart, I was Tom Cruise - but everybody else seemed to think of me as Rick Moranis.

Besides, climbing family trees and chasing "dead Germans" were taking over my life. Family history research was a heck of a lot more fun than having to wake up and stagger to the studio for a 5 A.M. make-up call. So, I made my choice - and, hands down, it was GENEALOGY!

But then, as fate would have it, NBC and *Unsolved Mysteries* made me an offer I couldn't refuse.

Here's what happened:

In their July 1994 issue, *OMNI Magazine* published a nice article about my new book *Psychic Roots: Serendipity & Intuition in Genealogy.* As luck would have it, the writer of the piece, Sherry Baker, had worked at one time in the past for the popular *Unsolved Mysteries* program. Thinking that my own story as well as some others in the book might be "naturals" for the show, Sherry pitched the idea to the producers. After hardly any time at all, deals were made, contracts were signed, and - good grief - I was back in show business.

I was ready for anything! And I was wary. After all those years in front of the camera, I knew that the unexpected was the norm, and that if anything could go wrong it often would. In fact, my whole career was a myriad of mishaps. For instance:

Of the eight movies I did for Disney Studios, my favorite role was in Walt's last personally produced film, *Blackbeard's Ghost*. Because of my rather unusual appearance (I was so skinny at the time, I barely photographed sideways), they asked me to do my own stunts.

That was their first mistake. The climactic moment of the film took place in a college stadium. It was quite a scene. Hundreds of extras, all yelling and screaming, urging me on to win a big relay race and bring glory home to the alma mater. The script called for me to seemingly run the race in mid-air, mysteriously held up by the invisible ghost of Blackbeard (played by the inimitable Sir Peter Ustinov). To accomplish this effect, the studio technicians attached me to their fabled "Mary Poppins wires" which gave the illusion that I was flying.

Unfortunately, Mr. Murphy's Law was in effect that day. Something went terribly wrong. I'm ashamed to say that I have the dubious distinction of being the *only* actor in Disney history whose wires broke mid-flight. I was racing the entire length of the sound-stage, ten feet off the ground, when I fell.

But I couldn't just fall, get up and continue like a normal person. Oh no - I landed right smack on poor Peter Ustinov with a thunderous crash and then proceeded to bleed all over his expensive pirate costume. But - not to worry. After being mopped up, sponged down, and re-wired, we repeated the scene ten more times until we finally got a perfect take.

OUCH!

But I suppose I was a slow learner. I was pretty-much like the man in the circus who swept up after the elephants and said ...

"What - and give up *show business*??"

And in my litany of disasters, I certainly can't forget *Day In Court*. This was back in television's infancy when some programs were broadcast *live* throughout the country. I had a courtroom scene where I played a young rock-and-roll singer. He believed his parents were trying to steal his money and was suing them to stop their chicanery. As the trial reached its emotional peak, I stopped the proceedings cold. Jumping up from my chair, I shook my fist at my parents and, at the top of my voice, screamed for all America to hear,

"YOU'RE NOTHING BUT A VUNCH OF BULTURES!!!"

They never asked me back on that show.

I wonder why?

But I guess my ultimate claim to fame in the blooper department took place years ago on the old *Tennessee Ernie Ford Show*. My singing partner, Dean Kay, and I were co-stars of the program, broadcast every weekday on ABC-TV. You may remember that we closed every show by singing a hymn. It was sort of Ernie's trademark - he had that wonderfully rich, bass voice and great sincerity that would send the chills down your spine whenever he sang. Although we had loads of fun and could cut-up on other segments of the program, it was an unspoken rule that we *never* kidded around during the hymn.

One particular day just prior to the closing, Dean and I sang a musical number from our then-current RCA album. We were dressed in casual outfits for that song, but then had to dash backstage for a quick change into the suits we were to wear for the hymn. Unfortunately, in the rush, I neglected to zip one very crucial part of my apparel.

Thinking that all was well, I ran onstage unawares and stood next to Ernie, ready to sing. We looked especially distinguished and dignified in our dark suits that day, standing with our hands folded in front of us against an illuminated cross as our backdrop. Immediately, the floor-manager began to count down, "5, 4, 3 ...."

At that precise moment, Ernie happened to glance over at me. He looked down, did a double-take, and whispered urgently out of the corner of his mouth ...

"DON'T WAVE BYE-BYE!"

But it was too late - we were back on the air, singing our little hearts out. I don't know how we got through "Peace in The Valley" without "losing it," but somehow we did.

The panic of that moment has sort of made everything a blur, but I do remember one thing: I kept my trembling hands clasped tightly in front of me, and when it came time to wave bye-bye ...

it was the *quickest* wave you've ever seen!

But in spite of these past embarrassments, I tried to keep a positive mind-set. After all, hadn't I stressed in *Psychic Roots* that "pessimists make lousy genealogists?" I kept telling myself *Unsolved Mysteries* didn't *have* to be another ride on the *Titanic*.

It started well. Sherry Baker had done her homework and was very familiar with all the stories in my book. We put our heads together and came up with six of the best that might translate well to television. I gave her the six genealogists' addresses and phone numbers to contact, and we were off and running.

Next, Mike Mathis, who was to be the director of the episode, flew down from Los Angeles to meet me at my home in San Diego. He had studied Sherry's breakdown of my book, and we spent the afternoon just getting to know each other and talking in depth about my own personal experiences in genealogy. A delightful man - savvy, sensitive, and funny - I knew in an instant I was in good hands.

I had expected that the show would be filmed somewhere in the Hollywood area. I even looked forward to working at one of my old studio stomping grounds and being able to inhale that wonderfully musty sound-stage smell again that I missed so much.

WRONG! Mike looked around the house, cased-out my large genealogical library, and decided they'd shoot my interview right there in my home.

At first, I was a bit reluctant to agree. Having had first-hand experience seeing coffee spilled, dents poked, and doors scraped on other location shoots in the past, I knew that some crews could care less about damaging someone's home. Sometimes things could go very wrong. In fact, I had heard from the horse's mouth the ultimate disaster story along these lines. It was told by producer Hal Roach at a dinner I attended in 1971:

In the 1920s, Roach Studios rented a house to use for the Laurel & Hardy film *Big Business* from a studio worker who was going on vacation. The script called for Stan and Ollie to engage in a tit-for-tat feud with an irate neighbor (their marvelously mustachioed "triple-take" foil, Jimmy Finlayson). The conflict built slowly, then grew to absolute mayhem. It finally culminated in the total destruction of the premises.

As the last scene was being shot, the man from whom they rented the house returned from his trip. All that was left to see was rubble.

"My God, Mr. Roach," he exclaimed. "*That's* not my house ... *My* house is the one *next-door!*"

CAN YOU IMAGINE!!??

But why dwell on location horror stories, I thought? And Mike did assure me that the *Unsolved Mysteries* crew would leave our house spotless and just the way they found it. So I gave the ok.

A few days before my actual interview was to be filmed, the location manager came by to take detailed still photos of our home. He canvassed the neighborhood and put out flyers announcing that "a national television show would be filming in the area, and that they were sorry for any inconvenience this might cause."

I crossed my fingers. My wife Bonnie and I live in the quiet San Diego suburb of Scripps Ranch, sort of an idyllic Southern California version of Mayberry, RFD. I sure didn't want the hubbub to disturb any local Aunt Beas or Opies!

But before I had time to worry, the big day finally arrived!

Three immense, unmarked yellow trucks pulled up in front of our house. The crew - "best-boys," sound-men, gaffers, and "go-fers" - piled out and started unloading what looked to be enough lights to illuminate the Statue of Liberty during the Bicentennial Celebration. A catering truck arrived. The chef proceeded to set up a complete kitchen and dining facility right there in our front driveway. It looked like he had tables and chairs to feed the entire Mormon Tabernacle Choir. Within five minutes, our front lawn reminded me of an ant-farm - everybody running around in organized chaos.

But - not to fear - Bonnie had prepared well. She had always been proud of our home, and, with her gift for interior design, had decorated it tastefully with lovely furniture and beautiful handpainted porcelains and antiques. By the time the crew arrived, it was immaculate and looked like something out of *House Beautiful.* "Gee," she told me, "our home is going to look so pretty on camera!" As a matter of fact, I thought she was more excited about seeing our house on television than about seeing me!

But when the director, cameraman, and crew finally came in the front door and started working, the real world of television production arrived with them. The favorite phrase of the day became, "LOSE IT!" Within a few minutes, the living room was emptied of most all of Bonnie's carefully arranged chairs and tables. The antique porcelains were quickly removed from their shelves, and all the other decorations and accessories were taken away. Our house began to look like it did on "moving day" before we had moved in! Even the chandeliers were raised or taken down so that they wouldn't be in the way of the booms and cameras.

The metamorphosis of the house continued. The windows soon were covered with blackout tape, hiding any possible view of our front yard or backyard patio. On the lawn outside, lights were placed on twenty-foot pole-stands to help illuminate the interior scenes. My desk, which I had tidied up so neatly, was purposely *un*tidied and put in disarray to make it look "used." And when a young pony-tailed member of the crew looked at the door to my genealogical library and said, "Lose it!" ... Bonnie and I both gulped.

My poor wife! I must admit that in order to get her to agree to the filming I'd minimized the traumas that the day might bring:

"Oh no, " I told her, "You won't even know they're here!"

Bonnie "covered" well and was her usual sweet and friendly self to one and all. She appeared to be nonchalant about everything going on around her. But it didn't take long for her to figure out what was really happening: I knew - and *she* knew ...

This was an INVASION!

As all this was going on, the neighborhood was waking up. The man across the street, whom we hadn't seen for two years, mysteriously decided that that particular day was *the* day of all days to hand-water his front yard. It was a great way to satisfy his curiosity and sneak looks at all the action going on. So he proceeded to water ... and water ... and water his lawn, until the flood started backing up the gutters in the street. At least he had a good view!

Another neighbor didn't receive the flyer announcing the filming. When she saw all the strange people with unmarked trucks moving things in and out of our house, she too wondered what was going on. So to try and get more information, she kept walking her dog back and forth on the sidewalk in front of our home. As night fell, exterior lights were shown through the windows to give the illusion that it was still daytime outside. Then our curious neighbor's suspicions *really* were aroused! She thought perhaps some gang might be in the process of robbing us. We found out later that only a chance conversation with another resident who knew about the filming prevented her from calling the police.

Amidst this zoo-like atmosphere, Mike sat me down in a chair, rolled the cameras, and began asking me questions about my book. To make a long story short, the interview went pretty well. I was secretly afraid that, because of my time away from the cameras, I might turn into "Mr. Mushmouth." But, after a few false starts and thanks to the director's skills, everything turned out all right, and they seemed pleased with the results.

But then came the dreaded BEDROOM SCENE!

In *Psychic Roots,* I told how I would dream occasionally of the Palatine emigrants' ancestral origins in Germany, and how those locales I dreamed about, in a few cases, proved to be the correct home villages when we finally found the families overseas. *Unsolved Mysteries* thought this was an important part of the story and should be dramatized on the program.

Filming *Unsolved Mysteries:* just another quiet day in the neighborhood

With *Unsolved Mysteries* director, Mike Mathis

Reenacting my introduction to genealogy on *Unsolved Mysteries:* opening the old trunk in my parents' basement (with the child actor playing "me" at age 8)

They knew that I had been a professional actor. So rather than have someone else recreate my experience, they asked me to play myself in the episode.

As my look-alike (Robert Redford, of course) was unavailable, I agreed. I guess you could say they got a "Hank Jones type." They wanted to shoot the dream sequence in our upstairs bedroom. So I donned my best pajamas, tousled my hair, and plopped into bed, waiting for the cameras to roll.

"Something's not quite right," Mike, the director, said. "It should look more natural, more real." He thought about it a minute, and then you could almost see the light bulb pop on over his head with inspiration:

"Oh Bonnie," he called. "Come here, will you? Would you mind taking off your clothes and putting on your nightgown?"

I'm afraid *I'm* the "hambone" in our family. No matter how hard Mike pleaded or cajoled, there was no way he could convince Bonnie to jump into bed and make her national television debut from under the sheets. I even offered her chocolates (her weakness), but she *still* refused.

DRAT! Once a lady, always a lady!

Next time they rerun the show again on cable-TV, take a look at that particular bedroom sequence. You'll see me there, leaning over the nightstand and writing down my dreams on a note pad. And next to me in bed, hidden under the covers, if you look hard - you'll see a very attractive *lump*.

No, it's not my wife ...

It's just three of our fluffiest pillows making their debut on national television!

2
A SAFE PLACE TO TALK

The response to the two airings of *Unsolved Mysteries* on NBC and subsequent broadcasts on Lifetime Cable Network was simply unbelievable! The mail poured in from viewers eager to comment on the program and add their own unusual experiences to the ones I was collecting for the sequel to my book. And Mary Pat Carney, Tim Rogan, Sam Lucchese, and all the others on the staff at Cosgrove-Meurer Productions couldn't have been nicer to deal with. They even referred all the telephone calls received on the *"Unsolved Mysteries 800 number"* regarding the episode to my publisher's own 800 number in Baltimore. That sure didn't hurt sales!

The feedback was good also on the other two stories that were dramatized from *Psychic Roots*: Carol Montrose's thrilling experience of chasing a hot-air balloon to a cemetery that eventually yielded an undiscovered relative's tombstone; and Dr. David Faux's remarkable tale of fantasizing about finding a portrait of his Victorian ancestor who had fought as a sergeant in India, and how he then unexpectedly came across just such a picture as he roamed through a castle in England. As both stories were so visual in nature, they translated well to the medium of television and really enlivened the program.

Before I go any further, now is probably a good time to give a bit of background about *Psychic Roots*. For those who haven't read it, the book began with my own story - how I started climbing the family tree at the age of eight, exploring a forbidden old trunk filled with family memorabilia in the basement of my parents' home. I went on to tell how genealogy had really hooked me from that moment on, and how nothing else seemed to matter to me as I was growing up.

Carol Montrose filming her story on *Unsolved Mysteries*

Dr. David Faux and his ancestor's portrait, as dramatized on
Unsolved Mysteries

But then some strange things started happening. I found that one tiny branch of my family tree descended from a group of Germans who were settled in Ireland by the British in 1709. They were called the "Palatines." From the moment of that discovery, it was as if the Palatines became my calling. While still an undergraduate at Stanford University, I wrote a book about them (*The Palatine Families Of Ireland*, published in 1965). I then felt compelled to move on and chronicle all the 847 Palatine families who bypassed Ireland and arrived in colonial New York in 1710.

This New York study began as peripheral research, but grew into an intensive twenty-year project. I guess you could say these courageous German emigrants had become an obsession - even though, to my knowledge, I was related to *none* of them who settled in New York. I soon dropped all genealogical research on my other family lines to concentrate solely on this one obscure group. It was almost as if I had a "mission" to tell their story and reconnect their families.

One of the major goals in my New York Palatine project was to document all 847 families in their German villages of origin. As such, my first foray into overseas research turned out also to be my introduction to what some have called "The Twilight Zone of Genealogy" - where unexplained events and serendipitous discoveries sometimes lead us to successful results in our searches. I had noted that many of these emigrants seemed to stay together in specific clusters of families upon their arrival in the New World. I wondered if this interaction might be attributed to common towns and villages of origin for these groups in Europe. To test this out, in 1973, I employed the widely esteemed German genealogist Carla Mittelstaedt-Kubaseck to go literally village-to-village for me looking for the 847 Palatines in areas where I'd theorized they might be found (oh, and in a somewhat diabolical afterthought, I added about 2,000 second-wave, later-arrivals for Carla to search for also).

I could really have cared less where to begin the European research - they weren't my families. I just wanted to find them all and tell their stories. But, obviously, we had to start *somewhere* looking for all these emigrants. So, just off the top of my head to get things rolling, I told Carla to begin her investigations for me by searching in the lovely Westerwald region at Hachenburg for Dieterich Schneider and his emigrant family, one of the 847. I don't know why I picked him particularly. But, for some reason, I'd always found Schneider intriguing and strangely fascinating whenever I would run across him in the old records.

To date via my project, over 600 of the 847 families have now been documented in their ancestral towns overseas as have well over 1,000 of the later arrivals to colonial America. And Rod Serling would be proud: the *only* family I find that I am directly related to is ... the Dieterich Schneider family of Hachenburg - my *first* choice selected *totally at random* out of all those thousands of families for Carla to look for in Germany!

Other uncanny events occurred. My very first visits to some of the locales in New York, Pennsylvania, and New Jersey where the Palatines eventually settled brought forth some very unusual happenings. Although I had never been to these places before, I would experience a strong geographic déjà vu - an unexplainable familiarity with my new surroundings. In several instances on a trip, I knew what was going to appear around the next bend in the road before we even got there! There was also a serene feeling of "being home" as I explored the areas where the Palatines had lived - an inner peace that is hard to define.

And then there were those *dreams* about the Palatine emigrants that I mentioned earlier. In some of these nighttime episodes, an emigrant would appear and let me know in no uncertain terms that I was looking for him in the wrong place in Germany. He would essentially say, "I didn't come from *that* place - our family originated from over here in *this* region!" At first I just tossed off these unsettling dreams as unimportant and tried to forget them. But they began to occur often enough that I really could no longer ignore them. I decided that I had nothing to lose, so I sent Carla to a few of the places overseas where the dreams suggested we look. And lo and behold - in several places, there indeed were the unplaced emigrants, almost waiting to be found! No wonder *Unsolved Mysteries* wanted these occurrences to be dramatized on their program.

These weird occurrences were very unsettling. I wondered if I was alone in all of this, or were others also having similar experiences as they climbed the family tree? To find out, I wrote to 300 of the world's leading family historians asking them to share any serendipitous events or intuitive nudges that had led to successful genealogical results. I always made it very clear that in no way was I negating or minimizing the proven and logical "scientific approach" to genealogy championed by my fellow Fellows in the American Society of Genealogists. I just wanted to know if - every so often - something *beyond the logical* had occurred in their research that had helped their investigations.

Surprisingly, over 200 encouraging and fascinating responses came in, filled with unexplainable, "off the wall" experiences that had amused or puzzled my correspondents over the years. Many of my colleagues also added their thoughts and comments regarding these events that were as intriguing as the experiences themselves! I was *not* alone! My growing belief that serendipitous events were indeed a crucial part of the research process was reenforced in letter after letter. These shared thoughts and experiences, so generously contributed by family historians around the world, made up the core and indeed the true heart of *Psychic Roots*.

I had envisioned a potential sequel, so, in the last section of the book, I urged readers to write me if they had any personal stories to share along these lines. When I inserted this invitation, I really didn't know what kind of response I would get.

I should have known. From day one, letters arrived from readers that not only echoed the experiences in *Psychic Roots*, but even went far beyond them! I was deeply touched by the comments that started coming in:

Jennifer J. Cummins of West Chester, Ohio, wrote:
"I am writing to tell you how much pleasure *Psychic Roots* has brought to me. Actually, pleasure is not a strong enough word. Your book has encouraged me in my genealogical pursuits. It affirms my feeling that I am 'meant' to do genealogy, and that others also have personal relationships with people that have died years before."

Carmen Boone de Aguilar of Mexico City volunteered:

"I can truly say that I have experienced practically all other 'happenings' described by the rest of your contributors. Not only has *Psychic Roots* become my 'procedures manual,' it has also become my alibi when non-genealogical-minded relatives and friends wince at my 'peculiar' interests - thanks a million for writing it!"

Vera W. Merritt of Los Angeles, California, told me:

"I would like to thank you for writing *Psychic Roots*. I seem to be a rigid, rational, and structured person. When I first began my genealogical research, these strange things started happening to me also: I couldn't explain them, and I thought I was going crazy or reacting in a very weird (unusual) way as I worked on my family history.

Your book has helped me to better understand these 'happenings,' and now I feel much more comfortable with them. I will continue to follow these feelings without the doubt or suspicion that I have had in the past!"

Jean Cheger of Bay City, Michigan, kindly noted:

"After reading the first pages of *Psychic Roots*, I found myself saying, 'Yes ... Yes ...' - because I have had experience after experience as you have written. I don't know why I bothered to write - except to realize how very much your book means to me. I don't know whether or not I will feel revitalized, but I do know your book has made a major difference in my life at this time."

The material in *Psychic Roots* did indeed seem to strike a familiar chord in many readers. I was delighted! But then something else started happening. The book itself became involved in some unusual occurrences, almost as if the volume took on a life of its own! These bizarre events were detailed by some of my readers.

My friend Ernest Thode of Marietta, Ohio, wrote:

"When you first wrote me preparing to write *Psychic Roots*, I tried to think of good examples, but was unable to think of anything that seemed really out of the ordinary. I guess that was because the out-of-the-ordinary seems so commonplace to me.

While I was reading *Psychic Roots* last night, my wife Barbara asked me if the book was anything new and interesting, or just what I already knew. At the moment she asked me that question, the book was open to pages 110 and 111. I had just read about Raymond Martin Bell and the Williamson family on those pages. Barbara's mother was a Williamson of that very line.

I was reading the one page of the book directly connected with Barbara!"

Loreley A. Morling of Swan View, Western Australia, remarked:

"The week before Christmas 1994 I was attending the annual lunch for volunteers at the Western Australian Genealogical Society (WAGS). Sitting next to me was a lady who used to be in charge of our local LDS Library but now lives in the country. She remarked on how often coincidences seem to happen in genealogical research. Currently she edits the Newsletter for her branch of the Genealogical Society and mentioned that she was considering having a section in it on coincidences. There followed a discussion on coincidences amongst several attending the lunch.

The next day I received notification from my public library that your book had come in for me. I had requested it months ago, and they had to buy it specially for me. It seemed a remarkable coincidence that it arrived just as we were talking about coincidences."

Ruth Merriman of the Family History Library in Salt Lake City wrote:

"I was telling some of the unusual stories that have happened to me to a co-worker, Keith Rose. He replied, 'Gee, you ought to send that story to Hank Jones.' After Keith told me all about your book, I made a mental note of it. A few days later, I looked up the call number and headed down to the main floor to take a look at it. To my dismay, it was gone. I searched all the shelves on the chance it was filed incorrectly, but no - it just wasn't there.

I threw up my hands and gazed heavenward in mock despair. And then - I saw something. There on the top shelf, lying on top of the books with just a corner poking out over the top, was *another* book. I grabbed a stool, reached up, and - you guessed it - *Psychic Roots!*"

And Dorothy Hall of Prescott, Arizona, said:

"I received a letter several days ago from my brother who is tracing our father's line. He wanted to tell me about a profound and vivid dream that woke him up completely - something he says rarely happens. He dreamed that he saw genealogical charts, records, and an undated marriage license giving the name of George Schneider and Mary Elizabeth Krutzinger. In the dream, my brother shouted at the people who appeared to have attended the marriage that the actual spelling of the name was "Kirzinger." What is weird is that we didn't know the name of George Schneider's wife, but now we're wondering if Schneider married a relative of my grandpa Frank Kirzinger? Of course there's nothing definite here, but we're certainly going to research that possibility now and see if we can find documentation to back this up!

It seems ironic he should be having such a dream while I was reading your book *Psychic Roots* at the same time, since neither of us have had such an experience previously nor talked about our ancestors influencing our genealogical research."

Patricia Stover Fair of Oklahoma City, Oklahoma, related:

"For several months, every time I sat at my desk, I saw the note I had written to myself reminding me to order *Psychic Roots*. I don't know why I didn't do it before, but, suddenly, just three weeks ago, I had the urge to get the order in the mail and finally did.

The following day, instead of doing our usual activities, my teenage daughter Wendy and I decided to watch tv. We looked at the schedule, saw that Disney's *Blackbeard's Ghost* was coming on soon, and decided to watch it. As the movie started, I saw 'Hank Jones' listed as one of the stars. Having just recently learned of your acting career, but not having any knowledge of what you appeared in, I told Wendy that perhaps this 'Hank Jones' of the movie was the same one whose book I had just ordered. Having never met or seen a photo of you, we watched - not knowing which character you might be. Then, when a particular young man came on the screen, I said to Wendy, 'I just know that's Hank Jones!' Unfortunately, the end credits matching the actor to the role passed by too quickly to verify my hunch.

I didn't think a whole lot more about it, and then *Psychic Roots* arrived last Saturday. I took off the wrapping, and there you were on the back cover. I was stunned! We were indeed looking at the same face whose character in the movie I was so sure was Hank Jones. And then when I saw that still from *Blackbeard's Ghost* on page eleven, there was no doubt!

Coincidence, lucky guess, or what?"

In telling their stories in *Psychic Roots*, many contributors mentioned their specific family lines and research locales. This led to a nice fringe benefit from the book that I never even dreamed about when I wrote it. As Miss Lou Duprey of Danville, Illinois, observed:

"Do you realize how much genealogy is in your book? I betcha there are going to be a lot of people reading it and finding something they have been looking for for years."

She was right! A clearinghouse had to be set up between the contributors to the book and my readers. Happily, lots of people were put in contact with one another via the pages of *Psychic Roots*. William L. Deyo of Fredericksburg, Virginia, reported:

"*Psychic Roots* has led me to some wonderful genealogical discoveries. Mr. Maurice Hitt was listed therein, and after a long process of tracking him down at his new Florida address, I found we were related. He was able to tell me my Hitt ancestry back to Henry Hitt who had come to America from Devonshire, England in 1665!"

Wilma Moore of Colville, Washington, wrote:

"Historic Resources, Inc. recently held a workshop here for the genealogical society of which I am a member. Even though I hadn't planned on attending due to my mother's illness, I had an overpowering need to check out the materials that would be available. Settling my mother down with her breakfast, I then went to where the workshop was to be held.

The first book I picked up (it was in the center of the table, surrounded by many other interesting things) was your *Psychic Roots*. It was though a magnet had drawn me to it. I then went on to select several other books and materials. When I returned home, for some unexplained reason, I put down the whole load without even checking out the packets of materials to see what was in them, and started reading your book. I have never read a non-fiction book from start to finish, but rather browse through them, reading sections that pertain to the issue of the moment. For some inexplicable reason, I quite literally could not put *Psychic Roots* down. I started wondering if there was a 'psychic' reason for it, maybe something was going to jump out of the pages at me.

I finished the book in less than two days, and then I did something else I never do. I read every entry in the pages of contributors. Sure enough, fifteen pages in, on page 220, something did literally jump off the page at me: 'Nancy Vollner, Michigan, was researching MUNSON.' My great-grandfather was Loren Munson from Michigan. Naturally I will be contacting Nancy. Being quite psychic myself, I truly believe there had to be some reason for the strong pull to your book and finding Nancy's research listed in it - other than a quirk or coincidence."

Sometimes, I didn't have to play matchmaker at all. People just sort of ran into each other on their own!. As George E. Flagg of Des Moines, Iowa, related:

"I had read in your book *Psychic Roots* that Fred Sisser III was a very prominent genealogist doing work in the Somerville, New Jersey area. So when I was in that town, I tried to find him in the local phone directory there. I had no luck in locating him and even checked city directories for that area all the way back to 1964, but with no success. I informed my wife that probably that gentleman had retired, gone to Florida, or maybe had left this world.

The next day we went to Trenton, New Jersey to do work at the State Library. On signing in, I was amazed to discover the name on the sign-in sheet immediately before me: Fred Sisser III! We talked, and he agreed to do some research for me.

Talk about serendipitous!"

As I tried to put together my thoughts and goals for this sequel to *Psychic Roots*, Nancy Maxwell of Rancho Cucamonga, California, wrote:

"I am the reference librarian at the Corona Public Library. I've had some weird research experiences and have wished for a 'safe place' to talk about them."

Nancy's words gave me the key I had been searching for in establishing the overall thrust of this book. So I offer this sequel as "a safe place to talk" - a forum for our unusual genealogical experiences.

Psychic Roots was largely drawn from the input of professionals in the family history field. Catherine A. Cissna of Jackson, California, thinks it's time our focus should be expanded:

"I have only one criticism of *Psychic Roots*, and it's not a true criticism. I realize that an endeavor to investigate this phenomenon must start somewhere. Other professionals in the genealogical community would seem to be a logical starting place ... and lend credibility to the subject when published. But I'm hoping that the sequel will include more stories from the grass roots segment of the genealogical community."

A good point well taken, Catherine. So now sit back, relax, open your hearts and minds, and enjoy *More Psychic Roots* - not only from the professionals -

but from the *grass roots* as well!

3
THE MYSTERY OF THE CEMETERY:
A FAMILY PLOT

"It was a *daaaark* and *stormy* night. The cold wind howled as it blew through the cemetery with ominous ferocity, making the crumbling tombstones shudder from its impact. A dark cloud covered what was left to be seen of the moon, causing the site to be enveloped in a shroud of shadows. The entire graveyard was filled with a foreboding sense of impending horror, as if the dead were preparing to rise again from their decaying wooden coffins and terrorize any unwelcome visitor.

No person would dare intrude upon such a scene ...

... Or would they?

Wait a minute ...

Someone *is* out there! I can see him now ... or is it a "her?" Whoever, they're on their knees, trying to balance a flashlight and a pen in one hand and juggle a notebook in the other. They seem to be struggling to copy down an inscription from one of the tombstones. Who *in their right mind* would be out there at this hour trying to do that?

Oh, of course ... I should have known ...

It's a GENEALOGIST!!!"

(From *The Fall of the House of Jacobus*,
by Edgar Coddington Poe)

To the layman, sometimes we family historians are viewed as "a half bubble off plumb." It's especially difficult for a civilian to understand the lure of the graveyard we feel. But to the avid family historian, the siren call of a potential tombstone rubbing or photograph is impossible to ignore. We'll easily drop mundane things (like making a living) in order to travel to far-off cemeteries just to find out where Great-Aunt Tillie was buried.

So, then, since a cemetery is almost a second home to genealogists, it came as no surprise that my mail was filled with stories that took place in that setting. As noted in *Psychic Roots*, the classic scenario is ... "I had never been to the area before and didn't know where to look. I drove to the cemetery, got out of my car, and immediately walked *straight to my ancestor's grave!*"

But there were such wonderful variations on the theme. Sometimes the cemetery itself was "missing." Dalton W. Mallory of Colonial Beach, Virginia, writes:

"I am presently working on a book about the family cemeteries in Westmoreland County, Virginia. I have been told that on certain pieces of land there was a cemetery, but no directions as to where to find it. In spite of this, I have gone to the piece of land and walked almost directly to the cemetery, without even knowing where to look. This has happened to me on numerous occasions. I have also been in a cemetery, looking for a certain grave and walked straight to it - even though I had never been there before."

Margaret Norris Heinek of New Carlisle, Indiana, wrote:

"My husband and I were in Franklin County, Virginia, looking for anything we could find on my Woody family there. We found a map of the early land owners, so I decided to see if I could find the area where the Woodys lived. I was told to 'drive three miles, turn left for about two miles, and left for another one and a half miles.' I was lost! But I saw a lovely house on a hill, and, for some reason, I went to the door to see if they knew anything. The lady didn't, but she did say there were tombstones in their cow pasture. We drove down in her truck, and there were the stones of my ancestor's brother and his wife! What a find! Martin Woody had served in the Revolution, but his grave had never been recorded on any Revolutionary soldier-burial list. We are amazed and delighted!"

Barbara A. Bennett, of Columbia, Maryland, Secretary of the National Genealogical Society, tells a marvelous "shaggy" cemetery story:

"When my Dad was a small child, my grandfather told him that his (grandpa's) grandma, who was his grandpa's first wife, was buried in a cemetery $1/2$ mile back in a field over north of Lick Creek in Van Buren County, Iowa. Over the years, Grandpa took several people over there, but my father never went because he wasn't interested. Grandpa died in 1980, and knowledge of the cemetery location died with him.

In 1988, Dad and I went to visit Grandma and take pictures of grave stones. Even though we didn't know the name of the cemetery where great-great grandma was buried or even what county it was in, Dad borrowed a plat book, and we set out on a search. We visited all the cemeteries shown on the plat map in the northern part of the county. We found many other relatives, but great-great grandma remained hidden.

We figured someone who lived in that area would be able to point us in the right direction, so we stopped at one of the houses. The woman couldn't help us because she had just moved into the area. She sent us to a neighbor who had lived there for 75 years. He didn't know of any cemetery like the one described, but sent us to the man who mows the cemeteries in that township. In Iowa, a portion of real estate tax is used to maintain the cemeteries. Every cemetery, including the defunct ones on private property, are mowed twice a year. Unfortunately, the cemetery mower wasn't home.

We temporarily abandoned the search and went to some cemeteries in another part of the county. While we were having lunch, Dad remembered an old fellow who lived in the part of the county we were searching, so we went to see him. He wasn't home, either. We went back to try the mower again, but he still wasn't home.

We decided to give up and head back to Grandma's. We noticed a hunter walking along the road. Dad stopped and asked if he lived around here. He said, 'No, I live in Stockport, fifteen miles away.' He asked what we wanted. Dad told him we were looking for a cemetery $1/2$ mile back in a field. The hunter said, 'There is one about a mile north of the county line in Jefferson County and gave us directions to the farm owner's house.

The farmer was home, and Dad told him what we were looking for. The farmer pointed out toward his fields and said, 'See that brown cow? Now look over here to that dead cedar tree. That's where the cemetery is.' He told us there used to be a road to the cemetery from the east, but it washed out years ago. He said, 'Now you go $1/2$ mile west, 1 mile north, then to the end of the gravel, then follow the fence south to the pond, and you're almost there.' In dry weather you can drive back to the cemetery along the edge of the field, but, of course, it wasn't dry. We parked the car and hiked through the mud back to the little hill the cemetery was on.

One of the first stones inside the cemetery gate was Harriet Latimer Bennett, my great-great grandma!

The next day, we visited one of Dad's cousins on the other side of the family, who lived in Jefferson County, and told her story of our search. She said, 'Why didn't you ask me? My husband used to be a township trustee, and I wrote checks to pay the fellow who mowed it. I could have told you where the cemetery was!'"

Gerald Ortell of Floral Park, New York, recounts:

"In the summer of 1992, we vacationed in Maine, combining a pleasure trip with visiting some of my wife Barbara's ancestral locations. When we arrived at the Laurel Cemetery in Saco, the office was closed and the cemetery street signs had been taken down. Somewhere in this large cemetery were the graves of Barbara's grandparents. We faced a long day. However, we got into the car and without stopping drove directly to the graves within fifty seconds!

The second graveyard we tried to find was quite a way out in the rural farm country near Parsonsfield. It was getting late, and we couldn't find it. On the way back to town, I said that I would go to the post office, since they know where everything is. Barbara said, 'NO! - we MUST go to the real estate office we passed because they will know.' She insisted we ignore the post office and turn around. I walked into the office, a converted home, and after a Maine razzing of 'but ya kant git thar frum heya' - I got directions. We had to go up a private driveway, thru their backyard, past a stand of trees, and up a mountain.

We arrived in the cemetery. Barbara scampered over a hill and within a minute or two she found the grave of Eliza D. Fox and other family members.

Months later in checking a 19th century atlas of York County, I was surprised to find that the real estate office had been the home of Barbara's ancestors!"

But it is in the actual finding of a long-sought-for grave that some real twists of fate can occur. Rose Young of Bellevue, Washington, remembered:

"While in Montana in the fall of 1980, my husband and I were researching my mother's family. My great-great grandparents were Manville and Lucinda Edwards, who had settled at Basin Creek, an area six miles south of Butte. A history of Madison County stated that, although some of the famly had lived fifty miles east of Butte at the little town of Silver Star, Manville and some relatives were buried in a cemetery at Basin Creek. We looked for the cemetery there, but were unsuccessful. We finally contacted the Butte Water Company because they had a reservoir at Basin Creek. An employee who lived there didn't know of a cemetery, but told us that four or five years ago during an excavation a tombstone had been dug up. The workers gave the tombstone to him because it had the same name as his - 'Morrison.' He kept it even though it didn't mean anything to him.

My great-great-grandmother Lucinda was divorced, and had remarried to a Lewis Morrison. She was supposed to have been buried at the Silver Star Cemetery, but here was her tombstone retrieved from under all that water at Basin Creek - the *only* old stone that was rescued! She died in 1887, but, due to the stone's submersion protecting it, the lettering was still sharp, and I could easily decipher her birth and death dates.

It seems to be more than a coincidence that I came along 93 years later, and Lucinda's tombstone was waiting for me with the information that I needed."

Carol MacKay of Calgary, Alberta, had a good one:

"I read your book and have to say that many of the examples of serendipity and intuition presented have also happened to me. I have often opened a book to the exact page where an ancestor's name appeared; stopped a whirling microfilm right at the exact page I was looking for; and knew exactly where to look for a gravestone in a cemetery when I had never been there before. All these things have happened to me, and more.

Usually these things happen when I am researching a client's family tree. While looking for a gravestone in the cemetery at Retlaw, Alberta, I fell into a gopher hole at the foot of a gravestone as I wandered the rows. It really gave me the willies, because when I looked up I realized I had fallen in front of the gravestone of my client's ancestor! The search was over!"

Carol goes on to tell how her husband's intuition - not her's - led to the location of a another grave:

"One time, my husband, James, had accompanied me to Queen's Park Cemetery in Calgary to photograph three gravestones for a client. We discovered the cemetery office was closed, and we couldn't get the location for the graves. We drove around the grounds for a while, marveling at how large this cemetery was and how we could never find the gravestone by just wandering around, as we had in other smaller graveyards. My husband then pointed to a section of the cemetery over a hill and said, 'The graves are there.' I laughed, but he insisted that was where they were. I told him we would have to come back the next day to get the proper location from the cemetery office. And that is what we did. As we drove to the location the office gave us on a cemetery map, we both realized we were heading in the exact direction where my husband had said they would be. When we finally found them, all three were very close to each other and in that very section of the cemetery. My husband looked at me and sang the 'Twilight Zone Theme' when we realized his intuition was *right!*"

Ruby Coleman can identify with that incident, "relatively speaking":

"I call her 'My Mother The Psychic.' For years she has entertained me with her bits of wisdom and, uncomfortably, these often became true. Some of my genealogy friends would like to borrow her!

A few years ago, I told her that I was trying to find my husband's ancestor's grave. Henry Eberhart died 25 February 1878 in Kansas, while looking for land. I had tried to locate his grave in that area with no luck. I knew that Henry had two children who settled in the county in eastern Nebraska where my parents live.

One summer day, I was visiting my parents. Mom and I decided to do some 'cemetery hopping,' and visited some rural cemeteries that were hard to get to and in bad condition. At the end of the day, we were no closer to finding Henry's grave ... just in case he had been brought back to Nebraska for burial. The results were negative.

A few months later, I was again visiting my parents when Mom decided we should visit an old, country cemetery she had just heard about from a friend. While we were driving to the cemetery, I asked if she had been there before or had asked if Henry was buried there. She replied that she had not, but had been told that Henry's descendants had lived somewhere in the area.

As we entered the cemetery, my mother paused, then walked over to the far southwest corner. She stood there, looked up at me and said, 'This is where Henry is buried.' I laughed and explained there were no stones or anything else to indicate that he was buried there. A little further in the cemetery, we found graves for two of his grandchildren. Then Mother walked almost knowingly toward a row of graves in the cemetery, pausing to look at the stones. She asked if I didn't want to copy those names and dates. They were names that meant nothing to me. She seemed annoyed that I didn't copy the information.

A couple of months later I discovered a cemetery plot map that showed that Henry Eberhart did indeed own a lot in that very cemetery. It was the *exact* spot where Mother had stopped and declared he was buried. A few months after that, I learned that the other graves were of collateral relationship to one of his children. Not direct relatives, yet all in the family. I still have no proof that Henry is actually buried there, but feel there is a good chance that he is in that unmarked spot. After all, Mother knows best!"

Sometimes not an adult, but a child helps find an elusive tombstone. Irene Burton of Wakefield, West Yorkshire, England, wrote:

"Some years ago, in the early days of my interest in the family tree, my sister and I scoured dozens of graveyards, thinking that tombstones were the only way, apart from parish registers, of finding ancestors. At one small country church, we mapped out the graveyard and searched every inch of it seeking the tombstone of our great-grandfather, who died in 1875. My mother knew she had seen the stone, and no alterations had been made to the graveyard since. However, we were unable to find it.

At that time we had to take my sister's youngest daughter with us as she was a mere tot, and, to keep her amused whilst we searched, she was allowed to push her little buggy up and down the paths. We were leaving the churchyard, disappointed, with the child ahead with the buggy, when it veered off the path and into a huge overgrown bush, disappearing completely beneath it.

When my sister had literally crawled under the bush, there facing her was our ancestor's grave ... We would never have found it otherwise."

My friend, Melinde Lutz Sanborn of Derry, New Hampshire, can relate to that tale:

"My husband, George, is one of those people who can enter a cemetery and walk straight to the desired gravestone, whether it belongs to his own family or to a stranger's. The only time I can recall when this uncanny ability has failed was when we went to visit the grave of Mercy (Short) Marshall, an ancestor of George's through whose descendants he picks up one of his *Mayflower* lines.

The Boston cemeteries have been transcribed any number of times, and George and I knew that a gravestone for Mercy was in Copp's Hill Cemetery, or at least there had been one at one time. With our daughter Ruthie in tow, we entered the cemetery, and George struck off, making what I expected was a bee-line for the stone. Being a descendant of Copp, I took a more leisurely approach, putting Ruthie down so that she could explore, and soaking in the surroundings of ancestral land. The stones were very interesting, some pertaining to families I had worked on, others with tragic tales.

George came back after a few minutes and told me he couldn't find the stone, which was a lot like saying that it hadn't survived. We stood near the top of the hill and determined to pace off the cemetery, looking at every stone, just to be sure. This took the better part of a half an hour because many of the stones were difficult to read. Finally, hot and exhausted, I went back up the hill to where Ruthie had plunked down and was happily pulling up grass. Sitting down beside her, we played for a moment, when I happened to get a better look at the little stone she was sitting against. A chill went through me as I realized that it was not just a footstone and that the names and dates carved into it were Mercy's.

Ruthie had gone straight to this spot when I first put her down, and had stayed near it all the time. She doesn't go to cemeteries much any more, being more interested in rock music and fashion, but I suspect that she has her father's talent for finding gravestones should she ever need it in the future."

Daniel J. Hay of West Clearfield, Utah, had yet another "and a child shall lead them" story:

"When my daughter Lauren was six years old, she went with me from Missouri to Nebraska to return a borrowed truck. I decided to combine the trip with some research in Kansas, since we could go right through the towns my grandparents and great-grandparents lived in. I particularly wanted to find the headstone for my second great-grandmother Lydia Amelia (Hoyt) Hay. She had died in 1879 when her son was only a few years old. Her husband remarried, and little was passed down about his first wife.

We arrived in Seneca, Kansas fairly late in the afternoon and got directions from the local gas station on getting to the cemetery. What I didn't know was that there are two cemeteries there, facing each other across the road. As we came over the hill and saw that there were two, I actually stopped on the road and, looking back and forth, said, 'Darn, now where do I go?' Lauren had been awakened by the bouncy road only moments before. She looked out the window and pointed at the nearest lane to the cemetery on the left, the driver's side. 'Turn here, Daddy!', she said. I did, slowly, and asked her as we went through the gate, 'But, honey, where do we go now?' The lane was grass covered, not graveled or paved, and the turns were long arcs of worn away grass. Although not a large cemetery, I had no records on where to look and had never been there.

Lauren, as I started to pass the first row to the right, yelled out, 'Right here, Daddy, turn right here!' I had thought to head to the next row which looked as if it had been driven on more often. But, with no other clues, for some reason I decided to follow her directions and took the first right lane. I told Lauren that we were looking for the stones with our last name on them and said, 'Where do you think we should stop?' She looked out the windshield for a moment as the truck crept down the lane. Then, looking at me with a big smile, she said, 'This is good.' I stomped on the brake pedal causing the truck to lurch to a sudden stop.

Getting out, I said to her that we could just start browsing around until we had covered all the sections. We went over a wide area, from stone to stone, until it began to rain. As we headed back to the truck, I told Lauren that I sure would have liked to find that old marker before it got dark. Lauren said, 'Daddy, what does it look like?' I again explained that her last name 'Hay' would be on it, and that it could be shaped like any of the ones we had already seen. Then, as we started to part to our own sides of the truck, she said, 'You mean this one, Daddy?'

There next to the road, in line with the front tire - *right where Lauren had told me to stop* - was a small marker for Lydia Amelia Hay. Lauren had found the stone for us, but we didn't know it until we were ready to leave. It had to have been serendipity. Sure, I have been researching since I was nearly fifteen, but Lauren had not. She knew nothing of where we were or who we were looking for. Even though she could barely see over the dashboard, she told me to turn at the crucial moments in our journey through the cemetery and then stopped me at exactly the right spot. She did it all! Now somebody tell me that she was not the recipient of a serendip-nudge, or, perhaps I received it because she was the guide!"

Simply following a hunch has led many a researcher to a remarkable discovery in a cemetery. Doris Powell Schultz recounted:

"After we found long-lost ancestor Nancy Ogilvie's gravestone, one of the only ones in that Ohio cemetery not broken and stacked, a certain feeling told us to take time to use a broken stone to scrape away sod nearby. There, four inches down, we found her husband's well-preserved stone to tell us he died on Christmas Day."

Edwin G. Rossman of El Sobrante, California, recalled:

"I was fascinated with your NBC *Unsolved Mysteries* program last night. You mentioned that about 200 genealogists had intuitions that led them to certain discoveries ... well here is case 201. I really don't believe in this stuff, and now I don't know what to think.

On 7 October, 1994, I visited the St. Thomas Lutheran Church's cemetery in Churchtown, New York where several of my direct ancestors are buried. Although I had been there many times before, I seemed to be attracted there once again. I found myself wandering in a circle, about in the middle of the cemetery, when I noticed an old gravestone in very poor condition. It was slate, patched up a little bit, and seemed to have the name 'Geor Ros' inscribed near the top. I have seen hundreds of these virtually unreadable stones, and never really bothered to take a close look at any of them. I left the graveyard that day and retired for the night.

The next morning I *knew* I had to return. I stopped by the local supermarket and bought a rubber squeegee and some shaving cream. I had heard about squirting the shaving cream on the stone and wiping it off with the squeegee to bring out the inscriptions, so here would be my first try. The inscription was in German, which I can't read, but I picked off the name of 'Georg Rosc(h)man' and the date of '1791' and assumed the '48' was part of 1748, which is the year of his birth. These dates coincide with both my family's and Church's records. The headstone inscription is not listed in any of the Columbia County graveyard registers. It was indeed my family!"

The tombstone of Georg Roschman (1748–1791), St. Thomas Lutheran
Church, Churchtown, New York

The "tipsy tombstone": George & Elizabeth Brown, Hopewell Cemetery,
Preble County, Ohio

My friend and colleague Marsha Hoffman Rising of Springfield, Missouri, had an inkling about one of her forebears that proved to be correct:

"I always look forward to the first visit to the cemetery where ancestors lie. By the time a visit is arranged, these people have become old friends from intense research into their lives. I felt I already knew Elizabeth Brown very well. One of the things I learned was that some time during middle age she became 'deranged,' and her husband left a trust fund to provide for her after his death. From the court records, it appeared she never recovered.

It was a beautiful day to visit the lovely rural cemetery located behind the old white church. The cemetery was larger than I expected and extended down a rolling hill. The oldest stones were in the back. We started toward them. Suddenly, I called to my husband. 'That's probably Elizabeth there. See, it's a little off!' The tipped stone indeed was that for Elizabeth Brown! In death - just as in life, she was leaning toward her husband - still depending on him to hold her up!"

Sometimes it appears as if we get a nudge from the Great Beyond, enabling us to find an old marker or stone. Peggy S. Joyner of Portsmouth, Virginia, contributed a moving example of this:

"One of my clients whom I'll never forget was 'Harry,' an English engineer, who wrote me in 1980 to request a search for his 'kinsmen' who came from England and settled in southeastern Virginia. Four orphaned children, three brothers and a sister, came from England in 1857. One of the brothers wrote a surviving letter to relatives in England in 1886 which contained enough clues to launch a search.

As my work progressed, my admiration for this family was apparently conveyed in my reports to Harry. His excitement mounted, and his pleasure was obvious in his replies. Eventually, I documented all three of the brothers and found they all fought in the Civil War for the Confederacy. They left no descendants. The one sister, Louisa, was a schoolteacher who married in York County and had one daughter who had no children.

This search produced a voluminous report to Harry. While all of the discoveries excited him, he became somewhat obsessed with details I could not find. He especially wanted me to continue the search for Louisa's tombstone. The name of a lady in Newport News 'who might know something' about Louisa's daughter was given to me. When I called her, she was not cooperative because, 'I am potting my geraniums,' she said. That comment delighted Harry.

The following summer Harry wrote that he was coming to the United States, and he wanted me to take him to all the places I had researched. He especially wanted to visit the 'Geranium Lady.' He had better luck than I, writing from England the day and time of our pending visit.

Harry and I spent a week retracing my steps before we went to see this lady who lived on the James River and was, after all, a gracious lady. She showed us a table that she said had once belonged to Louisa, but she could tell us nothing about her except she had often heard about the English lady in her family. She had been told long ago about an old family graveyard not far from her house on the banks of the James. She had never been there and wasn't sure where it was. She simply pointed.

I drove on each street that lead to the river and saw no graveyard. We came to the last road. As I drove slowly on the narrow road in the thick woods, Harry said, 'Stop, I see something!' He went into the woods while I turned the car around. He came running back to the car to say he had found a vandalized 1699 grave.

In 100 degree heat, we looked into an open grave and reassembled the pieces of the large, broken table-top stone which had once covered it. Harry began to read the long inscription on William Rosco's stone as I copied. Suddenly Harry began to shake, and he became very pale. His clothes were soaked with perspiration as he sat on the stone with his head buried in his hands. He would or could not speak. Finally, when he regained some of his composure, he said the stone had the man's birthplace at Chorley where Harry, too, was born!

The badly shaken Harry was convinced he had been led to the grave by his long deceased countryman. 'He has brought me over thousands of miles to find his vandalized grave,' declared Harry. 'My mission is accomplished.'"

Another experience along these lines came in from Elizabeth J. Kampcik of South Colton, New York:

"Being new at genealogical research, and having no living relatives to ask questions of about my Canadian ancestry, I decided one day to travel across the border from Upstate New York and visit the town of Brockville, Ontario, which is close by. I remembered hearing the Brockville name at some time in my life in conjunction with my family and was looking for traces of any relatives I might have there.

After a visit to the Mayor's office which brought no result, his clerk asked if I had checked the local cemeteries. I inquired as to how many there were, and she replied that there were eight or nine close to town, all in different directions, and wished me luck. I didn't know quite what to do or where to go, but I found myself in the westbound lane, without choice. After driving eight miles, I had come to the conclusion that I was not going to find any cemeteries on the road, and that I should turn back. Just then, I saw two cemeteries, one on each side of this busy highway. I quickly got out of the traffic pattern, pulled off to the right, and decided to inquire right there.

When I walked into the office, a woman giving a cup of tea to a man working on some files. When I explained I was looking for information on any relatives I could find, she became visibly exasperated, saying that 'ever since *Roots* on TV, everybody from the States was asking them to look up people.' She left, and the man in charge told me that, although I couldn't look at the old records myself, he would look up just one name for me, to see if he had any record.

I told him I thought my grandfather's name was Charles Amies, but that he had died when I was very young, maybe in 1927 or 1928. He pulled out a large ledger-type book, and laid it its spine on the desk. He turned to me and asked how to spell the name. As he did this, he let the book fall open - and it fell open to the very page bearing my grandfather's name! He looked at me again, sort of in disbelief, took the pipe out of his mouth, and said, 'Young lady, I have your grandfather!' The chills ran down my spine. The man then went to a file, pulled out a card, and told me that in the same family plot was my grandmother, a son and daughter-in-law, my grandfather's sister and her husband, brother- in-law and wife, etc.

Looking out the window in amazement at such luck, I asked him where in this big cemetery I would find this plot. He looked up the location and said, 'Would you believe that it's practically next to this building?' By this time, he was as happy to have found so much information as I was, and said he would show me. We walked outside to a tall red granite stone bearing the name of my grandfather's married sister. There was no way to spot the name 'Amies' on the stone unless you walked to the side. I could have walked right by it and never known my name was there! The family plot was in the sister's married name, and not my maiden name. Needless to say, I was very happy to have had this good fortune.

I don't know why I drove the direction I did, or stopped at this particular cemetery out of the eight or nine there, but I had gone directly from the States to the town where my grandparents were buried and had found them in a family plot that bore a different family name on the stone - so I think that is pretty remarkable. Call it luck, intuition, or what you will, but I'm still grinning!"

And Cynthia Drayer had an intriguing event occur also:

"I had journeyed to Warren County, Ohio to try and find an old Templin family cemetery that I found mentioned in a book. I knew it had to be located near the old family home, so I canvassed the area thoroughly. After finding a 'T' on an old cornerstone in the area which had been mentioned in some old deeds relating to the family, I walked through a densely forested area to a flat area at the top of a knoll. It had a beautiful view of the old farm lands and of a small creek below. But there were absolutely no gravestones there - just grass, trees, and lots of flat land.

I had come 3,000 miles to find this graveyard, not even really knowing who was buried there. I was beginning to think it had been totally destroyed, and that there was nothing left to see. I closed my eyes and placed my face in a small patch of sunlight that made its way through the trees. Under my breath I said, 'Please Richard and Elizabeth Templin - *please* let me find you if you are here. I've come so far, and I want very much to see you.'

When I opened my eyes, I looked around again. This time, in a far corner, almost to the edge of the knoll, I saw

... a fish tank! ... upside down in the tall weeds. What an unusual thing, I thought, to be up here on this knoll. I went over, lifted up the tank, and there was the gravestone of Richard Templin! I brushed away some of the dirt and grass, and there, along side that stone, was the grave of his second wife, Elizabeth Stilley Templin. Thanks to their guidance, I left with some very nice photos and some birth and death dates that I didn't have before. (I also should give some thanks to the person who had the foresight to place a fish tank over the tombstone: it had kept the weeds off and served as a better marker than the stone.)"

One never knows what will happen in an old cemetery "on the hunt." Sometimes, it can be the simplest of syncronistic experiences. As Doris Powell Schultz noted:

"A butterfly (my symbol for new life) came down and rested on my father's newly-covered grave, and flew off as I stood there."

Other times, it might be a spine-tingler, like what happened to Anna Neale:

"In 1979, I made arrangements to drive to three cemeteries in Pennsylvania to get pictures of my ancestors' graves for a book I was writing on my family. We had a terrible 'northeasterner' that weekend, and the rain pelted down in a torrential storm. I had no idea where the cemeteries were, let alone the exact location of my ancestors' stones, but I was determined to accomplish my task.

I arrived at Bernville, Pennsylvania and was able to follow a state map to find one of the cemeteries. The rain was falling heavily in small pellets when I arrived there. But just as I entered the grounds, the sky above the cemetery parted just like someone had parted a curtain, and there was no rain over this particular section. I quickly ran through the cemetery, camera in hand, looking for my ancestor, Abraham Stoudt. For some reason, I abruptly took a diagonal path at one point, and suddenly came upon the markers for Abraham and his wife, their final burial place in this very large cemetery. I quickly took the picture I needed and ran back to the car. The moment I entered my vehicle, the sky closed over again, and the rain started pouring down.

I then drove to another cemetery. It continued pouring buckets, and the wind from the storm almost blew me off the road. But the same thing happened again: just as I got out of my car, the rain stopped, the clouds parted, and I was able to run up the hill to find the stones honoring my ancestor, Reverend George Menning and his wife Catharine. As before, I took my pictures, ran back to my car, and then the rain started up again. As this all was occurring, I remember thinking of my deceased mother and saying to myself, 'My mother is helping me by parting the clouds and pushing them aside so that I can get my pictures.'

Did the spirits help me? I'm *sure* of it!"

Patricia A. Cramer of Silver Spring, Maryland, certainly had an unusual experience:

"For many years, my husband William S. Cramer had been searching for the grave site of his great-grandfather, John A. Cramer. He had been told that John (an immigrant from Bavaria) was buried in St. John's Cemetery in Frederick, Maryland. Both the newspaper obituary and the Church records indicate this was the place of burial.

When we could not find a marker in the family plot, Bill and I began searching the entire cemetery. We would each take a different section and read all of the markers hoping to find John Cramer; but to no avail. At least once a year we would make a thorough search. We knew that he was a Union veteran; so we looked for military markers, but there were very few and none with the name Cramer.

About two years ago, we were going through our same cemetery drill when I knelt down to take a closer look at a small plain marker hoping that it might be military, but it was for one of the priests who had served at St. John's church. I leaned back on my heels and said, 'John Cramer, where *are* you?' I looked up and there right in front of me was a military marker with the name John Cramer, Pvt., Co. A, 13th Md. It was in an area where we had looked many times before; however, for some very strange reason we had never seen this marker. My common sense tells me that we just overlooked it; however, my 'gut feeling' tells me that it was never there until the day I discovered it.

Two searches were made by the Military Reference Branch of the National Archives to find out when the stone was installed and who requested it. They could not find any record of the request. We have since made visits to the cemetery, and the stone is still there."

One never knows just how a long-lost tombstone will turn up. Margaret Norris Heinek of New Carlisle, Indiana, related:

"One patron of the library where I work came in all excited one day. She had just found the grave of her great-great grandfather in a place she had been going for years to decorate the graves of her mother's family. A rose bush that had gone wild was always in the way, and they would fuss about getting pricked with the thorns.

This spring, on her usual trip to decorate, a long stem caught on her skirt. She fussed and fumed and threatened to cut the bush out, but in pushing the stem back, she found the gravestone of her great-great grandfather! No one ever knew where he had been buried."

And Pamlea [*sic*] Langston wrote:

"About five years ago, I returned to England to do family research and visited the old church at Earls Barton. I had been raised nearby and remembered seeing the gravestone there of my great-grandmother Mary Ann Simpson, born in 1843, the daughter of Edward Simpson and Letitia Oram. At that time, I had no interest in family history but since my research had produced two Mary Ann's I wanted to see her stone again to resolve the problem.

When I got there, imagine my disappointment to find that, as in the case of many old churches, the stones had been taken up and placed around the outside wall to facilitate mowing; and a search of all the stones did not turn up that of Mary Ann. Disappointed, I was walking toward the gate and turned to take one last look at the old church. The grass had recently been mowed, and the ground was covered with grass clippings. I realized that I was standing on an old stone set flat to the ground. I knelt down and brushed away the grass. There was the name 'Oram.' I quickly brushed away more grass, and the crumbled old stone revealed the name '-h----s Oram, born 1782.' Mary Ann's grandfather and my great-great-great-grandfather,

Charles Oram! I had no idea he was even buried there. There were several ways that I could have walked out of that churchyard, but *something* had led me to walk over *that* stone!"

Sharon DeBartolo Carmack of Simla, Colorado, had her family history "baptism" amongst the tombstones:

"Most of my unusual experiences have occurred in cemeteries, so I find it interesting that I can also trace my start in genealogy to a cemetery. When I was about nine or ten, I was visiting relatives back east (New York) with my parents. Some close friends of the family, with whom we were staying, knew I had an obsession for old cemeteries, so they took me to one near their home. As I recall, it was approaching dusk, and we were about to leave when we noticed an old man copying down tombstone inscriptions. He said he was a genealogist. Our friends invited him back to their house, where he gave me my first pedigree chart and family group sheet and told me how to get started! Thinking back on it with adult hindsight, I wonder why our friends invited a strange man home with them, and why he accepted the invitation of strangers!

When I am in a cemetery, whether my ancestors are buried there or not, I get the most peaceful feeling and hate when I must leave. I also had this same tranquil feeling when I visited Ellis Island where my Italian ancestors first entered America.

One time, my husband and I were in Dade County, Missouri, searching cemeteries for his relatives. I knew one of his ancestors was buried in a particular cemetery as I had found the inscription in a book of cemetery transcriptions a few months earlier at the Family History Library in Salt Lake. The transcription was published a few years earlier, so the stone still had to be legible. We walked row after row after row and could not find that tombstone I was seeking. As it was a hot July day, we took a break under one of the only shade trees in the cemetery - my husband choosing a tombstone to sit on. Exasperated that I could not find the woman I was looking for and ready to start my row-by-row trek again, I 'happened' to look down and saw that my husband was sitting on the tombstone right next to his ancestor that I had been looking for!"

But Marsha Hoffman Rising may win the prize for "off-the-wall" cemetery experiences:

"It all began with a routine trip to the local genealogy society. The new quarterlies were on display. It won't take long, I thought. I will just quickly glance at the queries to see if any of them apply to my pioneer families. It jumped off the page!

'Help! Seeking descendants of Robert Sharp buried in Sunset Hill Cemetery, Warrensburg, Missouri. Decisions required about mausoleum.' It was my husband's second great-grandfather!

A telephone call that evening revealed that the roof of the mausoleum had collapsed damaging the coffins and exposing the crypt. The five bodies had been removed to the local mortuary, but the kindly funeral director did not know how much longer he would be able to keep them. The cemetery association was a private one and had funds only for maintenance, not repairs. The only descendants that had been located were not interested in the problem.

My husband, Dean, traveled to the ancestral home. The cemetery committee recommended the mausoleum be razed and the bodies buried. Law required that vaults be provided for the six evicted residents. This could all be provided at the bargain basement price of $6,000 - $8,000!! Concern, respect, and regard for our ancestors is one thing. But this was another! We could think of a few other things to do with that amount of money!

We contacted two other descendants. Neither were interested in providing funds. We contemplated how long it could take to find descendants who would contribute enough money to put these unfortunate folks in the ground - where they never wanted to be in the first place! Perhaps a compromise was possible. How about cremating the bodies, replacing the remains where they were, and fixing the mausoleum so that it would not constitute a hazard? The funeral director was willing, but he would need death certificates in order to cremate them. Only one of the deceased persons had lived into the death certificate era. Fortunately, my husband is a physician.

An image immediately developed in my mind - my husband, with stethoscope appropriately placed, bending over a pile of bones and pronouncing them 'really most sincerely dead' (as the coroner said in the movie *The Wizard of Oz*). Dean had a better idea. He called the Bureau of Vital Statistics. It wasn't easy to find a way around the rules, but we finally located a reasonable bureaucrat. We would need notarized statements that Dean was indeed a bona fide descendant, and that he took responsibility for the disposal of their remains. We provided all the family statistics for the funeral director, produced the notarized statement, and for $600 he agreed to handle the matter.

But, before the remains became ashes, Dean wanted to be absolutely sure that the people who were supposed to be there were indeed the ones who were. He made another trip to the ancestral home, camera in hand. So, if anyone is interested in seeing how well preserved someone remains after 120 years in a mausoleum, I will happily provide photographs!"

I'VE SEEN THEM, MARSHA ...
<u>YUCK!</u>

4
READ ANY GOOD BOOKS LATELY?

There's something about a genealogical library that really gets to me! Particularly the older ones. Quite honestly, you can keep the sleek antiseptic "techno-perfect" new buildings: they look like they were cast from the same sterile mold.

I prefer a library with some seasoning: sturdy dark-wooded furniture illuminated by user-friendly lighting; *open* stacks, crammed to the ceiling with countless volumes - each one a potential "Rosetta Stone" that will unravel a long-confused family line; a helpful staff - older than God - who really know where the bodies (and books) are buried; large tables big enough to handle any number of pedigree charts and family groupsheets sprawled out on top of them; and more than enough microfilm and microfiche readers to accommodate the eager clientele. And call me "kinky," call me "crazy" - how I love the musty *smell* of the older repositories. There's nothing like the pungent aroma of ancient books to get those research-juices flowing!

And as in *Psychic Roots*, the serendipitous stories centered around libraries, books and microfilms just poured in for this sequel. There were lots of "and the first book I looked at ..." experiences. Dawne Slater-Putt, Reference Librarian of the Historical Genealogy Department at the marvelous Allen County Public Library in Fort Wayne, Indiana, wrote:

"When I began as *Periodical Source Index (PERSI)* project supervisor at the Allen County Public Library in 1989, the project already was three years old, and many of the 'good' periodicals (translation: the ones that may have contained information about my ancestors) already had been indexed.

My husband and I had recently rafted down part of the Snake River, so I chose *Snake River Echoes* from Idaho as my first periodical to index. That makes about as much sense as choosing a winning sports team by the color of its uniforms, nevertheless, it was my reason. I had no belief that any of my family had been in Idaho. The only family connection I had in the West to my knowledge was a fourth-great-grandfather who was at the Gold Rush, then returned to Ohio.

But the *first* article in the *first* issue of the *first* volume that I opened to index contained an article on the brother of one of my Pennsylvania ancestors, a man who had disappeared from my research with no trace prior to my opening that periodical. It mentioned his parents' names, which I had been given, but had not been able to confirm before that finding. Now I had two separate sources listing the father's name and the mother's maiden name.

I cannot explain why we sometimes are 'given' information. It takes my breath away when I think of what I would have missed had I not chosen *Snake River Echoes* to index. I think our ancestors are closer than we know. Perhaps they are, as I have heard at funeral services, only 'in the next room.'"

Elise Baker of Taneytown, Maryland, had her twist to this:

"When I was a teenager, my great-grandmother Bell Quigley (Bowman) Emery gave me papers about her husband's family, the Emerys, who settled in Newbury, Massachusetts in 1635. I enjoyed reading about them, but I never had the urge to get more information about them, or any other ancestors, until my daughter was born.

I had just begun research when one day I was taking a lunch-time walk with a friend in Baltimore. Our walk took us past the George Peabody Library, and I suggested we take a look inside. We signed in, I walked up to the third bay, and at eye level was *The Descendants of John Emery of Newbury, Massachusetts*. I returned to work, called the publisher to obtain the author's phone number, called her that evening to order the book, and I was hooked!"

Doris P. Schultz told her version:

"Researching at the DAR Library in DC one day, heavy snow began falling, and the driver in our group said we must start home. She laid the book she had been using on the table, discouraged that someone had removed (!) the pages that she needed. I said, 'I've never searched in that town (about which the book was written), but it is near where my ancestors resided. Can I take time to look at it?'

Believe it or not, the book fell open to the page that listed my ancestor's birth! I would not have had time to search an unindexed book, but there it was! An unexpected piece of information that led in a new direction and later orphans' court records that proved my line."

Shirley York Anderson of McFarland, Wisconsin, communicated:

"I was looking for the parents of Catherine Stuart who married Benjamin Brown in Sterling, MA in 1786. I had found some possible fathers in the probate index, but nothing firm. One afternoon, I had about two hours to kill while waiting for my husband. I decided to spend it at the State Historical Society. I had no notes with me and no plan of attack as I usually do. My first stop was the shelf where the books are filed awaiting reshelving. There in all their glory were the bright red volumes of the *Stewart Clan Magazine*. I took them all into the reading room, found myself a comfortable chair, and began to browse. I set the books in the chair next to me and picked up whatever came to hand.

The first two happened to be later volumes. I began to come across the name Solomon, one of the names I had found in the probate index. Something made me become more deliberate in the volume that I selected. I decided to start with Vol. 1. I soon found Catherine and her husband Benjamin. She was the daughter of Solomon Stuart. The entire male line was shown in bits and pieces throughout the first two volumes. I had just enough time to locate and copy them before it was time to go down and meet my husband."

And Barbara Nichols of Longview, Washington, added her genealogical two cents to these episodes:

"During a recent research trip to Salt Lake City, I found myself frustrated in not being able to pursue my research on my Shepard line. I had been very unsuccessful in learning the ancestry of Sally Shepard, who supposedly had married William Shoen in the late 1700's. Not only was Sally or Sarah Shepard a common name, I didn't even have a clue as to the state of origin.

As I often pursue genealogy in a non-traditional manner, I found myself literally walking up and down the book aisles. For some reason I'll never know, I stopped at the New Hampshire section and randomly chose a book from the shelf. The book, *History of Dublin*, seemed to almost magically open to a page with the name Shepard on it which stated, 'by an Act of the General Court, the name Shepard was taken by this family instead of Hogg.'

It was my family! It seems that a son of the Hogg family was adopted by a benevolent gentleman named Shepard from the State of New York and educated by him. The Hogg family was so indebted to Mr. Shepard that the entire family took the name of Shepherd. To complicate matters, Sally Hogg was already married to William Shoen before her maiden name was legally changed.

The chance finding of that particular book amongst the vast volumes in Salt Lake City has opened up a whole new world of research for me."

I think Margaret S. von Kempf of Palo Alto, California, speaks for many of us when she simply states how this seems to work:

"In July 1991 while browsing the Maryland book shelves at the California Genealogical Society, a thin, bright yellow volume said, 'Please look at me!' I took it off the shelf and checked the index, and - lo and behold - there was my Ernst Wilhelm Kafferoth!"

Attention should be paid to these discoveries, however. Just ask Elissa Scalise Powell of Wexford, Pennsylvania:

"While living in Massachusetts, I became interested in tracing my family tree. My neighbor and I were rank beginners when we visited the Worcester Public Library.

I only had Pennsylvania, Ohio, and West Virginia roots, so I asked the librarian to see their collection of Pennsylvania books to begin with. She advised me that they were in the closed stacks, but that she could bring us a couple of books to examine. She brought me two books, one of which was of interest - so I made a note of it.

The other volume listed a Sarah Perine, one of my ancestors, but with the wrong husband's name (I knew she was married to Edward Pritchard Southworth); however, all the other facts of this Sarah seemed to fit. But being my first foray into a genealogical library and not even thinking about the possibility of a multiple marriage, I didn't write this reference down.

To this day, I regret not being more receptive to my first serendipitous moment in genealogy. I have gone back to that library several times over the succeeding years, but have not been able to locate that book, nor the one I did write the reference down for - in case they came off the same shelf. But that one has disappeared as well!

The Angel of Serendip was snubbed (or is it my ancestress who thinks she has been insulted?) and will not present the material to me again. How does one apologize?"

The old chestnut of "looking for one thing, finding another" certainly held true in this arena also. Ask Helen M. Imburgia of Boothwyn, Pennsylvania, who told of this occurrence:

"Sometime in the first year of my research, I went to the courthouse in Media, Delaware County, Pennsylvania. I was looking for the death records of my great-great-grandparents, Bridget (Norton) McIntyre, and Patrick and Mary (Maynes) Tuttle.

I approached the clerk at the desk and told her what I was looking for. She took a big docket down from the shelf and placed it on a high counter top. She asked the name of the person I was researching. I said, 'Bridget McIntyre!' The clerk inserted her right hand into the pages, lifting them up into the air. She proceeded to explain to me how the book was indexed, while she thumbed through the pages on the left looking for McIntyres. I was standing to her right and being very curious started to read the page she was holding up in the air.

Well, to my amazement, what did I find but the name of Patrick Tuthill, indexed under 'Patrick' not 'Tuttle.' The clerk, at random, had inserted her hand into the P's and to the exact page my great-great-grandfather's name had been incorrectly entered! Had this not happened, I never would have found it.

Would you say now, I had a leprechaun sitting on my shoulder?"

Dr. William B. Saxbe noted:

"I was in a county courthouse in western Ohio last week, in the dusty basement vault, looking at chancery records from the 1820's. The record I sought was not on the expected page - because I had pulled down the wrong volume - but on the page to which I opened there was a suit brought by an ancestor of mine (on a completely different line) from another county 100 miles east, acting as administrator for an unknown brother. The eastern county's courthouse had burned down in 1875, and there was no record of the family or the administration left there.

As will genealogists from now on, I thanked God and thought of you. Why should this have happened?"

Sometimes the "wrong" book turns out to be the "right" one. Gerald Ortell of Floral Park, New York, writes:

"I was researching my wife's colonial Bishop-Bragg-Pullen lines from Rehoboth, Massachusetts in the New York City Public Library. A page brought me a book I didn't ask for: *History of Winthrop, Maine*. This fortuitously turned out to be where those lines moved after leaving Massachusetts.

Two years later in the same room, I was researching her Scottish ancestors in Perthshire. An incorrect book was again delivered to me. I looked through it once, I looked through it twice and found nothing in it. But I remembered what happened before. I stared at the book for five minutes. I tried a third time. I found nothing about Barbara's family, but I did find a listing for the Testament-Dative of my ancestor, James Drummond of Drumdowie, who had returned to Scotland from Poland (famine caused a significant 16th century Scottish migration to Poland). No wonder I couldn't find his will in Cracow."

The strangest things have been known to drop out of the least likely places. Family historians might be well advised to keep a lookout and cover their heads to protect themselves from these barrages of genealogical manna. Frederick E. Bitting of Fair Haven, Vermont, related:

"On one of my visits to the Montgomery Co., PA Historical Society, I randomly pulled a book from a shelf and, on opening it, a letter fell out. It was to the Society from a Russel Bitting in Miami, Florida. I wrote to him, and we were able to help each other in extending our mutual lines.

But why did I pull out that particular book? Why was that letter in it? Why did it fall out when *I* opened it rather than someone else?

WHY?"

Mollie Bradley Howard of El Paso, Texas, recalled:

"The search for my orphaned father's family started after my retirement. Mail and phone efforts to locate the Syracuse, New York and San Francisco, California orphanages that Dad mentioned were fruitless. Two years ago, I spent several days in Syracuse with no apparent success. However, with spare time before flight departure, I visited the Syracuse Public Library. I was about to leave there empty-handed when a vigilant librarian insisted that I examine books of obituaries.

The *first* item to appear was a LOOSE CLIPPING that was not an obituary: it was from the 13 June 1913 issue of the *Post Standard*, and featured a letter which was headlined, 'Boy, Lost 25 Years, Writes Letter from the Philippines Seeking Parents.' It was written by *my father!* Dad had found a copy of the Syracuse newspaper in his barracks' day room. It contained an item announcing the 50th wedding anniversary of a Syracuse couple, and he wrote to them asking for assistance. He related a story I had never heard, about having become separated from his mother on a downtown street and having been taken to the orphanage. A woman he did not know claimed him, told him his name was Arthur James Bradley, and took him to Montana. I suspect that my father's letter drew some kind of response, because the letter lacked details that he knew later."

Sadie Langlois Cutchen of Spanish Fort, Alabama, had a classic occur:

"The red three ring binder lay there, gathering dust for two or three years - unnoticed, unused. Flat on its side, it was an unshakable item - solidly resting on top of the book shelves about seven feet from the floor.

A friend, thinking I might have use for a book no longer in print, had copied the whole thing and sent it to me. It was useless in my own research, but I still couldn't bear to throw it away; so I climbed on a stool and placed it completely out of the way. I promptly forgot all about it.

One night, while on the Prodigy network, I came across a request for help with a surname that I thought might be in my collection of Louisiana colonial research books. After a thorough search of my own books, I replied that I didn't locate the surname, then resumed other work of my own. When I finally decided to call it quits for the night, I left the book I was working with open to my family information and placed a map I wanted to copy the next day on top of it.

As luck would have it, the next morning my husband and I were in the car ready to back out of the driveway, when I suddenly remembered the map. I dashed back inside to get it. I walked to my desk and saw the same type red binder open, sitting there just as it had been left the night before. But I didn't see the map on top of it. I glanced down at the book and was puzzled: It definitely wasn't the book I had worked with earlier. After a few years, you *know* your books. The printing was unlike any of my books. Still puzzled, I started to turn a page, and a name close to the bottom of the page almost leapt out at me!

It was the name I had seen on Prodigy and hadn't been able to find. I was completely baffled. After a few moments, I happened to look upward toward the ceiling ... and it hit me like a bolt of lightning ... the dusty red book was gone!!! It had mysteriously appeared on my desk on top of my family book and map from the night before. I began to tremble, got goose-bumps up and down my arms, and my heart was pounding. Back in the car, my husband looked at me in awe as I sat there trying between sobs and shaking to tell him what had happened.

Later, I decided to face the laughs and teasing, and told the story on open line when I again contacted the person who had posted the query on Prodigy. I got a bit of razzing from my Prodigy friends, but NO ONE LAUGHED! Wonder why? I think it's because we have all learned to expect the unexpected and the 'strange happenings' that seem to be a real part of genealogy."

Serendipitous experiences weren't limited to books. Genealogists using microfilms had their share of extraordinary events also. Marsha Hoffman Rising of Springfield, Missouri, observes:

"Serendipity may provide us with the answer to a problem. Or, is that ancestor begging to be found?

Some time ago, I sat down next to a woman at a microfilm machine. She immediately said, 'I hope you have as much luck as I'm having.' For those new to the field, in genealogical terms that meant, 'Please let me tell you what I found.' She was looking for a great-grandfather on the 1860 census of Madison County, Georgia. She said she had been looking for him for years with no success. But she wanted to try once more. She rented the reel of microfilm containing Madison County, and started at the beginning. Eureka! She found him! There was no doubt that she had the right man as he had an unusual name, was the right age, and his twin brother was with him.

BUT, the county she was searching was not Madison but Macon, which had been placed on the microfilm reel ahead of Madison. For those of you unfamiliar with Georgia, Madison County is in the northeast section near the South Carolina border, and Macon is in the south central near Alabama!

Was that an ancestor shouting, 'Look! Here I am'??"

Margery W. Shaw of Evansville, Indiana, wrote:

"My maiden name is Schlamp, and I have rather complete information on six generations of Schlamps in Vanderburgh County, Indiana, but have never been able to hop across the ocean and discover the Schlamp German ancestral village. Naturalization, church, and census records all give 'Hesse-Darmstadt' as the place of origin: that's like finding the 'state' without a clue as to the county, city, town, or village.

One day at Willard Library in my hometown of Evansville, Indiana, I studied a microfilm on the records of St. Johannes Evangelical Church, long extinct. I have found a Phillip Jacob Schauss, son of Jacob Schauss and Dorothea (Schlamp) Schauss, baptized in 1821 in Wonsheim, Kreis Alzey, Hesse-Darmstadt! For the first time, I had the name of a German village where a Schlamp had resided.

I traipsed to the local LDS Family History Library and looked on the microfiche index to discover several microfilm numbers listed for Wonsheim, which I ordered. Three weeks later, I sat down at a microfilm reader to peruse the first film. I quickly spun the handle and stopped on a page early in the reel, only to look down and find three Schlamp surnames staring at me. I carefully recorded all of the Schlamp data on the film and rewound it to record the exact titles and records and microfilm number I was copying. Lo and behold, I was reading the Evangelische Kirche records of *Wollstein*, not *Wonsheim*!

Checking the microfilm index again, I discovered that Wollstein immediately preceded Wonsheim in the alphabetical listing, and I had miscopied and ordered a microfilm number from the line above Wonsheim. It is easy to understand my mistake. It is not so easy to explain why the mistaken records were the ones I needed - but did not know I was looking for!"

Shirley York Anderson of McFarland, Wisconsin, reflects:
"It isn't often that I chuckle reading a genealogy book, but I sure did with *Psychic Roots*. Thank you for the fun and insights. I agree with you that there is something more happening than just good research techniques, although it is difficult sometimes to tell the difference. The elation from success is just as real for either cause.

I have two rather elusive ancestors with unusual first names, Waffe Rand and Partridge Richardson. Although they should stand out, I was having difficulty finding them in the records. Except for both names beginning with 'R', there was no connection between the two (one was the gg grandfather of my maternal grandmother, and the other was the gg grandfather of my maternal grandfather). The only locations I had for Waffe Rand were his baptism and possible first marriage in Sussex Co., MA, and his

Revolutionary war service from Worcester Co. The birth and marriage of Partridge Richardson are recorded in Middlesex Co., MA and his later children were born in Saco, ME - but I didn't know where he was in between. After much digging, I found that one of his son's birthplace was given as Salem, MA in Essex Co.

I decided to check Essex Co. Land Records for Partridge to see if he had owned any land in Salem. He hadn't. But the film that had the Richardson portion of the index also covered Rand. And there was Waffe Rand, buying and selling property in Beverly. The Beverly VR, which I would have never thought to check for him, provided me with more details on his children and with the death of his second wife."

Ruth Merriman of South Jordan, Utah, writes:

"I work as a librarian at the Family History Library in Salt Lake City. I was helping my sister-in-law with her genealogy years ago. She is part Chippewa, and I was searching the Indian census rolls from the White Earth Indian Reservation in Minnesota. Because the census takers spelled the names phonetically, it was hard to find names spelled the same way twice. Besides that, you had to practically sound them out to figure out what the census taker had actually heard. The names appeared like this: 'Oooh-be-tay-quay,' etc.

I was beginning to despair of ever finding her ancestor, a minor chief named 'White Cloud' whose Chippewa name I didn't know. I *did* know his wife's English name. As the microfilm rolled in front of me, I became very sleepy and eventually passed out. I awoke with a start, saw the film continuing to roll, and stopped it immediately. There on the very frame where I stopped was 'Wah-bon-ah-quod' (White Cloud) and his entire family!"

Roberta Wagner Berman of La Jolla, California, had two stories that occurred while using microfilm:

"I was in the Family History Library viewing a microfilm of vital records for the town of Lomza, Poland searching for the Wapniewski family. I went through the entire film. While I was rewinding, I stopped three times.

Each time I stopped, I looked up at the screen and discovered a record I had missed. A careful recheck of the microfilm revealed no further records on this family.

A few weeks later at the Federal Archives in Laguna Niguel, I wanted to find a family in the 1910 census for New York City (Manhattan). These records are not soundexed, but I did have an address. There are fifty-three microfilms covering Manhattan, so I decided to pick one at random to see if I could figure out how the addresses work and hopefully find the correct film without having to look through all fifty-three. The film I picked at random was the correct one."

HMMM. THERE SEEMS TO BE A PATTERN HERE!

5
SERENDIPITIES & SYNCHRONICITIES: SOME CLASSICS

I wasn't even looking for Aunt Tillie, but there she was ... in a record where she shouldn't have been! I just sort of tripped over her while researching an entirely different line!"
(A comment guaranteed to be overheard with regularity at any genealogical gathering)

That remark is "old news" to any seasoned family historian. To paraphrase my old friend, the late Dr. Kenn Stryker-Rodda, almost as many genealogical cases are solved by serendipitous discoveries as by rational thinking! Proof positive of this is the quantity and quality of such experiences that were contributed for this sequel to *Psychic Roots*.

A classic example of such an event was sent in by Charlotte Megill Hix of Mill Neck, New York, who then added some reflections on this entire area:

"I had spent years looking for proof of an old family tradition that said that my great-great-grandmother, Widow Elizabeth Johnson, was the mother of Sophia (Johnson) Vanderbilt, wife of Commodore Cornelius Vanderbilt. One day in the Staten Island Institute while looking for an entirely different family, as I was browsing through other books, my proof literally jumped off the page at me - proving the old family tradition!

I have never really thought too much about serendipity and intuition, but reading your fascinating book has made me think about it. I have known for years that things happen for reasons unknown to us. My family always said that my mother had ESP, and believe me, I didn't get away with very much while growing up. She always seemed to know what I was doing and with whom.

My spur of the moment purchase of your book has led me to some very interesting *rethinking* of my genealogical experiences."

Linda Stufflebean of Alta Loma, California, can relate to Charlotte's experience:

"I was at the Los Angeles LDS Library looking at Arkansas records for information on the Hamby family. They had nothing whatsoever to do with the Sturgell family of Missouri, Ohio and Virginia, whom I had been studying for a long time.

After twelve years of getting nowhere, I stumbled on the third marriage of my Isaac Sturgell in Pope County, Arkansas while looking in the records there for the unrelated Hambys!

There is no way to explain it."

Jennie Howe of Gloucester Point, Virginia, recounted:

"It was only after all four of our family had graduated from Virginia Tech that we finally checked out the historical 'Howe House' at nearby Claytor Lake. Hoping to find some information that might connect it to my husband's Howe ancestors, we were very surprised to find that it was my *Hite* grandmother who was connected to Howe House, not his family at all. A double treat was to learn that the old house was also linked to the family who had recently purchased my grandparents' homeplace two hundred miles away!"

My "kindred spirit," Jane Fletcher Fiske of Boxford, Massachusetts, contributes:

"One morning about fifteen years ago, I went to the Library at Providence College, where the Rhode Island Court Records were then stored, to try to find some information for my book, *Thomas Cooke of Rhode Island*, which was published in 1987. The records, in large cardboard cartons, were not quite in complete disarray, but close to it. It was quickly apparent that I would never find anything I was looking for, so I gave up on Cooks. The archivist was willing for me to browse, however, so I picked out a box that had records from the 1750s, sat down, and pulled out one of the tightly folded cases.

As I opened it up and began to read, I discovered that inside was a copy of the will of my ancestor Gov. Henry Bull of Newport, who died in 1694. This copy had been made as evidence in a court case in 1755. The officially recorded copy of the will, in the Newport Town Council & Probate volumes, was lost in 1779 with many other Newport records that had been carried away by the British in a ship that ran aground in New York Harbor - Austin, the authority on early Rhode Island, wrote in his *Genealogical Dictionary of Rhode Island* (1887) that there had been references to a will left by Gov. Henry Bull, 'but a copy has never been found.'

Today, I have a book of over 1100 abstracts of Newport court files nearly ready for publication, and certainly the inspiration for all the work which has gone into it came from that serendipitous discovery the first time I dipped into the records at Providence College."

Donna Porter's experience happened when she was doing client work:

"On 21 August, 1993, I was in the Family History Library in Salt Lake City working on a client's line - the Hinds family of Jennings County, Indiana. In a book of will abstracts for that county, I noted one entry indexed for a Hinds on a particular page. When I turned to the page and perused it, I studied it several times, but no Hinds was to be found.

But what I did find was data on the estate of Henry Kyle Sr. who died in 1849, administered by Abraham Showalter and John Kyle. I was taken aback, because I had been looking for the parents of my ancestor Henry Kile for the past thirty years. My Henry died in Franklin County, Indiana in 1865, and among my granduncles were John Kile and Abraham Showalter. I left my client's work to pursue this some more, and found much in Jennings, Franklin, and neighboring Ripley County records on the Kiles!

I had found my great-great-grandfather! It just goes to prove something that I had known all along: that counties surrounding those our ancestors lived in should be investigated for genealogical material also."

A serendipitous find doesn't necessarily have to be momentous and earthshaking. "Eurekas" are not always necessary. Frederick E. Bitting of Fair Haven, Vermont, was simply browsing through a newspaper:

"I always stay at my brother's home in Lansdale, Pennsylvania while doing research in that area. I had spent many visits there, unsuccessfully trying to connect my great-grandfather Edmund Thomas Bitting, to the emigrant ancestor of 1723, Henrich Bitting.

On one particular trip, the evening before I returned home, I picked up the local paper while waiting for my brother to complete whatever he was doing. I flipped over the few pages of the paper and, as I started to turn to the last page to fold it and put it away, a small ad at the top of the page caught my eye: 'The will of Edmund Alexander Bitting will be probated ....' The name 'Edmund' stopped me, as my great-grandfather was so-named, I have an uncle 'Edmund,' and my own middle name is 'Edmund.'

Serendipitously running across this notice eventually led me to my long-sought-for relations. I located the survivors noted in the will, established our connection as cousins, and was able to track down the old Bitting Family Bible going back to 1817.

All because I happened to glance through a local newspaper while waiting for my brother!"

Good grief! Someone even tripped over *me* serendipitously! Shirley Beaton of Iroquois Falls, Ontario, confided:

"I had written several letters trying to reach you to obtain your *The Palatine Families of Ireland*. Each time my letters were returned because of insufficient address.

On Friday January 6, 1995, I was watching "Unsolved Mysteries" when the program mentioned a genealogist by the name of Hank Jones and referred to German refugees who went to Ireland. I was sure, at long last, I had found you - the same man I had been trying for so long to find."

Sometimes the discovery of an old family treasure can bring forth an amazing story. Elizabeth Burrelle-Fowler of Sherman Oaks, California, related:

"I have always been interested in genealogy, but, for the first part of my life, I pursued a career as an actress/model and put family history aside. The only relative who really knew all the family lore was my maternal grandmother, Mable Sweyer Jones. I must have mentioned to my Grandma that at some time in the future I would work on our family tree, but, tragically, she died before we could ever discuss what she knew.

Years later, I was injured on a set and had to stop working to recuperate. With so much time on my hands, I finally started my research. And oh how I longed to speak to Grandma Jones! Sometimes, when I was particularly frustrated, I would pray to her and ask her for help. She seemed to answer me, and I felt her presence strongly.

Last Christmas, I visited my favorite cousin who, on Grandma Jones' death, got a chest of old family photos that had belonged to her. Until I started doing interviews with family members (very important!), I hadn't even known those photos existed. I had thought that my cousin was just going to let me see the photos, but, when I arrived, they *gave* them to me for Christmas! I was practically shaking when we pulled out the old chest to open it. It was aged brown heavyduty cardboard with a cloth strap around it, and a musty smell clung to it. It was beautiful to me! We lifted the lid and began pulling out unbelievably old photos, some dating back to the mid-1800's.

But, then, something very unusual happened! I pulled out one of the larger ones and turned it over, and there on the back - written in *MY* HANDWRITING - was the name of our ancestor. "Hey," I said to my cousins, "This is *MY* handwriting. How ...?" I started lifting other photos out of the box and, on over half of them, my distinctive scrawl told us who we were viewing. I was speechless! I sat there stunned, while I tried to figure it out.

Finally, I had a vague recollection of visiting Grandma Jones a couple of years before her death. I had been working in New York on a soap opera and had flown over to Erie, Pennsylvania to see her. While relaxing in the parlor on a cold afternoon, she told me that her eyesight wasn't as good as it once was. Grandma noticed how big and legible my handwriting was and asked me to write certain names she would give me on the back of the photos - which she would hand me, almost secretively, 'backside up.' I was rather bored with my task, but dutifully did as she requested. I must have suffered from a deplorable lack of curiosity, because I never once turned the photos over. What an idiot! That would have been the perfect time to ask all the questions I had. But I didn't.

By the time I finally saw those old pictures, I was the only one in the family who knew where all those people in the photos belonged on the family tree. And, other than Grandma Jones' small writing, mine is the only other handwriting on the pictures. It's as if they were always meant to end up in my possession. So, in a round-about way, she has ended up sharing her treasures with me anyway."

Another good photo story was submitted by Annette M. Havranek of Rolling Meadows, Illinois:

"My grand-uncle, my grandmother's only brother, Joseph H. McCarthy, was a Sergeant in the Army for 25 years, beginning in 1918. Most of that time, he was stationed at Fort Sheridan, Illinois. After I started doing research, my husband and I said we'd have to visit the museum at Fort Sheridan to see where Uncle Joe had spent so many years. Many times we planned to go, but something always came up to prevent us from making the trip.

One Saturday morning, we decided, 'Why not go to Fort Sheridan today?' So we did. The museum was not too large, a couple of rooms re-capping its history from the beginning. Guns, swords, uniforms, and miscellaneous war items were everywhere, and, of course, pictures of the men and women who had been stationed there. Remember, this was an old fort, and tens of thousands had made it their home over the many decades. After browsing through some rooms, I noted there was one last cabinet set back in a corner I had better look at, because it was time to leave.

In that last cabinet was a picture of my Uncle Joe, in his baker's hat, taken with the rest of his unit! I was so surprised and very pleased and astonished. Out of all the people to pass through the fort those many years ... there he was!

Joseph H. McCarthy (3rd row, 5th from left, with his baker's hat on) & his unit at Fort Sheridan, 1934

We asked the curator if we could get a copy of this new-found photo in the case and told him how unusual we thought this find was. He told us that it was even a weirder coincidence than we knew: every two months, the pictures were changed. Chances of this happening again were next to none. It was a good thing we hadn't gone earlier and those other trips were cancelled, because we never would have encountered Uncle Joe's photo.

Uncle Joe was kind of a loner and very reserved, never getting or wanting much attention - or so I thought. Well, he sure got our attention that day! It was an experience I won't soon forget!"

Susan Droege of Germantown, New York, sent along a clipping from a column by Wes Keeler in *The Independent*, Columbia County, New York, dated March 31, 1994, which tells an equally unusual tale:

"Years ago, Mary LeBrecht of Hartsdale, New York, accompanied her husband on a Midwest sales trip. As she was browsing through a thrift shop in Peoria, Illinois, she found an interesting old Family Bible printed in 1833 which once had belonged to one Orin Doty. Although not related to the family, for some reason Mrs. LeBrecht purchased the old book. She always had been fascinated with old books and thought perhaps the Bible might find its way back to the Doty family.

She eventually gave the Bible to her daughter, Lindsay LeBrecht, who, when she left home at the age of 19, inadvertently took the Bible with her. In the next twenty years, Lindsay moved seven times, and the Bible went with her every move.

It was on her bookshelf when a miracle occurred. Lindsay was doing sales work for a manufacturer of mountaineering equipment when she received a telephone call from Sgt. Dale Doty of the Tulare County, California Sheriff's Department, who wanted to buy some rope for a search and rescue unit. When Sgt. Doty spelled his name for her, Lindsay immediately thought of the old Bible. She told Sgt. Doty about it, and - sure enough - his grandparents had come from Peoria.

'This is really bizarre, but I think I have your Family Bible,' she told him. She agreed to send it to him. The Dotys used the Bible to establish their descent from Edward Doty, a native of England who arrived in Plymouth Colony in 1620 on the *Mayflower*. The entire episode was a classic example of coincidence and 'good timing': Sgt. Dale Doty was making the purchase call for someone else who normally took care of such matters. And Lindsay LeBrecht took the Doty telephone call the day before she left the company for a new job.

'It was such an overwhelming feeling,' says Lindsay. 'So many things lined up like dominoes to make it all happen. I'm really happy the Dotys got their Bible back. That was my mother's intention from the first!'

Liz Kelley Kerstens of Woodbridge, Virginia, had an experience that is among my favorites of all those shared:

"In 1983, I began to redevelop an interest in genealogy. I picked up a copy of Gilbert Doane's *Searching for Your Ancestors* and read it cover to cover. It had been about four or five years since I had done any digging into my family tree. One of the suggestions in the book was to start with what you already have in your possession. Well, this posed a bit of a problem because I was in the Marine Corps and was stationed in Austin, Texas at the time. My parents had not yet entrusted me with valuable family documents to cart around from duty station to duty station.

What I did have with me was my post card collection that my mother had started for me when I was six or seven years old. Over the years, I had amassed a sizable collection of post cards (about three or four thousand, but I've stopped counting). I decided to look through the post cards to see if there were any clues to my family. I remembered that the post cards that my mother had started my collection with were very old and were from my grandmother and other family members.

After digging through endless piles, I came to a post card that seemed rather thick. Upon closer inspection, I found it was actually two post cards stuck together. I gently pulled them apart, and a folded piece of paper fell out. The paper turned out to be the original marriage certificate of my great-great-grandparents Jesse Cook and Deborah

To all whom these presents may come—

I George E. Tiffin one of the Justices of the Peace of the County of Monmouth do hereby certify that I have this day joined Jesse Cook and Deborah M. Tallman in the holy bands of Matrimony.

Given under my hand and seal this 21st day of May in the year of our Lord one thousand eight hundred and forty eight

George E. Tiffin Justice

The marriage certificate of Jesse Cook & Deborah M. Tallman, 1848

Mahala Tallman from 1848! The paper was in perfect condition, with just a couple of minor stains. It also had an original paper seal attached. I have since found verification of this event in several places, including the *Monmouth County (NJ) Marriage Records, Book D.*

What a start for my genealogical quest! I have always felt that my ancestors were watching over me that day and guided me to that marriage certificate. More amazing, is that those postcards had traveled with me from duty station to duty station and had been handled and sorted since my childhood. And yet the certificate was in near perfect condition when I found it! I've always wondered how the certificate got there in the first place."

I like John L. Scherer's story too:

"My great-grandfather, James T. Betts (1869 - 1944) was a professional photographer. I tried to assemble a collection of his photographs, but realized that many that 'should have been there' were still missing.

In March of 1993 in my capacity as a curator of decorative arts, I acquired a tiger maple chest of drawers in an old antique shop in Saratoga Springs, New York. After loading the chest on the moving truck, I decided to take a look around the shop to see what else might be of interest. I let out a whoop when I spotted a photograph of my grandmother, Mabel Betts (1893 - 1964), in an old frame. I immediately purchased it for one dollar. It was so strange to suddenly come upon my grandmother looking out at me from that framed photograph - what are the odds of that?

The dealer then directed me to her other shop at Hartford, New York where she thought more Betts photos might be found. Sure enough, there were stacks of them, and I bought several for one dollar. I have a hunch that my grandmother and great-grandfather did not like the idea of those unidentified photographs ending up in a dusty old antique shop. Knowing that I would be able to identify them and would treasure them, they directed me to them.

I am sure that this was no accident. It was a setup!"

We genealogists should be made to wear kneepads to protect ourselves from tripping over unexpected sources so often.

Barbara Roberts Baylis of Dallas, Texas, remembered:

"In Strafford County, New Hampshire on a research trip one year, we were working in the courthouse. It was late in the day, and as we were walking out of Probate Court we passed the file box of records to be refiled.

Much to our surprise, we found a file with the name 'Hannah Marston' on the front. We knew this lady to be the granddaughter of the man we were searching. It was if the file was calling to us. Looking through this will written some eighty years later than our search had taken us, we found Hannah to have died without issue and therefore naming all her living first cousins and their parents (the object of our search).

When we shared our experience with the clerks, they told us the file had been used that day by a title searcher."

Ruby Coleman didn't even know she'd stumbled over something important, until much later:

"Several years ago while doing research in the Family History Library in Salt Lake City, I meticulously copied cemetery records from an unindexed book. They pertained to my relatives who lived in Washington County, Virginia. Once home and putting my notes in order, I discovered that I had copied all of the Richardsons in the county. I could not imagine doing this, as I had no known connection to a Richardson family, particularly in that county.

It was over a year later that I finally secured a marriage record for my great grandparents who married in Washington County. The family records and Family Bible show that they were Fleming Mays and Deborah Denton, who were married on 8 August 1861. And I found out it was a second marriage for both of them: she was married previously to a Richardson and had had one child before his death.

There it was: RICHARDSON! What a shock to see that surname on the old marriage record and remember how I had copied all who bore the surname from the cemetery listings - even though I was unaware I had any relationship to that family!"

Joyce M. Tice of Marathon, New York, had a "triple-whammy" happen to her:

"In May of 1992, I went to the Historical Society in the county in Pennsylvania where all of my father's ancestors settled and in which my parents still live. One pair of my great-great-grandparents are Joseph W. Holly and Mary Wood. (Joe was always special to me: he died 11 August, 1894, fifty years to the day before I was born on 11 August 1944). In the file in the society was a four-year-old letter from a woman named Alice Ellingsberg of Fargo, North Dakota, who said she had Joe Holly's 1880 diary.

With my heart in my throat, fearing someone else had claimed it first, I called her in Fargo. She still had the old diary: she had found it several years before when she and her father were cleaning out the old house her grandmother had lived in prior to its demolition. Just before leaving the old home for the last time, she went back to say goodbye to the house. Up in the attic, she found the little diary lying on the floor and, fortunately, had recognized its value. I went to Fargo, met Alice, and was able to read the diary from cover to cover.

On the weekend I came back from Fargo, my parents made an unusual discovery. They lived in the home that once belonged to Joe Holly. It had been gutted for remodeling in the time they've had it, so it's very difficult to think that there could be anything in the house they would not know about. But that same weekend they found the 1912 diary of my grandfather Tice on the banister upstairs. My father had never seen it before and had no idea it existed. There is not to this day any explanation of how it got there.

In the meantime, I had become friends with another woman, a cousin on my Wood line, who is also working on the genealogy of the area. It is a small rural township, and, as we have discovered, nearly everyone is related. Within the last few months, her cousin found the 1946 to 1950 diary of their grandmother, Carrie McConnell Beardslee.

Now we have three diaries from the neighborhood. The interesting thing is that all three of these people lived at one time or other in the *same* house. They are not related to each other except through marriage though all are related to me."

Serendipitous events often are also synchronistic. This term, coined by Dr. Carl Jung, refers to seemingly unrelated coincidences which have special meaning to the person who experiences them. I love these occurrences the most. They sometimes celebrate the pure wackiness of the Universe! Witness a story from my friend, Nick Vine Hall of Albert Park, Australia:

"I have experienced an event of syncronicity against odds that would be hard to lengthen. About 1965, on my way home from the office in the evening, I was sitting on Wynyard railway station in Sydney, waiting for my usual train. Sydney at that time would have been a city of three million people.

I looked up and saw an old school friend approaching, whom I hadn't seen for years. His name was 'Huntley Gordon.' Then, out of the corner of my eye, I saw another acquaintance, whom I vaguely knew from somewhere in my distant past, named 'Gordon Huntley.'

I waited until they passed the spot where I was sitting, both exactly in line with my seat, then I sprang up and said, 'Huntley Gordon, meet Gordon Huntley!'

How about that!!?? That *has* to be longer odds than there are stars in the sky!"

Dr. William B. Saxbe has a similar tale involving a name:

"I spent my Christmas vacation in 1968 working at the Albert Schweitzer Hospital in Haiti. My 90-mile trip into Port-au-Prince at the end of that two weeks took me south along the coast. It was a perfect tropical day, in brilliant sunlight, with spectacular vistas of the ocean, the mountains, and the coastal plain with its plantations and villages. Suddenly, I had a superimposed - and totally incongruous - mental image of the Red Hand of Ulster.

Let me explain what that is, but first state that I am not given to visions, that I have no known family connection with Ulster, and - beyond having read the legend some years before - that I had no great knowledge of, interest in, or recent exposure to Irish mythology. The Red Hand of Ulster is the device on the field of the flag of the Irish province of Ulster: a red hand set in a yellow hexagon. It commemorates the bloody deed of one Hugh O'Neill, legendary founder of the ruling dynasty of the province. He was challenged to a footrace, the winner to become king. He soon fell behind, and it became apparent that his opponent had supernatural help. Hugh was about to be beaten when he stopped, drew his sword, and cut off his hand. He threw his severed hand across the finish line (different rules then!) and won.

Well, I recognized the hand and the hexagon when they appeared in my mind's eye, but was completely unable to explain their momentary presence. I thought no more about it, rode on into town, checked in at my hotel, and was soon sitting beside the pool with a rum punch. Seated next to me was an American couple in their forties, just arrived there on holiday, who were 'thee' -ing and 'thou' -ing each other. I surmised that they were Quakers, and we soon fell into conversation. They were from Philadelphia, as had been their forbears for a couple of centuries, and he was a psychiatrist at the clinic there. We had a pleasant talk with each other.

On rising to leave, I introduced myself: 'I'm Bart Saxbe,' I said.

'Nice to meet you,' he replied, 'I'm Hugh O'Neill.'

How's that for uncanny?

(P.S.: He had two hands.)"

A certain name haunts Deb Boardman of Clarks Summit, Pennsylvania:

"I took over our family genealogy from my brother and quickly became obsessed. It took several years, but I finally went back one generation and was introduced to my ancestor, David Hunt. I found the large cemetery where he was buried and made an appointment with the records keeper to help me find his stone. But I arrived earlier than expected and drove down the winding roads of the cemetery while I was waiting. Amazingly, I found David's stone within a few minutes and thought this good fortune would continue. It didn't.

After exhausting all the obvious sources for information on David Hunt, I located distant relatives in other states, but they never returned my letters or calls. It got to be a joke: 'I know who is related, because they never respond!' I was desperate and frustrated, as I somehow felt a mysterious special bond with David.

But each time I seem to be at a dead end, the name 'David Hunt' keeps popping up in the strangest places:

1) I was on the phone with my mother one day while we were snowed in, and we began 'channel surfing' with the remote to break the boredom. Then 'David Hunt' appeared on tv: he's the British official in charge of employment.

2) My husband asked me if I saw David Hunt in the Sunday paper. He said he had read an article about a David Hunt doing research at the Smithsonian.

3) But the strangest one was when my husband received a letter at work from a salesman with the name of David Hunt. I contacted him and his father (also named 'David Hunt'). They were supposed to forward some Hunt information on to me, but they never did. (They must be related!)

I believe David is trying to tell me something: maybe not to give up. Come to think of it, finding information about your book was a fluke too!"

My friend Dr. Helen Hinchliff of Salt Spring Island, British Columbia, reported an uncanny synchronicity in her family. Her paternal immigrant ancestor William Hinchliff died 15 February 1899. His son William Elias Hinchliff died 19 February 1921. He had a son William (born 2 January 1892) who died young on 17 February 1893. A fourth William Hinchliff, a nephew of infant William, passed away 18 February 1994.

It's evident that something quite unusual occurred during this 101-year period from 1893 to 1994: *every* male who bore the name "William Hinchliff" died during the span of just four days. Furthermore, no other identified descendant of immigrant William Hinchliff died during the month of February. Helen tells me that this "coincidence," discovered by her first cousin Peter Hinchliff, a son of the William Hinchliff who died in 1994, enabled him to better accept his father's passing; he felt there almost seemed to be an inevitability to his demise at that certain time of the year.

While doing genealogical research, Jean Cheger of Bay City, Michigan, made a discovery of significance to herself:

"I was cast as 'Granny' in the musical 'Pippin' - shortly before I became involved in genealogy. I then found out later that I had portrayed my own ancestor!

Things like that have a mystical aspect that we can't really fathom."

Doris Powell Schultz has had unusual events occur in connection with her immediate family. Besides noticing the butterfly that landed on her father's newly-covered grave as mentioned earlier in the cemetery chapter, Doris reports:

"An alarm clock that my grandfather gave to my father stopped on the day Grandfather died, and it could never be made to run again. It helped us make a permanent record of his death date."

I've had many strange synchronicities pop up in my own life also. One of the wildest took place years ago in the mid-1960's. I had just arrived in Hollywood from the San Francisco bay area and was looking for a young-adult church group to attend. Someone told me that Roy Rogers and Dale Evans had helped organize just such an organization for young people in the entertainment industry, so I decided to go check it out.

The initial meeting took place at the old Hollywood Knickerbocker Hotel, a musty relic of the past that had seen better days and was now well past its prime. Our group met in an interior room of that ancient building that was chock-full of people when I arrived. I felt rather claustrophobic, I remember, because the room wasn't air-conditioned and had no windows for ventilation. The heavy drapes hanging from the four walls made the site seem even more oppressive. I must say, when they closed all the doors, I wanted to leave.

I'm glad I didn't! The guest of honor that night was Elmer Bernstein, the famous film composer. Bernstein was wonderful! He spent his part of the program regaling us all with marvelous stories about his life in music and demonstrated some of his compositions on an old grand piano in the room. At the climax to his talk, he announced that he "would now play a piece he wrote for the score of Cecil B. DeMille's classic movie *The Ten Commandments*." It was the beautifully majestic theme that was used whenever God was spoken of in the film.

The *very* moment his hands touched the piano keyboard something amazing happened. That closed room came alive! A whoosh of air from nowhere rushed through the entire facility, as the heavy drapes against the walls billowed forth and flapped wildly. This intense burst of energy continued on for a good fifteen or twenty seconds. And just as suddenly as it started, it stopped. In an instant, it was over.

There was a silence from the crowd that you could cut with a knife. And then, someone in the back row chuckled. Soon the room was filled was cascades of laughter as we all began to appreciate what had transpired.

"God's Theme" indeed!

Yes, synchronicities rear their lovely heads often. My daughter Amanda Jones has figured in several. She's now in her early twenties and always has been quite instinctual, very in tune with her sixth sense. A correspondent on the Palatine Wager family, Steve Spicer of Gary, Indiana, sent me an ancestor chart recently. Lo and behold, one of his relatives was named Amanda Jones (1835-1914), author of the groundbreaking *A Psychic Autobiography*, published in 1908. She was a real pioneer in the field, writing for *Harpers, Atlantic Monthly,* and *The Century*. And her father was named ... (gulp) "*Henry Jones!*"

But if synchronicities are "coincidences that have meaning to the person who experiences them," then the "Amanda Jones" synchronistic pattern continues. I recently received a big batch of viewer mail forwarded on to me from "*Unsolved Mysteries*" regarding the *Psychic Roots* episode. It was accompanied by a nice note from the young woman in charge of coordinating and cataloguing all the mail response to the program.

Her name was (you guessed it!) ...

"Amanda Jones!"

Sherry Suib Cohen touches on all this in her excellent article "Miracle Alert," in the March 1996 issue of *New Woman Magazine* and in her forthcoming book, *Looking for the Other Side: A Skeptic's Odyssey*:

"Why is it that we just happen to meet the people we meet just when we need to meet them? Why is it that we find the article on Ireland just when we've been thinking about going to Ireland? Why is it that Christopher Reeve portrayed a paralyzed cop in a movie - actually learned how to *be* a paralyzed person - just before the riding accident that paralyzed him?

Is it possible that there's a sort of universal plan behind all of these 'accidental coincidences?' Synchronicity shows us that there is a higher intelligence at work, a plan, a poetry to the universe.

Now, more than three decades after Carl Jung's death, quantum physics offers scientific evidence for synchronicity. Research by physicists like David Bohm points to everything being a seamless extension of everything else.

If everything in the universe - past, present, and future - is indeed connected by some force, E.S.P. and synchronicity start to seem logical."

And on it goes. Dorothy Hall of Prescott, Arizona writes:

"My husband was born and raised in Texas, and I in Kentucky. We met at a neighbor's house during World War II. Even though we had very few dates before Harry went overseas, it seemed instant compatibility and love - a feeling that remains after forty-eight years of marriage. Perhaps, if I am to believe your book, there is a reason.

I had often envied the fact that my husband's mother and other relatives had done extensive research on their family, one line going back to Col. Richard Lee of Virginia in the 1600's. I started late in genealogy, but in three short years I have been able to trace and document most of my mother's line back ten generations. I have found that members of my grandmother's Brumley line lived in the same Virginia counties in the 1600's where my husband's ancestors lived. Some of the Brumley documents and wills were witnessed by these same Lees. Furthermore, one of my husband's great-grandfathers, Col. Thomas Lee's sister, Leticia Lee, married a Col. James Ball, who became the guardian of my great-great-great-grandmother Susanna Holloway.

What an amazing coincidence that a boy from Texas and a girl from Kentucky married, only to find out forty-eight years later that their ancestors were acquaintances and neighbors three hundred years ago!"

Elaine Moss of Oconto, Wisconsin, had a synchronistic experience:

"For quite some time, I had been searching for the ancestors of my great-great-grandmother, Mary Ann Shaw Eble. Her father's birthplace was listed as Pennsylvania in the 1850 census, so I started writing to various historical societies in that state in the hopes of finding those ever-elusive forebears.

Before I go to sleep at night, I 'program' myself to dream of one certain ancestor. Needless-to-say, Mary Ann is almost always on my mind. One night, at the point where I had almost drifted off to sleep, I smelled the over-powering fragrance of roses. I woke up my husband to ask if he smelled it. He replied, 'No' (and probably wondered what on earth I was talking about). I chalked it up to a freak incident, but remember thinking that perhaps Mary Ann had liked to wear rose-water fragrance.

The next day in the mail, I received a reply from the Monroe County Historical Society in Stroudsburg, Pennsylvania. And enclosed in their material was the genealogy of Winnefred *Rose*, the great-great-grandmother of my Mary Ann Shaw! I was both stunned and thrilled! It became perfectly clear to me at that point that the smell of roses was the foretelling of a wonderful event. It also was fascinating that Winnefred Rose was Mary Ann's great-great-grandmother, and Mary Ann is *my* great-great-grandmother!

I've since documented Winnefred Rose back to a family of early New Amsterdam: she was baptized Wyntje Roosa there and assumed the name Winnefred Rose in 'Pennsylvania. Since then, there have been many other 'psychic' events in my research. I often go on 'feeling' more than anything else, and the proof always shows up later!"

Kathryn L. Burgess of Old Chatham, New York, tells a lovely tale:

"I agree with you and many of the contributors to your book that we are frequently led or misled, according to what our guiding spirits want us to find. I had been looking for the English home of my Ingraham family for many years, to no avail. My husband and I are inveterate tourists, and on one trip, we decided to go to the Cotswolds in England. He gave me a choice of three places to stay, so I said 'Moreton-in-Marsh,' and began to research the area.

In a local secondhand bookshop, I came upon a copy of 'Highways & Byways in Shakespeare Country,' which sounded good and the price was right. I took it home and began to read. On page 7, there was a description of the church at Great Wolford, going on to describe how the Ingram family was enfeoffed in Little Wolford, 'antiently,' being granted use of the land by the Barons of Stafford ca. 1202! Here was a travel book I'd bought to learn about the countryside, and found an ancient seat of the very family I had been looking for in every other place!

Well, we flew to Heathrow, picked up the car and drove to Moreton-in-Marsh, arriving in mid-afternoon, tired out from the flight and the long drive. It was cloudy and cool, so we decided on a nap before touring the village. When we awoke, an hour or so later, and threw back the curtains, there was a beautiful rainbow!

Next morning we drove out to Great Wolford to the church. In the first row of stones in the churchyard there were all members of a family called 'Rainbow!' Inside, we found the stone in the floor of Hastings/Hastang Ingraham, with the family arms displayed on it. What an exciting thing to find! In the village, they sold us a large sheet of paper and crayons to make a rubbing, which I still have.

After a trip to the manor house to learn more of the family history, our journey continued. As we drove back to spend the night at Oxford on our way to Heathrow and the flight home, all we saw in front of us on the trip, one after the other, were a series of rainbows, all the way!

I'm delighted with your book, because so many people find the magic of working with genealogy, and need reassurance that it isn't always just in their heads!"

THERE *IS* A MAGIC TO GENEALOGY, ISN'T THERE??!!

6
TALK ABOUT TIMING!

"Being in the right place at the right time is an important part of genealogy!" notes my old friend Schuyler Brossman of Rehrersburg, Pennsylvania.

But often *we're* not in control of the timing! It's almost as if we were all actors in some divine play - not really in control of our own destiny - moved around on stage by the whim of an unseen director. And let me tell you: judging from all the new "off the wall" experiences coming in, that celestial director - the Great God of Genealogy - has a pretty good sense of humor!

Talk about timing! Ernest Thode reflects:

"I have been the Local History and Genealogy Librarian at the Washington County Public Library in Marietta, Ohio since August 1992. Last Saturday, August 14th, a local patron came in looking for records of an obscure cemetery in Washington County called 'God's Knob' or 'Knob' or 'Point Pleasant' or 'Gobbler's Knob.' A few minutes later, in came some people from Martins Ferry, Ohio, about 70 miles away, looking for the same cemetery!

At the same time, a Mrs. Lois Turney from Chesapeake, Virginia came in to do research on her Finch and Perdew lines. But her husband was suddenly taken ill and had to go into intensive care in the local hospital, so she was in and out of the library during visiting times. That same afternoon, in came Tommy Perdew of Belpre, Ohio, familiar with all her local families. They exchanged ancestor charts and visited the previously unknown cemetery where some of her ancestors are buried.

And if that is not enough, in came our local Civil War historian, Jerry Devol, with only four of his Finch index cards out of the many thousands in his files. They were for the very Finches that Mrs. Turney was researching. Why did he bring precisely those four cards on that day?

These three 'coincidences' all occurred in one afternoon, within about fifteen minutes. But this does not seem at all unusual to me: just another day at the office! When I first started work at the library, I was struck by the number of serendipities. Now I just accept them and 'go with the flow.' Surely something remarkable is going on, and I don't presume to know what it is. I am a pragmatist: I don't care what it is, but if it works, for goodness sakes, let's use it!"

Ernie had another incident involving Jerry Devol happen along these lines:

"One afternoon, Jerry Devol was in our Washington County Ohio Public Library doing research on Civil War soldiers and local history, and in came his distant cousin Howard Jones from Louisiana who was working on resolving his Devol and other New England lines. No big coincidence here - just two separate Devol researchers.

Another Devol cousin, Mrs. Van Morris, then arrived with her husband. They were from Clarington - about 45 miles from the library. (Incidentally, Van Morris was my wife's high school band instructor.) Three - now that's a coincidence.

Then in came a young woman with a pre-school daughter wanting to see about having some old photographs identified. This is right up Jerry Devol's alley - he is a postcard, stamp, and photograph collector - so I introduced her to Jerry. She said, 'My maiden name was Devol!'

Four Devol researchers in one little library at once - for separate reasons. Nothing unusual here - just another day at the office."

John T. Humphrey of Washington, D. C., commented:

"I really enjoyed reading *Psychic Roots*, and it occurred to me that maybe I should add to your, I am certain, accelerating 'cache' of evidence. I have experienced many of the same things that you and others speak of in your book: letters suddenly arriving from two or more people in different parts of the country looking for or providing information on families I have not worked on in years.

One experience that sticks in my mind was a trip I made many years ago to the Monroe County, Pennsylvania Historical Society in Stroudsburg, which is about 250 miles from my home in Washington, D. C. It was a hot summer Sunday, and the only other person researching at the Society that day was a young man who had also travelled about 300 miles to do some work. I was doing some additional research on Nicholas Muffley, who had arrived in Philadelphia in 1737. The other gentleman that day was working on his ancestor, Christian Jakey, who arrived on the same day in Philadelphia. In fact, Christian Jakey, listed as 'Cresten Yaki,' signed the oath list immediately after my ancestor Nicholas Muffley.

Fortunately for me, this gentleman had information on the Swiss origins of both of these families!"

Donna Valley Russell, from New Market, Maryland - one of my favorite fellow Fellows - recalls:

"My husband George and I were in Portsmouth, New Hampshire for a meeting of the American Society of Genealogists on 17 October 1993. At our business meeting, the Donald Lines Jacobus Award for an excellent compiled genealogy published in the previous five years was awarded to *The Ancestry of Emily Jane Angell*, by Dean Crawford Smith and Melinde Lutz Sanborn.

After lunch, George, Tim Beard, and I were wandering around town, and Tim, being a librarian, wanted to visit the local library there. While he talked to the librarian, I wandered over to a group of about 50 file card drawers and pulled out one at random.

I opened it to a card which was for the book we had awarded two hours earlier."

And, as we've seen, sometimes the darnedest things can happen at a cemetery while doing research. Schuyler Brossman relates:

"Doris Seirer from Washington State learned that her ancestor, Jacob Seirer, lived in Tulpehocken Township, Berks County, Pennsylvania. Although she didn't know anyone in the area, she decided she would make the long trip and see if she could find his grave.

It just happened that I was in the old part of the cemetery, putting flags on veterans' graves for Memorial Day, when she came walking down the path and asked, 'Do you know where Jacob Seirer is buried?' I told her, 'Right here!' - for, unbeknownst to her after coming that long distance from Washington to Pennsylvania, she had walked to within 20 or 30 feet of his grave.

If I had not been in the cemetery, she never would have found it, for she could not read German (and no one else in town is interested in such things). Also, if she had come fifteen minutes later, or fifteen minutes earlier - she would have missed me. But the real payoff was when I told her, 'Would you believe it - *I'm* a descendant of Jacob Seirer also!!'"

Edwin C. Dunn adds this to our collection of cemetery lore:

"In 1920 in the rural North Carolina neighborhood where my maternal grandfather lived, a cotton gin boiler exploded one October morning, killing six men, including one of my uncles and great uncles. In 1991, I was visiting in North Carolina from my home in New Mexico when I decided to drive the approximately forty miles from where I was staying to visit the cemetery where the two men were buried along with many others of my late mother's family.

I was copying inscriptions all alone in the rural cemetery when a car drove up with three women who got out and walked to a spot in the back of the cemetery. After a few minutes, I had worked my way around, and they had started back in my direction towards their car. We exchanged greetings, and I told them what I was doing. The older woman began to ask questions, and it turned out that she had known all of my mother's family, although it had been sixty-five years since any of them had lived in the immediate neighborhood.

Her father had been one of the men killed in the explosion, and she told me about the triple funeral of her father, my uncle, and my great uncle which had been held in the old church across the road. I had never heard about that event, and never would have, except for the chance encounter on that afternoon almost 1800 miles from my home."

Cynthia Brott Biasca of Fremont, California, can identify with just how important timing can be in tracking down our ancestors:

"Your book *Psychic Roots* has spoken to me loud and clear and demands a detailed response. For years, I have been looking for the father of my great-grandfather, Oliver Brott/Bradt. Early on in my research, I felt I needed assistance from a professional genealogist. The New York State Library had sent me a list of certified genealogists and, at random, I chose one from Rensselaerville, because I knew some Bradts had lived in Rensselaer County. Her name was Hilda Olsson, and I sent her a resume of what little we knew about Oliver Brott/Bradt.

I had a friendly response from her, stating that she only did research in Albany County; only then did I learn that Rensselaerville was *not* in Rensselaer County, but in Albany County. Discouraged by this poor start and now involved in my own research, I dropped the idea of using a professional to help me.

Six months passed, and my sisters and I were planning what were to become annual or biannual week-long genealogical trips to New York. Then, out of the blue, came a letter from Mrs. Olsson: 'Are you still looking for Oliver's father? I don't know his father, but I know his mother - she was Sally Congdon!'

By my writing to the wrong place at the right time, a wonderful serendipity had occurred!: The President of the small Rensselaerville Historical Society had been offered a box of old research notes by Charlotte Luckhurst that no one had wanted. Mrs. Olsson was one of the people who had volunteered to go through the material and catalogue it. While doing this, she happened to run across a one-sheet memo with data on my family. Even though it was six months after my initial letter, she remembered the Bradt name, and sent the information on to me.

Eventually this 'wrong place at the right time coincidence' led to my discovering an entire line of Congdons and Northups in Rhode Island and documenting nearly every last one of them."

Cynthia goes on to add:

"I, too, think I have some of the powers you describe - particularly picking up the phone and calling someone who either is about to phone me, or has some information I need (or vice-versa).

Kenneth Bradt is one of the guiding lights of Bradt family research. Many people have written him with Bradt information as they have me, and we have shared with one another. Within a few days in 1980, three people had written Ken Bradt wanting to locate long-lost cousins or, in one case, a half brother-in-law. About the same time, I had an overpowering urge to look up Bradts in the Houston telephone book. I had called one 'Brott' several years ago, but never 'Bradts.' There were four, and I chose one. He was a retired gentleman who knew little of his family except for two things: his father was Lewis, and his uncle was Leonard; and he had a half brother, long dead, and wondered if that man's wife Phoebe was still alive?

I promised to see if I could help him. Two days later, I received copies of some old letters that had been sent to Ken by a professor at MIT, one of the above correspondents looking for cousins, and one of the letters written by the man's father years ago that mentioned relatives Leonard and Lewis Bradt, who were brothers. The woman who was looking for her husband's half brother turned out to be Phoebe, and the fourth person was a cousin to all of them. At the Bradt Reunion held in 1987, all four had a joyous personal reunion.

But what made three people independently write Ken Bradt at the same time? What made me go to the phone and call a particular Bradt at that same time?"

This dovetails into what Helen L. Harriss of Pittsburgh, Pennsylvania, had to say:

"For about three years, I've been working for a client on the many branches of his family - a very early and distinguished line in the southwest part of this county. I'd visited the area where they lived and the burying grounds, etc. Then I got a research project for another client - not known to him. Her ancestor had lived next to or near his families, attended the same church, witnessed each other's wills, etc., so we are sure they knew one another.

Then last spring, I was asked to do some research for a church history on the family of one of their early rectors. They also were neighbors, also witnesses and executors of wills, etc. Yesterday, I mailed a report to a client with information on *her* ancestor - still another neighbor, also obviously closely involved; I came home from the post office, and found that the mailman had left a letter requesting help on still another resident of that little community - all there in the late 1700's, all friends; some intermarriage among their children.

Can you believe that there is not something more than chance that all of these people would contact the same researcher to find out about their ancestors who were neighbors and obviously friends 200 years ago? It has been an experience for me - a chance to learn about a whole community!"

A valuable resource would have been lost to Gwenn F. Epperson of Provo, Utah, had it not been for good timing:

"Some years ago, I had a very strange experience. While my husband and I were driving through upstate New York in search of genealogical information on my Mickel line, we passed Mickel's Grocery Store in the small town of Carlisle, New York. We decided to stop and ask the owner, George Mickel, if he had any family records.

To our surprise, Mr. Mickel said a man, also researching the Mickel family, stopped at his store many years before. The man left three pages of information on the family which Mr. Mickel kept in his safe. Only the week before we came, he had decided to destroy the records, as he was not interested in family history. However, for some strange reason, he put the material back in his safe.

He kindly gave us a photocopy of the material. At that time, I could not tie the records with my own Mickel family, because I was researching the wrong immigrant ancestor. Thanks to you, Hank, and your German researcher, Carla Mittelstaedt-Kubaseck, I later found that my Mickels or Michaels descend from the immigrants 'Johann Nicolaus Michel of Heselock and Anna Barbara Schönin of Reiskirchen aus dem Buseckertal (Buseck Valley)' who were married in the Evangelical Church at Wiesbaden, Germany on 31 January 1708. They were found on the 'Fourth

List of Poor Palatines who arrived in St. Catherines, England, 11 June 1709' and then sailed to New York.

Mr. Mickel's records follow my family from Johann Nicolaus Mickel and Anna Barbara Schönin in America down to the nineteenth century and have been very helpful in organizing my Mickel history."

Phyllis Lewellen Brose of Ramona, California, had an incident happen to her similar to the one experienced by Dr. Helen Hinchliff in *Psychic Roots:*

"In 1992, my husband and I decided to take our family vacation in Colorado. I had a lingering wish to know more about my family history, particularly my Pool/Poole line, My great-grandfather was William Howard Pool, a wagonwright and blacksmith in Boulder in the 1880's.

We visited the museum of the Boulder Historical Society, where I was able to drop off some Poole family photos to add to their collections. The director was most appreciative of this and then took me around the corner to the museum's newest exhibit, saying, '*Look* at *this!*' Its centerpiece was a large photo of five men standing in the doorway of 'W. H. Pool's Wagon Shop.' And there, right in the middle of that old photo, was my great-grandfather, William H. Pool.

The director looked astonished as he explained, 'We have over 110,000 pictures in our collection. I plan these exhibits months in advance, and picked this one for today's exhibit a long time ago. I didn't think about putting this particular photo up until this morning, and here *you* are! If you would have come yesterday, you wouldn't have seen it!'

That was day one and my first lesson in what it is like to dig into one's family history. It catapulted me on a genealogical journey that has been more exciting than any ride even Disneyland could come up with! In the last three years, I have had so many similar 'coincidences' that I now almost take them for granted - but each one is a new, refreshing surprise. I know that my successes are the result of quite a bit of hard work and an unlimited amount of help from other genealogists. But I am always aware that there are other forces at work too - and I can't wait to experience the next 'coincidence.'"

I loved the two stories that Judith A. H. Meier of Norristown, Pennsylvania, contributed:

"I have had many occasions of serendipity, intuition, and just plain spookiness in the almost eight years I have been employed as Assistant Librarian at the Historical Society of Montgomery County, in Norristown, Pennsylvania. For example, for a number of years, there has been a great deal of interest in the clockmakers of Montgomery County, and two well-researched articles have been published in our Bulletin about them. We are always on the look-out for more clockmakers to add to our list.

One day last year, I was helping a patron locate her ancestor in a duplicate tax book of Springfield Township. There for the first time I saw the name 'Joseph H. Jackson, clockmaker,' listed for several years. I was so excited that I spent the rest of the afternoon trying to gather data on this man so that I could pass it on to our 'clock man.'

The next day, the president of our Society came in and asked me if I had ever heard of Joseph H. Jackson. I replied that I had just discovered him yesterday, and that I had some photocopied documentation of his activities on my desk. Our president had been visiting a small local historical society near Springfield Township and had been asked about Jackson. A query had been received from the Stephen Decatur House in Washington, D. C. A tall clock signed by 'Joseph H. Jackson, Flowertown' was part of the furnishings of the Decatur House. Since Flourtown is partly in Springfield and partly in Whitemarsh Township, the Decatur House people had sought the advice of the Fort Washington Historical Society in Whitemarsh.

Our president and I were amazed that we had both come upon Joseph H. Jackson on the same day. 'About what time yesterday did you run across his name?' he asked me. 'About 2:00,' I answered. 'That's when I was at the Fort Washington Historical Society,' he replied!

I was so unsettled by this whole experience that I told my pastor about it. 'If *you* felt this way, can you imagine how Joseph H. Jackson felt?' was her reaction!!"

The other experience Judith shared also involved our old friend, Father Time:

"For the past four years, I have been collecting the names of black Civil War soldiers who lived in Montgomery County, Pennsylvania. One day several months ago, an elderly black Baptist minister came into our Society Library looking for information about his grandfather, Harry James, recognized as Norristown's first African American policeman. Very little information was known about this gentleman's grandfather, and that which was published in newspapers occasionally was sketchy.

I knew that Harry James' father-in-law had served in the Civil War because the old soldier's records were already written up in my on-going project. I had no idea who Harry James' parents were, however, but something struck me as I was searching through old Norristown business directories trying to follow Harry James backwards in time. I had just received in the mail that morning the pension record of a Civil War widow, Harriet James. I had not even opened the large envelope. Harriet James had appeared in Norristown just prior to the 1870 census, and I knew absolutely nothing about her or her soldier husband.

When I opened the National Archives envelope and went through the many pages of photocopied documents, I discovered that Harriet's deceased husband was Michael James, they were from Lancaster County, Pennsylvania, and they had several young children, among whom was a Henry. When I compared Harriet James' Norristown address in the pension records with her address in the business directories, I discovered that Harry James the policeman was the same as Henry James, the son of Michael and Harriet James of Lancaster County. I had found the parents, birth place, and birth date of the old gentleman's grandfather as well as a great deal more information about the rest of the family.

The elderly minister was awestruck. Why had he chosen this day to come to our Society? Why had the mailman delivered that envelope to me the same morning? He was so moved by the experience that he asked everyone in the library to join hands with him, and he said a prayer of thanksgiving and blessing.

It was a moment I shall never forget in all my years of helping people find their ancestors!"

There's just no "textbook way" we run into fellow-researchers. It can run the gamut. Barbara K. Stone of Northford, Connecticut, recalls:

"My aunt had told me she would like to join the D.A.R., and I promised her I would look up our ancestors. To help me, she gave me everything she had in her possession, including the Civil War discharge papers of my great-grandfather, Emory S. Gould. I planned to research back from him. In August of 1993, a letter from the State Archives was received containing much on Emory Gould, including an enlistment card showing a New Haven address.

Although I normally wouldn't go to a library late on a Friday afternoon because of traffic and having to cook dinner, I felt I *had* to see if he was listed in the New Haven census at the Wallingford Library. I was reading the census on a microfilm reader at the library when the librarian seated a man at a microfilm reader that I had used the week before. Although I don't usually speak to strangers, I told them the reader took poor quality photocopies. So the librarian then seated the man at a reader next to me. After some time, he said, 'It is very difficult when you are hunting for Goulds.'

I couldn't believe it! Here was a man hunting for another Gould. He was from Vermont, worked in Stratford, Connecticut, and was only in the library because a person wasn't working where he first looked for information in Wallingford at a retirement home. He was told to go to the Wallingford Library! After hearing about my aunt wanting information to join the D.A.R., he went to his truck and gave me papers for our ancestor who served in the Revolutionary War. The man, Roland Gould's ancestor, William Gould, born 1759, was brother to my ancestor, Asa Gould, born 1760. Both lived in Warwick, Massachusetts.

I still can't believe this happened! It was as if they wanted to be found!"

And Arthur G. Sylvester of Goleta, California, recounted:

"Almost all of my experiences fall into the logic or intuition categories - perhaps a little lucky, but never have I had anyone show up at the foot of my bed in the middle of the night, had a book fallen off the shelf, much less to the right page, nor have I bumped into the single person in all the world who knew the identity of a long sought ancestor.

But a few weeks after I started my quest for information on my Maine Sylvester family, I found a brief obituary telling how one of my father's great-uncles had become a successful farmer in the central part of the state. I telephoned the town clerk of the little town and asked if she knew any Sylvester people. Yes, and she named some of them and allowed as to how she had seen one of them backing out of his driveway that morning.

But she also told me of a Richard Bradford in another town who knew something about the family. Now my grandfather left Maine in 1904 and was virtually unknown to the rest of the family ever since. So when I called Mr. Bradford, he nearly dropped the telephone. He turned out to be my first cousin, and it seems he had just written to the last address he had for my father (who had died ten years before, and had moved from that address fifteen years before). The letter was returned as 'undeliverable,' so he gave up ever establishing contact with my end of the family at all. Then he received my call just one day later! He still shakes his head in disbelief. Contact with him opened a myriad of connections for me, a couple visits with him were trips back in time, and his stories have given me many clues to the family's history that really died with my father.

To be sure, I may have encountered him eventually, I may have been able to discover some of the family stories myself, and I may have found particular gravestones without his help. But he and I believe that my hunch about contemporary Sylvesters still being in Maine, that the town clerk would mention him, and that my telephone call should come only a day after he had given up on ever hearing from my grandfather's line again, smacks of coincidence - perhaps serendipity. Or is it merely beginner's luck? Or another case of ancestors helping us to discover them?"

Sometimes the timing of events is so precise, it's downright scary. Ruby Coleman had such an occurrence:

"One evening I sat down to browse through a new genealogy book, a listing of family histories in the NSDAR

Library in Washington, D. C. Thumbing through the book, I spotted an unsual name - one of the surnames that one of my genealogy students had been researching. Even though it was late in the evening, something compelled me to call the student. She said, 'What would you suggest I do with this title and information?' I told her to instinctively do what she should or had learned from the class.

Naturally, she could have called me back and asked me to order photocopies of pages from the book (since I am a member of the DAR). But, she didn't! The information I gave her consisted of the title of the book, author, place of publication, and year. The place of publication was a town in Illinois, and the year was a fairly recent one.

Shortly after ten that evening, the telephone rang. My student apologized for calling that late, but had great news she needed to share. Armed with the information, she called telephone information for the town in Illinois and asked for the author's number. Her first thought had been to wait until morning to call, but something compelled her to place the call right then and there. After several rings, a lady answered the telephone. My student explained the nature of her call and asked for the author by name. What transpired is amazing.

The author was deceased. The lady who answered the telephone was his daughter who lived in California. After the man's death, the family kept the house intact, telephone and all. They used it when they traveled back and forth between coasts. She was on her way home to California and decided to spend the night. Her alarm was set for a very early morning wake-up. She explained to my student that nobody would probably be back at the house for close to a year. The lady had her father's books and genealogy and promised to share it with my student once she got back to California. And, yes - it was my student's own family line.

This was a case where the compelling telephone calls were made. Had we waited, it would have turned out differently. Is this following a hunch, or is something pushing us in the right direction?"

Another uncanny story came in from Keith F. Rose of the Family History Library at Salt Lake City, Utah:

"In 1978, I was in Europe on business and, although my time was limited, I decided to try to go to the hometown of one of my German ancestors in East Germany.

I had approximately two months warning before going so I asked the travel agent what my chances would be of getting into East Germany for a day or two to do research. She indicated that they would be slim to none; we would have had to apply for a visa a month earlier, but if we were determined, we should check with a travel agent in West Germany when we got there. This I did and was told that it would take a minimum of three weeks to get it. Inasmuch as I was there for only $2^1/_2$ weeks, I felt that it was a nice thought, but didn't hold out much hope.

After completing my business, my wife and I were visiting Vienna, Austria. We decided to go to the East German Embassy there and see if they could pull any strings for us. The diplomats were very kind, but told us that it would take three days to obtain the necessary visa. It was Thursday, and our flight was leaving on Sunday. Three days would not do it. Somewhat as an after-thought, our German friend suggested, as we were about to leave, that we just drive up to the border; perhaps they would be able to accommodate us. Filled with hope, we headed for the border.

Arriving at the border of East and West Germany on Friday afternoon, we were welcomed by armed guards and stern officials who took our passports and asked us where we were going and why. We weren't sure we would even get our passports back, let alone be allowed to cross the border. After an extensive wait, we were told to go to the travel bureau, located there at the border, change some money into East German marks, and make hotel reservations. After a three-hour wait, we had our visas and were on our way.

We traveled to Karl Marx Stadt and stayed at the Hotel Moscow. We were told to check in at the police station the next morning to have our passports stamped indicating that we had been there. By the time we left our hotel, cleared the police, and traveled to the small community where we wanted to research, it was already early afternoon. Still feeling somewhat hopeful, we drove up to the parish church and parked.

As we got out of the car, we were met by a kind gentleman asking if he could help us. We explained that we desired to see the parish registers to find information on my ancestry. He said that he normally did not come to this parish on Saturdays. He was the parish clerk for several parishes in this area, and he would come to this specific parish only one day a week, and it was not Saturday, the day we were there. For some reason, he told us, he felt a need to go to this particular parish on this particular day! He said that we were very fortunate that he was there; otherwise, we wouldn't have had access to the records.

Still, with much of the day gone, we felt that we had an impossible task before us to search all of the records that would be of value to my family history. Once in his office, he asked me what name I was looking for, and in what time period. When I told him, he pulled a small card file off the top shelf of his book case, where the parish registers were housed. He thumbed through the file for a couple of minutes and finally produced a large filing card that had not only the name of my ancestor on it, but the name of his wife, children, parents, birthdates of everyone and where they had migrated from. Within a couple of hours, we had all the information on my ancestry available from the parish records.

I felt as if somehow my ancestors were working in concert to co-ordinate my arrival with the parish clerk, and once there, everything was prepared for quick and ready access. I believe that there is, indeed, a power greater than us that helps direct our efforts."

WHERE HAVE I HEARD *THAT* BEFORE!!??

7
IT'S A SMALL WORLD AFTER ALL

The charming *Small World* rides at Disneyland and Disney World are among the most popular amusement-park exhibits in the country; and the tune played as you travel through the various countries represented is as charming as the colorful dolls encountered along the way. This particular exhibit has been a favorite of my daughter, Amanda, since she was three years old and still is very special to her. The only downside to the rides is trying to get that doggone, repetitive lyric - "It's a Small World After All" - out of your head after you've left the park. They should put a big sign up over the entrance saying:

"WARNING! THIS TUNE MAY BE HAZARDOUS TO YOUR SANITY AND IS DIFFICULT TO REMOVE FROM YOUR BRAIN!"

But the message the song bespeaks is a universal one. Its truth is reenforced via the strange goings-on that seem to occur often throughout the genealogical community. Witness the many letters that arrived telling of unusual experiences along these lines. Some family historians even started their genealogical searches with a "Small World" story, such as Betty Bowman of Newark, Ohio:

"When initiating my research three years ago, on my first visit to a LDS Family History Library a woman helping me on the computer was scanning several names I had given her. Discouraged, I was ready to quit when I gave her the name 'Sublette.' Startled, she said we were related. At her suggestion, I contacted the Detroit Genealogical Society and received a book on the Sublettes going back to Sedan, France in 1600. They were Huguenots driven out by the Catholic king and ultimately came to

Virginia in the early 1700's. I was descended from a male member of the first family there, and the LDS woman was from his sister."

And Joan A. Griffis of Danville, Illinois, President of Illinois State Gen. Society, recounted a similar tale:

"When our family was transferred to Danville, Illinois twenty-one years ago, I hadn't even KNOWN about genealogy. I 'happened' to meet a wonderful lady (because I responded to her offer on the radio regarding gardening) who took me under her wing, so to speak, because I was new in town. She took me to all kinds of meetings and eventually introduced me to the genealogical collection at the Danville Library. That was the beginning of the addictive hobby I'm involved with today.

Sadly, my mentor, Bertha Kamm, passed away two years after I met her. I have since learned that she and I are related. We both have a common ancestor, Obadiah Ayers of New Jersey!"

Genealogy classes often are arenas for serendipities and surprises. Deborah Brown wrote:

"About five years ago, I signed up for the National Archives week-long seminar about how to use records there. On the first day of class, we were all given 3X5 cards and told to write down the name of an ancestor and some pertinent information. Then we were told to put our cards in a box, and during the week, we could go look in the card file and see if we could make any connection.

I don't know why, but I chose one of my ancestor's Henry Miar's granddaughters, Elizabeth Myers Shoemaker, whom I didn't know much about. From my family papers, I knew that Elizabeth and her husband Michael Shoemaker had moved from Hardy County to Licking and then Franklin Counties in Ohio in the 1830's. This came from letters that she wrote back to her brother, John Myers, who had inherited the farm in Hardy County from their father, Johannes, who was Henry's youngest son. Then there was about a twenty-year gap between letters, and the last letter was from Steuben County, Indiana in 1854. Elizabeth wrote about a child who had just gotten married, and a little bit about her other children. That was all I knew about her.

At the end of the first day, one of my classmates came up to me and said, 'I noticed you put a card in the box on Elizabeth Myers Shoemaker. But, it's probably not the same one,' and she just shook her head and started to walk away. But I put my hand on her arm and said, 'No, wait. Tell me about her.' The woman looked up at me and then began telling me about her ancestor, Elizabeth Myers and her husband Michael Shoemaker, who had left Virginia in the 1830's, moved to Ohio, and then on to Steuben County, Indiana. Well, you know the rest - I had found another cousin! I got a big grin on my face, and I said, 'I have the letters that she wrote back to her brother in Virginia.' My new friend couldn't believe it, until the next day, when I brought in copies of them. We exchanged information and have kept in touch ever since."

And Ruby Coleman added her classroom story:
"One evening, while teaching my genealogy class at our local college, I began my discussion of late 19th century passenger lists. As my own ancestors all came to America before the Revolutionary War, I contacted a friend to borrow her copy of the page of the passenger list upon which her Nebraska German ancestor appeared. It was one page from the manifest of the ship *Kaiser Wilhelm*. Immediately a lady in the back of the room raised her hand in excitement. She announced that *her* ancestor had also sailed on the *Kaiser Wilhelm*. I explained that the ship made several voyages and gave her the date from the sheet I was holding. She came forward and proudly pointed to a name at the bottom of the sheet ... her ancestor. My friend's ancestor and the lady's ancestor had journeyed together and their names were very close on the manifest.

That evening I returned to the college to teach another class in advanced genealogy. Once again I began my lecture about passenger lists. One of the students raised her hand when I showed the sheet from the manifest of the *Kaiser Wilhelm*. Suddenly, I realized it was happening again! This student also had an ancestor on the *Kaiser Wilhelm* and on the same ship which transported the other two ancestors. And, she had a photograph of the ship.

It is understandable that the three ladies with Nebraska ancestry might have ancestors who came from

Germany during the same approximate period of time. A bit
less understandable that they would all come on the ship
Kaiser Wilhelm ... Less understandable that they would
have been on the same ship on the same date. Even less
understandable that the three ladies would have heard of
their connections through a class in the 1980s in North
Platte, Nebraska."

A visit to an ancestral locale can sometimes bring forth
unusual events in the "Small World" category. The Reverend
Harry R. Fletcher of Freeport, Illinois communicated:

"My great-grandfather, George Willis Waterbury, left
a note saying that his father, Solomon Waterbury, born in
N.B., Canada in 1788, had two sisters: Polly (later
discovered to be Mary) and Nancy (later discovered to
have been Ann) who married two Eastmans and went to
Canada. While looking into my Palatine forebears' old
stomping grounds in St. Lawrence County, New York, I
noticed a sign saying something about Cornwall, Ontario. I
asked my mother if she thought we ought to just wander
around and see what was over there.

The *first* person I saw was a very sprightly older
gentleman, and I asked him if there were any families by
the name of 'Eastman.' He said, 'Well, what a coincidence!
That's my name, George Eastman!' I told him that he
might be a distant cousin of mine, and that I was from the
States. He replied, 'Oh, you must be related to Mary
Waterbury.' I was astonished, and asked, 'How do you
know about her?' He said, 'Well, I ought to ... she was my
grandmother. Would you like to see her Bible? It's right
here in the house.'

That's not exactly scientific genealogy; I just had an
impulse and there it was! I've come to be a believer in
special feelings, and sometimes I wonder if we are being
pointed or directed somehow."

Paul Bachmann of Flint, Michigan, remembered:

"I was looking for all the living descendants of the ten
children of Iddo Blashfield. I'd confirmed them all except
the possible issue of Horace, the 7th child. One allied line
of this branch was a Mitchell family, which was listed in

the 1910 census of Coldwater, Michigan with a son Donald, aged 2 years among the family.

I went to Coldwater to research the family and had some success at the County Clerk's office, but nothing earthshaking. I decided to take a break from my investigations and have lunch at Irma's Restaurant, which had been recommended by someone at the local barber shop. When I was finished with my meal, I asked the waitress if she knew any Blashfields in town. She said no. Almost as an afterthought, I asked her if she knew of any Mitchells. She pointed to a booth exactly opposite to mine on the other side of the rather narrow room.

I went over to the booth, introduced myself, and met Donald L. Mitchell aged 82 - the little boy listed in that 1910 census of Coldwater and a living descendant of the one branch of the ten children of Iddo Blashfield that I hadn't been able to find previously.

Did we celebrate! The waitress told me later that actually the Mitchells only eat at that restaurant occasionally, which makes our contact even more amazing."

Doris M. Newbery of Belmont, California, had a thought-provoking experience:

"Seventeen members of my father's family, the von Mengdens, went to Germany for a reunion. One of the events was to take a day trip to visit the different areas where the old family had lived and worked. The family place of origin was Mengede, now a suburb of Dortmund. We rented a large bus and took off from Koln.

When we arrived at Mengede, the bus driver didn't know the route to the old church. He stopped on the street leading into town where there was a row of apartments that had their garages under the building, facing the street. There was but one garage door open, and this is where the driver went to ask directions. The German man asked why a tour bus was interested in the old church in Mengede. The driver responded that we were mostly Americans, descendants of the old von Mengden family, and were interested in seeing the church.

The German man became very excited and said that he had in his apartment many ancient photos of the old town and even some of the old von Mengden family home. Would we like to see them? Of course, we said. We enjoyed looking at them, and then he said that he knew another gentleman who had been commissioned by the city to look into the history of the town and the von Mengden family. Would we be interested in making an appointment to meet the man and find out what he knew? The appointment was made and later that day we met the gentleman who had been doing all the research. Thanks to him, we were able to trace our family back to the year 900!

How often do you have all those years of family history handed to you, completely documented? And all the result of a 'chance' selection of a person from whom to ask for driving directions!"

Dr. Raymond Martin Bell, of Washington, Pennsylvania, wrote:

"I told my great aunt that I had finally proved that we were related to a family in an adjoining county.

She said, 'Yes, we used to visit them!'

I said, 'Why didn't you tell me?'

She replied, 'You never asked me.'"

Yes, getting in touch with a kindred spirit researching common lines seems to happen in a myriad of ways. Ruby Coleman again contributed another gem to ponder:

"One morning in late June of 1991, I was in Salt Lake City using the Family History Library. As the early birds have first choice for microfilm readers and computers, I got there at 7:15 A.M. before it opened. When I arrived, there were a few people on either side of the entrance, sitting on the retaining wall. I struck up a conversation with a very nice couple there and eventually learned they were from Pinole, California.

That rang a bell. A distant cousin to my mother lives in Pinole and does genealogy. I had been writing to this woman, Evelyn Tharp, for a couple of years. However, I decided not to say anything, even though I was tempted to ask the lady if she knew Evelyn Tharp. My thought was that maybe they belonged to a genealogy society together.

The lady asked me where I was from ... Nebraska. She then began asking me about research in Nebraska, naming a cemetery where she needed information. I gave her the name and address of a Nebraska researcher who would probably look up information for her.

About that time, the doors opened. They claim at least 3,000 people walk through there daily. Because of the crowds of people we did not see each other again.

I thought about that lady all that summer and into the fall. As Christmas approached, I mailed Evelyn Tharp a card and letter, noting that they have very nice people in Pinole. I went on to explain that I had visited with a researcher from Pinole at the library in Salt Lake City, giving her a date in June.

Evelyn mailed me a Christmas card, stating, 'It was *me!*' She recalled being there on that date, visiting with a lady from Nebraska who gave her information on writing to a person for cemetery information. I called her on the phone, and we quickly agreed it is a small world. Perhaps we should wear name tags.

Over two years later, on 10 August 1993, I was once again doing research at the library in Salt Lake City. Arriving that Tuesday morning early, I joined a group sitting on the wall waiting for the library to open. Not far into our conversation, I thought one of the group looked somewhat familiar, so I asked where she was from ... 'Pinole, California. My name's Evelyn Tharp,' she replied. As soon as I told her my name, she let out a scream, and we were in each other's arms.

How many times could this happen? We did not plan it even though we have written to each other since our 1991 meeting. I had no idea she would be there, and she had no idea I would be there. We met several times during the day and laughed about our 'chance' meeting ... same place, same spot on the retaining wall.

They say you go to the library in Salt Lake to find your relatives. I go to *literally* find my relatives!"

Yes, the strangest things can happen at the Salt Lake Library. Just ask Horst A. Reschke, a contributing editor of *Heritage Quest* Magazine:

"I was doing research at the Family History Library one day, when I observed a group of tourists trying to communicate its wishes, in German, to an elderly attendant, without too much success. I was able to help, since German is my native tongue and more than forty years have not diminished my ability to speak it.

The tourists introduced themselves as the *Fraatz* family, Mr. Hermann Fraatz, Mrs. Maria Fraatz, and their teenage son, Daniel. Since their research focus was on the village of *Ebergötzen,* near Göttingen, Germany, I thought they were natives of the *Eichsfeld* region. However, when Mrs. Fraatz mentioned Hannover, my ears perked up.

'Are you from Hannover?' I asked. She said, 'Yes, are you?'

When I answered in the affirmative, she wanted to know where, in Hannover, I came from. I said, 'from Döhren.'

'Me too,' she marveled, 'what street?'

'Am Lindenhofe.' This seemed too much for Mrs. Fraatz.

'What was the house number?' she practically shouted.

'Nr. 2A,' came the reply.

It was then that she announced in the most incredulous voice that her sister, Mrs. Helga Bonn, lives in that house, the house in which I was born!

Needless to say, we had much to discuss and compare. Mrs. Bohn is a widow, but her late husband, Fritz, was my childhood playmate. In another unusual twist, I had just talked by phone the night before we all met to Mrs. Dora Menzel from Hannover, whom I had known since I was in knee pants; her maiden name was 'Fraatz.' Subsequent research showed the two families had a common ancestor.

Upon her return to Germany, Mrs. Fraatz wrote me that, 'Our meeting that day for us, too, is so remarkable, that I keep telling the story time and again. Through this encounter and genealogy I have already met many nice people. And do you know what my husband said when we were planning our journey and were considering the option of making a side-trip to Salt Lake City?

'What do we want in Salt Lake City? We don't know a soul there."

Strange events don't just happen in Salt Lake City: any genealogical library is a potential seedbed for the unusual. Lula E. Clarke wrote in *The Pioneer Wagon* periodical:

"For several years, I'd been hearing about all the research materials that were available at the Mid-Continent Public Library in Independence, Missouri. One day I decided to check it out, just to see what I could find. I was very busy looking at microfilm when I heard a lady's voice next to me say, 'Look at that. He should have been hung with the rest of the tribe.'

Turning to the lady, I asked, 'Where is the family you're researching from?'

She said, 'It's the the Eddings family of Douglas County, Missouri.'

I asked, 'What's the first name?'

She replied, 'My grandmother's name was Serilda Isabell Eddings.'

I just sat and looked at her for a moment, then finally told her, 'My grandmother was Mary Ann Eddings. Your grandmother and my grandmother were sisters.'

Believe me, I was really excited that day I left the library. No one had ever told me it could be *that* easy to find members of my family at Mid-Continent Library!"

Michael J. Evans of Newport, New Hampshire, recalled:

"My wife and I were in a second-hand bookstore in the little town of Goshen, New Hampshire, about five miles from home. I was looking through the history section, along with another fellow. We began to converse, and I told him of my new interest in genealogy. He also had an interest in the subject, and as the conversation continued, we learned that we both had lived in New York State at one time. He was from the Mohawk Valley area; I asked if he had ever heard of a place called 'German Flatts.' I told him I had learned about an ancestor named Jacob Wohleben, who had lived there.

We exchanged names and telephone numbers. A couple of weeks passed when one evening the telephone rang, and it was Doug Fay. He was most excited; he had been working with your books *The Palatine Families of New York - 1710*, and he discovered that his ancestor Dieterich Steele had married a Margaret Wohleben! We were cousins! His ancestor, Dieterich Steele, was an executor of my ancestor Johann Nicolaus Wohleben's estate. We have become close friends. How odd that we'd both be found in a used bookstore in the tiny village of Goshen, New Hampshire, one autumn day.

In these last four years, I have had many strange experiences like those described in *Psychic Roots*, and had begun to feel a bit strange at times! I am glad to know that my gift is not so unusual, and that there are others who have experienced so many of the same oddities that I have. My ancestors are alive for me; not just names and dates and places. My work grows and grows and continues to dominate my life as I know it will until my time comes."

Sister Donna Rock, C.S.J. of Lorain, Ohio, wrote:

"I thought I was a loner where serendipity is concerned until I read your book on the topic. For fifteen years, I and a number of relatives have been seeking information on our ROCK roots. Much of our family research centered upon Somerset, Franklin, and Bedford Counties, Pennsylvania, so I decided to make a visit to the Old Bedford Village, an historical location which tried to recreate the lives and times of its early citizens. I was making my way around the various buildings where different occupations were being demonstrated. I was about to pass up the one where quilting was being shown when I was prompted to go in, in spite of the fact that I had often seen my grandmother working on quilts in the past.

Upon entering the building, I found myself face to face with a lady in the dress of the period working on a quilt. We were quite alone. We soon struck up a conversation and as soon as she began to speak to me, I had the *strangest* feeling that I should know her! In the midst of our talk, I informed her that I was in Bedford in hopes of finding information for my family tree. She inquired of me what family I was researching and, to my utter amazement, she informed me that her maiden name was ROCK also! From what she told me about her family, I was able to trace her line back to the 'old' Peter Rock who appeared in the Bedford County, Pennsylvania tax record in the same year our 'young' Peter Rock appeared in Somerset County, Pennsylvania - 1820. I feel we'll be able to make a documented connection between the two soon.

When I first got started on my genealogical journey, my mother was quite apprehensive. She didn't like me studying about dead ancestors. She was afraid they would come to get me. Well, in a certain sense they seem to have come, but I'm still here - determined more than ever as a result of your book to find the connections!"

Florence Lavender Moore of Edmonds, Washington, wrote and told me:

"While living on Whidbey Island, I was using a copier at the Island County Courthouse. A county employee noticed the names on the photos I was copying (the album was a loan from relatives). When she saw the name 'Peck' she remarked that she knew a Peck family in Oak Harbor who had a book on the Peck family. Since the name is not unusual, I didn't follow up on her lead for several months. But when I finally got around to getting in contact with the family, Mrs. Peck was kind enough to let me examine the book. I was amazed to find my husband's grandmother's name and several generations of her ancestors!"

Here's what Janet Rosenbaum of Kennesaw, Georgia, had to say:

"About a year ago, I decided I would try to write about my life in order to better understand myself and to explain my life to my sons. In trying to understand myself, I discovered I needed to understand my parents and grandparents as well because they, to a large degree, made me what I am. This, of course, began my journey into genealogy.

After my initial searches, I decided I should check the library in Brownsville, Kentucky, where many of my ancestors have lived. On the day I arrived, the copier was broken, so I sat at a big table scribbling fast and furiously from the old books. I was so absorbed in my research that I was barely aware there were other people in the room. I'd been there about an hour when I heard someone say, 'Excuse me, may I ask what names you are researching?' I looked up and replied, 'Yes, I'm working on Merediths, Lindseys, Blairs, and Elmores.' The woman who had gotten up the nerve to approach me was obviously astonished. She replied in an awed tone, 'Those are my families too!'

We both had goose-bumps. Kathy later told me that she just had a strange feeling that she should speak to me that day, and we're both very glad that she did. Kathy and I found we are cousins, yet we'd never met before that day in the library. In later get-togethers, we were even surprised to find a family photo showing Kathy's father with my father!"

Sometimes a "connection" can be made from an unexpected source, far afield from the genealogical arena. Wayne Barksdale Goss of Rockwall, Texas, wrote:

"On the morning of 27 May 1994, after a four-day genealogical research trip to East Baton Rouge Parish, Louisiana, my car developed engine problems while I was trying to leave the Zachary Little Farms area. The engine would die and had to be started over again at every stop sign or when the traffic slowed down. I managed to get to a service station in Baker, but they were unable to service a BMW and advised me to go across town to Netterville Auto & Paint Shop. After many starts and stops, I finally arrived at that establishment - only to be told that they also couldn't service my BMW. Exasperated, I called for a tow truck to tow me into Baton Rouge to the BMW Service Center there.

While waiting for the truck to arrive, I struck up a conversation with Jerry Kilroy, whose phone I had used to make several of my calls. As his father had recently died, he told me that he too had begun an interest in genealogy. Our conversation eventually led to some interesting facts. As a boy, he had played on 'corn rows' which Buck Zachary, who owned the property, said were unmarked graves on the Hardscrabble School Tract. Jerry Kilroy's grandmother had taught school for many years at the Hardscrabble School and her family still owned about 200 acres across from the Tract.

This news was very interesting, because for thirty years my cousin had been unsuccessful in locating a Barksdale grandfather who was supposedly buried in Hardscrabble Cemetery. Jerry Kilroy then gave me directions to the old Hardscrabble School location. My tow service then arrived and took me to the BMW Service Center, where a computer check revealed absolutely nothing wrong with my car. I was advised to continue my trip to Dallas and not to worry - everything was fine! I shouldn't have any problems at all, which I didn't. No problem whatsoever after I took the car to see Mr. Kilroy and unexpectedly got the long-sought-for information on the Hardscrabble School.

Later research at the East Baton Rouge Courthouse proved Jerry Kilroy's directions to the Old Hardscrabble School to be correct, and I have since found a deed donating two acres of land to the School, which names this grandfather's brother a competent witness."

Barbara Vines Little of Orange, Virginia, conveyed a good story:

"A few years ago, a client, Bob Parkinson of Silver Spring, Maryland, told me of a chance encounter that produced genealogical paydirt:

'At a house party in Greenville, West Virginia near where some of my ancestors lived, our hosts threw a square dance for us. During an intermission, I happened to chat with the caller. I asked him if he knew where Bradshaw's Run was. I told him that I had two forebears who had lived in Monroe County, one on Bradshaw's Run and the other at the junction of Indian and Hans Creek.

He told me he lived at the latter location, and that two years ago while mowing a knoll in back of his home he had run across three grave markers, only one of which could be read. It was a marker for Jesse Green, an ancestor of mine. On the Sunday following, this obliging chap took me up the knoll in knee-deep grass, and we found the marker. There was no way I could ever have discovered it without that chance encounter!'"

"Small World" experiences continue to pop up at the drop of a pedigree chart. Anne Neale remembers:

"I wrote to the Postmaster of Lawrence, Kansas inquiring about my Deitzler family who once resided there. After sending me some general information, he referred me to a friend of his who lived in the town and was 'into genealogy.'

The lady, Mrs. Spencer, was most kind and went to the courthouse for me to see if she could find any land deeds or court records for my George W. Deitzler. Among the old items she discovered was a land map dated 1850 showing where Deitzler had lived. Would you believe that Mrs. Spencer was living on the *same piece of land* where George Deitzler had resided 145 years ago? I was in awe and dumbstruck. What are the odds of something happening like this, where the ancestor you are inquiring about back in 1850 actually lived on the very same plot of land that the lady you meet 'by chance' to do research resides upon today? Amazing!"

Helen S. Ullmann of Acton, Massachusetts, had a similar event occur:

"In 1984 we were in Oslo, Norway, and, being LDS, we decided to attend church in the ward on the west side of the city. During Relief Society (the women's meeting), I asked if anyone lived in Asker, a community two towns southwest, on the Oslofjord, because my great-grandmother had lived at the farm called Reistad there.

To my astonishment, the woman who had just taught our lesson said, 'I live in that house!' She invited us to come out and visit. The rest of my family was leaving for America, but I spent a week with my father's cousin in Baerum, just west of Oslo. I told them about the coincidence, and a few days later we drove down to visit the farm. Of course, the house was much changed from the 1840s, but the general floorplan and heavy oak beams were from that time. And it was delightful just to be there in that beautiful location. I love to see my dusty archives come alive in three dimensions and all colors of the rainbow. Even if my ancestors themselves aren't there, they were almost all farmers, and the texture of the landscape brings them to life.

Just as we were leaving, the lady said, 'Wait a minute.' She ran back into the house and came back with a coin. 'When we were cleaning the attic when we arrived, we found this coin. It dates from the time your family was here. I want you to have it.'

The little 1840 $1/2$ skilling coin is now among my favorite family heirlooms."

And Nancye Kent Perry of Eaglemont, Victoria, Australia, sent on this tale:

"My maternal grandfather Alfred Leahy was a pioneer in the township and district of Shepparton in North Central Victoria. In the early 1870's, he was elected to Shepparton's first council, at that time known as the Eastern Riding of the Shire of Echuca. Upon that first council of Echuca's Eastern Riding there sat three councillors, Alfred Leahy, James Campbell JP, and one other.

In July 1972, my husband and I moved to our present address in the Melbourne suburb of Eaglemont, and in 1973 we met John and Linda Campbell, neighbors living but a few houses down the road. In the course of getting to know one another, John Campbell mentioned Shepparton, and it turned out that it was his great-grandfather James Campbell who sat with my grandfather Alfred Leahy on that first council.

Exactly one hundred years later, to me it was a most eerie experience realizing that our two forebears must have been close associates in those far-off days. It would be intriguing to imagine that perhaps our respective forebears are chuckling over having arranged our meeting after all those years."

Richard H. Benson of White Bear Lake, Minnesota, noted:

"I must note the similarity of our interests in genealogy. I was twelve, not eight, and the trunk was in my grandparents' attic, not a basement. However, I came across Civil War diaries, old family papers which went back to 1812, and a host of other documents. I still have copies of letters I wrote to county clerks, which started, 'I am a twelve year old boy trying to trace my family history.' That usually got some extra help.

Some unusual coincidences came to light some twenty-eight years ago when I was married. I decided to trace my wife's family as well as my own. This, by the way, does make you somewhat of a hero with in-laws. We all know that migration patterns are similar, but those of my paternal ancestors and my wife's are amazingly so. My John[1] Benson came to Massachusetts in 1638. My wife's

Thomas[1] Read was in Massachusetts by 1637. In 1723, Isaac[3] Benson left Massachusetts for northwestern Rhode Island where he became a member of the Smithfield Friends. In 1746, Jonathan[3] Read left Massachusetts for Smithfield, Rhode Island where he became a member of the Smithfield Friends. Elihu[6] Benson was in Danby, Vermont as a single man in 1778, moved back to Rhode Island where he married and moved with his family back to Danby in 1798. John[5] Reed moved to Danby, Vermont in 1804 and to Western New York in 1818. Deuteronomy[7] Benson moved from Danby to Western New York in 1816 and on to Michigan in 1835. My wife's father came to Michigan in the 1930's.

Smithfield, Rhode Island and Danby, Vermont are pretty small towns. This is not a case of our ancestors leading us to the right page in a book by some psychic means but something more significant!"

Cynthia Marie Bernadette Drayer of Portland, Oregon, remarks:

"I am adopted, and it sends chills up my spine to see the many parallels between my adopted and biological families. For example, I can look at a Quaker marriage certificate in Pennsylvania and find the signatures of both my adopted and biological ancestors listed, side by side, at the same ceremony, in the same place, on the same day. And I have common ancestors in both my adoptive and biological families via the marriage of Arthur Barrett to Lydia Chambers: my adoptive sister Donna and I are biologically-related 8th and 9th cousins on two Quaker lines!"

But the most moving stories in this area are those that told of actual reunions of long-separated relatives. Donald L. Smith of Macedonia, Iowa, wrote:

"My favorite story occurred in my research on my mother's family. My Uncle Carl, his wife Jessie, and friends of theirs toured Florida in the 1950's. They pulled off the interstate for lunch at Clearwater in the Tampa/St. Petersburg area of perhaps a million people. While sitting at the table, Uncle Carl mentioned that he had a cousin living in the area ... a cousin he had never met ... who had moved from Valentine, Nebraska to the Tampa Bay area in the 1920's. He mentioned her name and wondered how he would go about finding her.

He looked up and the waitress had tears in her eyes. She said, 'She is my mother, and she will be here in fifteen minutes to pick me up from work!'

Almost unbelievable, isn't it? ... but true!"

Daniel J. Hay was kind enough to contribute this poignant episode:

"Shortly after I moved to Utah and before starting my company, Advanced Resources, Inc., I was in the Family History Library for an afternoon of research. At the same table I was using, a young mother and her newborn were occupying the other side near the end.

An elderly lady sat next to her and heartily talked up a storm about some of her ancestors she couldn't locate. During their sharing of what appeared to be lineages of their husbands, the elderly lady took up the baby to cuddle and rock it. After admiring the little one many times, she finally indicated she was going to leave.

Putting the baby back, she commented that it looked a lot like her own granddaughter whom she had not seen in twenty years. Then she took a note pad and wrote her name and telephone number for the young lady and said, 'When you're in town researching, give me a call, and I'll help with the baby.'

The young woman smiled as she took the proffered slip and read the name. But then her face turned to one of shock. She turned pale and nearly shrieking cried, 'Oh my God! Grandma!' She hurled herself at the eldery lady and wrapped her arms around her, sobbing, 'I'm Myrna.' Both of them stood there wrapped in a crushing embrace with tears streaming down their faces as they sobbed in an eerie silence. I think the only sound at the table was from the three others there and myself, who were fighting back tears and sniffling noses.

Can anybody say that their reunion was from pure scientific procedure or from experience that subconsciously guided them to a 'find'? No, I think not. This was pure serendipity at work that brought happiness so easily.

I later saw the young woman again and introduced myself. I asked after her grandmother and was told, with great sadness, that she had died in her sleep, two weeks after their reunion."

KLEENEX, PLEASE.

8
SHIRLEY FARANO'S STORY

Just as Dr. Joan K. Mitchell's experiences required a whole chapter in *Psychic Roots*, some of the new stories also needed telling in their entirety. When a big packet of material arrived in the mail from Shirley Vilim Farano of Lake Zurich, Illinois - the editor of the quarterly of the Chicago Genealogical Society - I was so enthralled I didn't want to waste any of it. So in order to do her story justice, I've decided to include just about everything she sent me, as I feel her story is so remarkable and told so well.

Shirley writes:

I apologize for the length, but it seems that anyone courageous enough to write this book deserved the whole story. I hope in some way it helps your project. It seems that these things could be happening to thousands of people, but who would ever openly talk about it? Certainly, only my immediate family and a very few friends know anything at all about these events. Maybe you were 'meant' to know, because once I began to write it all down, it all flowed on - even those things I hadn't thought about for years.

For example, your description of 'flying' in very early childhood struck me. I never thought I would hear of another person who experienced this. I too had a very similar experience, but with another twist. It always happened in the middle of the day or before bedtime when I was perfectly awake. Also it only occurred in my room. I covered a distance of about eight or nine feet from the doorway to my bed, where I liked to land! I was between the ages of five and seven when it began and ultimately ended. Even then I wondered if this was real, so I experimented. Sure enough, I could never jump that far. But I can distinctly remember all the times I could stand in the doorway and float, gliding over to my bed!

By now, there must be many times you've heard, 'I know just what you mean!' And here I am writing it again, after exclaiming it to myself throughout reading your book. I was happy to see your request to share experiences at the back of the book. There have been so many times I wondered what was happening and what it all meant. I'm happy to know so many people share these types of experiences.

After reading about so many experiences in your book, I think that the one twist that makes *my* experience(s) unique is that they seem to have continued throughout my lifetime as well as affecting lives of other people, apparently for the same purposes. Usually, the pattern is that an experience occurs to me and then, several years later, I find a distinct correlation in an ancestor's life. Other people seem to be affected when the timing is right! After several years of research, this pattern emerged to me. *I wondered how many times you can have coincidences before they are no longer coincidences!* And how specific can a situation be before it is no longer by chance?

Because of the chronology of these experiences, I should describe these events in the order they occurred. I've come to believe that 'someone (or more) out there' wanted me to know about them, their lives, share their interests, and, in one case, to be remembered and thank those from his old Chicago neighborhood. Those are my strongest intuitive feelings about why these things happened.

During my early childhood, my greatest love was ballet and the music that accompanied it. My greatest joys were taking my ballet and violin lessons. My favorite ballets were the *Nutcracker Suite*, followed by *Swan Lake*. Beethoven was a favorite composer. My sister and I enjoyed many other activities, but these were above them all to me. My Dad even took me to orchestral concerts in grade school, an activity unheard of on my block of seventy baby boomer playmates!

Oddly, I became very adamant about my violin playing, and very specific that I wanted to play violin, not viola, which my mother preferred. Also I insisted that I wanted to play first violin and carry the melody. The instructor wanted us to practice only chords and what I considered background. I was dissatisfied with my instructor, and wondered where all the good violin teachers were. I wanted to create my own pieces, and not just play lessons. Since you don't know me, I must tell you that this was very much out of character for me. I'm still known as a very easy- going person, and my parents are among my best friends. Around this time, I also wanted a piano, my second favorite instrument. I became quite frustrated because my mother didn't want to buy a piano for various reasons.

I was between six and eight years old when this all occurred. At the age of twelve, I began to be interested in family history. I first learned that my great-grandfather had been the church organist and excellent piano player in his village before coming to America. I thought that was quite a coincidence, considering my love of piano, and how I was already collecting classical music, especially Beethoven, Tchaikovsky, Dvorak and the Slavonic Dances. This was an interest I had to pursue on my own, since none of my friends were interested in classical music. We only enjoyed rock music together.

It wasn't until I was about forty years old that I learned another great-grandfather was an accomplished violinist. Not only that, but so were his father and two of his brothers. In fact, his father was a violin teacher when he first came to America and is listed as one in the Chicago Directories of his time.

The oldest brother taught violin to his younger two brothers and led an orchestra/band in Chicago. One of these brothers attended the Prague Conservatory of Music, travelling back to Bohemia from his Chicago birthplace. He then toured throughout Europe in concert, became friends with Tchaikovsky and played in concert with him. Upon returning to the U.S., he toured the country in concert, became an instructor at Chicago College of Music, a Director at the American Conservatory of Music in Chicago, a member of the Chicago Symphony Orchestra - as first violinist!! - and persuaded Antonin Dvorak to appear and play at the Chicago World's Fair in 1893. He finally opened his own school of music one block from the Art Institute in downtown Chicago. The school was highly successful, and his own two sons taught violin and piano (!!) there. He also began and led a Beethoven Society and Quartet, and was known as a supporter of Bohemian classical music, promoting the Bohemian composers.

He authored textbooks on violin techniques and composed music. Among his biographies, many passages attest to this brother's special gifts as a teacher of music.

This information absolutely stunned me. It was ironic to think the violin teachers I had so wished for in childhood were in my family! I had only one year of violin before my childhood violin teacher left the school, and there was no replacement. We later moved to the country, and there was no orchestra at all in school - only band. And then there were so many parallels to my own deepest interests that I had a strange sensation that I was reading about a description of my own personality (without the great accomplishments he had achieved!).

I decided at age seven to become a teacher, loving reading, encyclopedias, and even holding classes for my friends! As a babysitter in junior high and high school, parents told me their children wanted no one else to babysit, so when I was on vacation they couldn't go out. I did graduate college intending to teach, but the baby-bust years turned my career in a different direction.

Since junior high years, I had longed to travel throughout Europe and to study there in college. My violinist ancestor and teacher, Joseph Vilim, had studied in Europe and toured Europe more than once. Since my junior high years, I have taken several trips throughout Europe. Also, since that age, I always joked that I should have been born a century earlier. I always had an affinity for things one-hundred years before my time.

This whole scenario is not without a good ghost story as well. This happened one night in February when I was fifteen years old. I woke at 2:00 a.m. because of a rather loud and merry conversation in our kitchen. The lights were on and actually made my room quite bright. My room had a powder room between it and the kitchen, with two sets of bifold doors (a walk-through bath), and the doors were not fully closed. It was so bright that I walked over to my mirror and combed my hair without turning on a light. I intended to go to the kitchen and meet these happy people!

As I walked over to the kitchen (never thinking it was physically impossible for the kitchen light to be that bright in my room), I hesitated suddenly as I became self-conscious of being in a nightgown in front of people I didn't know. I stood there and observed that there were two men sitting at our table. Both were smoking cigars, one had his back toward me and was wearing a brownish suit. The other had his side toward me, and the ash tray I had washed that evening on the table in front of him. This one sat in a distinctive way, leaning off one leg and back on the chair. They were speaking to each other in some other language. I kept thinking I could understand it if I just listened harder, but all my efforts couldn't make sense of it. The syllables all sounded so familiar, yet I couldn't understand a word. Suddenly, one of them said, 'Shhh ... she's awake now.' This was clearly in English, and the only thing I could understand. They were silent for a moment. I looked up and noticed a great amount of cigar smoke swirling around in circles around the back door area in front of me. The smoke impressed me as I took special notice of it, and how much there was. Oddly, I smelled nothing and thought nothing of that! I then decided I didn't know these people, so I decided to turn around and go back to bed, as they continued their merriment.

The next morning I asked my mother, 'who was visiting in the kitchen last night?' She gave me a weird look. No one in the family heard or saw anything. My mother then questioned me about everything I saw, said she could not explain anything, and that I should talk to grandmother. I found this all pretty strange, but my grandmother did have thoughts about it. I also noticed the ash tray was on the table where I had seen it the night before. But I had been responsible for the dishes the evening before, and knew beyond a doubt I had washed it and left it on the counter by the stove. I also noticed that by standing where I was the night before, I would not be able to see one of the men where he was sitting. The refrigerator was blocking the view of that chair.

My grandmother had experienced psychic phenomenon before and felt that the man who sat oddly in the chair was her father-in-law, Joseph Zacek. He sat exactly that way due to an accident while working for the Belt Railroad when he came to America. It resulted in his leg being amputated below the knee. She had me sit the same way I saw him do it and questioned me several times before deciding she was right about the identity of this mystery guest. This was the first I knew anything of my great-grandfather. My grandmother could not determine who the other person would be. But this great-grandfather spoke Bohemian as well as English, and preferred his native language when socializing. If my hunch is right, the other person was my second great-grandfather, also of Bohemian background, and the father of our violin teacher, Joseph Vilim.

It was about twenty-five years later that I learned anything about this other ancestor. Joseph's father was also a violin teacher, who turned to saloon ownership near the time of the Civil War. I could then imagine well the lively conversation in his tavern, thinking back to my ghosts. His tavern served as the meeting place for the 85 founders of St. Wenceslaus Church in Chicago - the first Bohemian parish in the city. He is listed as one of the founders of this group in Chicago records. The church records show he was a popular sponsor for baptisms. The census shows his tavern and estate were financially successful. He was involved in many neighborhood activities as documented in books written by this Bohemian group about themselves. He donated a large sum for a start-up Bohemian language newspaper. They had tremendous pride, spirit and courage which has totally captivated me.

Even more intriguing, I learned that the older Vilim brothers owned a cigar manufacturing business in Chicago before the great fire of 1871. After that time, they moved to Green Bay, Wisconsin and continued to be merchants and cigarmakers there. When this second great-grandfather became ill and couldn't work, I found records of his wife running a cigar shop (later turned to a toy shop), and in 1880 they lived above a building that contained a cigar shop downstairs, the census listing her (not him) as selling cigars.

The study of this family has dominated all my available time and resources for family history. I don't know how this happened since I started by giving equal attention to all lines. My original intention was only to trace all direct lines as far back in time as I could go. I wasn't at all interested in collateral lines. I was just curious because I liked history. I was willing to stop when I found the villages of origin just before coming to America (I am sure you are already chuckling). Oddly enough, the only family lines where I have successfully traced to the 1700's are the Vilim and Zacek lines - the two Bohemian lines from those two kitchen visitors.

Completely unintended, I have become involved in preserving whatever material I can find on this neighborhood and group of people. I feel compelled to find all their names, businesses, and biographical information to document them for future descendants to find. I have walked the streets where this old neighborhood once existed even though it is no longer really safe to do. Without trying, I come upon people today who are descendants from neighbors of my great-great grandparents. Some were in the same social club together in the mid-1800's.

One man started up a correspondence with me. His family was from this old neighborhood. He happened to mention a Czech Old Settlers book he preserved from his grandmother. It was virtually unknown to genealogists, and wasn't in any library I could find. I am publishing it in the quarterly of the Chicago Genealogical Society, of which I am editor, to ensure its accessibility. This is really another example of this compelling desire to tell the story of this group. None of my ancestors were part of the indexed membership roll of this Czech Old Settlers group, yet I had to print it. I couldn't rest until I did.

Recently, I found a passage in one of Joseph's biographies that said his mother, brothers and friends helped him to go to the Prague Conservatory of Music. I know his father became too ill to work when he was fairly young. Were these the neighbors who helped him to go to school in Europe and make possible his wonderful career? Even when very successful, Joseph kept close ties with the neighborhood, often performing at ethnic functions. My research showed he disappeared from Chicago in 1915 when he moved out west. Even my great aunts and uncles couldn't find him. They were children then, and their parents told them nothing about Joseph's move. Does he need to say thanks now, or let us know what became of him? Or is the whole neighborhood group asking for recognition now?

Joseph Vilim

Shirley Vilim Farano

As I continued to trace my great-grandfather's brother, Joseph, I finally found he had settled in Coronado, California. My sister, who had moved to San Diego when her husband unexpectedly had been transferred there, also became captivated with my project of finding more on the violin teacher. One day, she and her husband walked into a used bookstore to browse. Her husband, now aware of her family interest in music, noticed a book sticking off a shelf. He opened the cover and found a bound collection of 'The Musical Leader,' a turn of the century musical publication. He turned to the first page - and it contained a picture of our violin teacher, his sons, and a feature on their violin school. Upon reading the book, she found articles published over a period of time which filled in all the missing years from the time they left Chicago for the west.

I can't help feeling this volume originally belonged to Joseph Vilim's family. I recently visited the family plot at the cemetery in San Diego. When I sat down to look at the area, I noticed three pine trees, each of a different variety. They were the same three pine trees I had drawn in an 8th grade art class! This was my first trip to California, and I believe these types of pines only grow in that climate. Yet, I clearly remember that 8th grade drawing.

My sister's husband has now been transferred out of California. She was the only member of the family, aside from the music teacher Joseph, to leave the Chicago area in the 150 years we've been there! Is it just a coincidence that she moved within a few miles of this old family branch just when my research was beginning to lag because of my geographic location? She found real estate records and other documents in places they had no reason to be. And she found the 'Musical Leaders' - or they found her.

And what about Joseph Vilim? Why did information about him always pop up no matter what else I was looking for? Why did I feel compelled to keep searching for *more* biographical data on him, even though I had amassed a great collection of facts about him already? When I finally saw his picture and what he looked like, I was surprised: it was *me* looking at myself when I wore no makeup! His hair even curls in the same place and in the same way - with one exception. His is on the left side, and mine on the right. It feels like yin and yang.

Finally, a strange pattern emerged after completing my Chicago family research. It seems that every major interest and/or hobby I have become involved with on any scale, was an occupation of a Chicago ancestor! And the same is true of my son and his two great-grandfathers on my side.

Here is a sampling: I have refinished all the kitchen cabinets in our house, all the woodwork, and done antique furniture as well. I own a woodworking text - the only woman I know who does. Joseph Kieserg was a carpenter and furniture maker. I sewed nearly all my own clothing in high school, and slowed down only because of career time demands (and genealogy!). My great-grandfather was a tailor for Hart, Schafner and Marx when he came to Chicago. I loved foreign languages in school and studied French, Spanish, Latin, and German. The g-grandfather-tailor spoke eight languages fluently. I had a strong fear of trains most of my life, once even being frozen in fear when stuck on a crossing as a pedestrian when the gate bells began to ring. My great-grandfather, Joseph Zacek, lost his leg below the knee when working on a train that rolled forward. When visiting Europe, I always visit every church I can. My g-g-grandfather, Joseph Kieserg, built churches. I love horses, and own two. My great-grandfather, William Goy, was a teamster in Chicago. When I tried to think of something to study in college where I could be outside instead of in an office, I seriously considered a surveyor (the only woman to do this). My great-grandfather, Charles Vilim, was a surveyor in Chicago.

My son decided to become a mechanic and airplane prop repair tech. He fishes for sport. His two g-grandfathers on my side (Vilim and Zacek) were mechanics for AB Dick Company and Western Electric, and they both fished as their only sport. The one at Western Electric supervised a department of seventy. My son, at age twenty-five, was supervising his area. It is a coincidence, too, that if those two kitchen ghosts were Vilim and Zacek, they represent the only two family lines I was able to trace out of Chicago and into the 1700's so far.

I think I know the feeling of 'being led' to family history as you wrote in your book!"

I'LL SAY YOU DO, SHIRLEY!

9
"OM" IS WHERE THE HEART IS

Thomas Wolfe was *wrong!*

You *can* go home again. Ask most any genealogist who has journeyed back to an ancestral locale for the first time. It's almost as if our forebears have set out a welcome mat heralding our return!

I certainly felt this serene feeling upon my initial visits back east to "Palatine Country." As I noted in *Psychic Roots*, I often experienced a strong sense of geographic *déjà vu*, an unexplainable familiarity with my new surroundings even though I had never been there before. Sometimes I would know what would be around the bend of the road before I even got there.

Others echoed these experiences. Lee R. Gandee of W. Columbia, South Carolina, had a carbon copy of my own feelings:

> "As a boy, I lived in West Virginia with the couple that reared my orphaned and abandoned mother. At the age of fourteen, I went by bus to Florida to visit my real father. When we neared Columbia, South Carolina, I began having a déjà vu experience that was so intense that, between Columbia and Lexington, I *knew* what would lie around the next bend in the road. At one point, when the bus stopped to let off passengers, I rose from my seat to get off because I recognized the place as where my family lived. But it was not my family in this life!"

And Patricia Stover Fair observed:

> "On my very first visit to Aaronsburg, Centre County, Pennsylvania - where my paternal grandfather Andrew William Stover had gone to spend summers with his

grandparents - I had an eerie feeling: I felt that this was *where I belonged.* Soon, after much research, I was to learn that Aaronsburg had been home to my Stover ancestors for over two hundred years. No wonder I felt like I belonged there!

There's another weird part to this story: I have a strong desire, when the time comes, to be buried in the old Stover cemetery in Aaronsburg. My family thinks I'm crazy!"

Catherine A. Cissna remarked:

"I grew up in Southern California, but never felt any particular connection to the place. In 1974, although living at the time in an area that suited me well enough, I suddenly began thinking about where I'd rather live if I had the choice. I thought about the Gold Rush area in the northern part of the state, talked it over with my husband, and relocated in 1977 to the Mother Lode. That first day of residence here I was overcome by a feeling I had not experienced before ... that I was 'home' for the first time in my life. I felt connected to the area somehow. I then started recording headstones in Amador's cemeteries in this area in March of 1979, hunting out the old, obscure graveyards and going through mortuary, death, and newspaper records for the region.

The project has become somewhat of an obsession, having now spent sixteen years and more than 30,000 hours of my own time chronicling the pioneer families in this area that I feel is 'home' to me!"

Ruby Coleman of North Platte, Nebraska, observed:

"A Methodist minister friend of mine was not a genealogist. But he began to tell 'strange things' that had happened to him. One was when he was in a strange town, yet felt it was familiar. He knew suddenly that one of his ancestors - a great grandmother - had lived there. While in that town, he went to the local cemetery and found her grave. He had no recollection of knowing that she was buried there. He said it was almost as if he had been there before or was willed to know that she had lived there!"

Bill Hull of Canton, New York, recalled:

"I was driving a charter bus through Rhinebeck and Red Hook, New York one time, and felt a strong affinity for both communities. I later learned that my Scherp/Sharp Palatine ancestors lived in the vicinity.

I had a similar thing happen while driving a milk truck on a route up Beech Plains Road in Pierrepont, New York. As I passed the local cemetery there, I had a very special feeling about the place. Years afterwards, I learned my great-great grandfather was buried there."

Helen L. Harriss of Pittsburgh, Pennsylvania, contributor of so many wonderful and unusual occurrences to the first volume, noted:

"On a trip to England, Scotland, and Wales which took me near the homes of my ancestors I did feel a wonderful sense of peace while there, of closeness to them, and of the 'rightness' of it all - whether that feeling was of my making or their gift to me, I do not know."

Charlotte Reedy of Springfield, Tennessee, had this to report:

"I enjoyed very much your *Psychic Roots.* I bought the book to see if it would confirm what I had experienced or thought I had experienced - and that is exactly what it did.

I grew up in Springfield, Tennessee and, like most families in the South at that time, mine took Sunday afternoon drives around Robertson County. Even that early in my life, I knew that there were particular areas in the county where I felt contentment. There were other areas that I found boring and in which I felt no interest at all. It was not until I returned to Springfield after several years in Virginia and started to research my own family background that I realized that the very areas which I so loved to visit - Coopertown, Cedar Hill, Adams - were the very areas where my 'early family' had lived. I found little or no trace of my family in those areas which were not interesting to me as a child.

Since then, I have had several 'place connection' experiences as well as other 'coincidences' that are more than coincidences."

The particulars of these "going home" stories are delightfully intriguing!   Barbara Roberts Baylis of Dallas, Texas, wrote:

"My experience happened in Strafford County, New Hampshire where my Roberts ancestors settled. The first research trip we made to New Hampshire, I booked a room in a bed-and-breakfast in Chocorua. At the time I didn't know this establishment was just down the road from the home my Roberts ancestor bought in 1824.

As we climbed the three flights of stairs and entered our room, much to our surprise, the wallpaper that greeted us was an all over pattern of 'Roberts Genealogy.' (I have enclosed a copy of the picture I took of the wallpaper.) It was a 'welcome' to the world of Roberts ... and in subsequent trips I've taken the line back to Thomas Roberts of Dover in 1632!"

Alice Strom of Reno, Nevada, can relate to Barbara's tale:

"The feeling that those 'on the Other Side' take an interest in our research and let their presence be known to us in mysterious ways really came home to me when I visited New England last year. I traveled to Bennington, Vermont to do some family history research. I was looking for data on Fanny T. Morgan, a relative who died there in 1952.

I called a Bed and Breakfast placement service, and they booked us in a room in The Safford Manor, located right on Main Street in Bennington. My research was very successful in that I found the graves of Fanny and her parents (and my great-great-grandparents), John and Anne (McIlroy) Tomlinson, in the Bennington Park Lawn Cemetery. The probate packet at the local courthouse yielded the details of Fanny's relationship to her ten heirs and identified all my great-grandfather's siblings.

But the real surprise came when I visited the library and learned that Fanny's husband was William R. Morgan, a descendant of the Revolutionary War soldier Joseph Safford, and that Fanny and William had lived in the big house on Main Street now converted into a Bed and Breakfast."

The Roberts wallpaper at the bed & breakfast inn

Dorothy Milne of Don Mills, Ontario, had a memorable visit to an ancestral town:

"When my husband and I visited Plymouth, Massachusetts in 1993, I noticed that the Howland House was open for tours - it had always been locked before. I asked my husband to give me thirty minutes to have a quick tour and, patient soul that he is, he agreed and dropped me off at the front door.

A tour had just started, but the lady at the door told me to follow the group, and I would be able to hear the early history of the house at the end. It was all most interesting, and then the guide and I walked towards the old part of the house. 'What brings you to Plymouth?' she inquired. I replied that my children are descendants of Kenelm Winslow and Thomas Rogers.

The tour guide the introduced herself. To my amazement, her name was Kathleen Rogers Winslow, and she was also descended from Kenelm and Thomas. After comparing family notes, Kathleen drove me up Rexhame Hill in Marshfield to the home built by Winslow in 1642, now a private dwelling.

What a thrill!"

V. G. Johnson of Independence, Missouri, remembers what happened to her friend Pastor David Folkerts of Calhan, Colorado:

"During a visit to Germany in 1985, Pastor Folkerts wanted to visit the Ostfriesland village of Walle where his great-grandfather Jurgen Folkerts had been born in 1860. Upon arriving in the charming village, several serendipitous events eventually led him to discover a 'Widow Folkerts,' who graciously received and entertained him. Old pictures were looked at, and Folkerts names on Bible records were scanned. Even though no real family connections could be figured out, the Folkerts name (and a strong family resemblance) bound them all together.

Just prior to Pastor Folkert's departure, Widow Folkerts remembered something. Hidden away behind a door that always stood open against a wall was an embroidered wall hanging. It showed the family tree of her husband's Folkert family. It was a wedding gift she and her husband

had received many years earlier, and showed five Folkert
brothers. And there in the lower right-hand corner of that
old family tree was Jurgen, who, she remembered, was a
brother who had gone to America. They never knew what
had become of him.

But Pastor Folkert knew: it was his own great-
grandfather, Jurgen Folkert!"

Kathy Staples of Bath, Ontario, Canada, had some fun with
a recent visitor:

"Last summer, a chap came into our Loyalist Cultural
Centre asking, 'What is this place?' After telling him that
we were an historical house and research library telling
the Loyalist story, he proceeded to say that he was
beginning to research his family who had settled in the
Bay of Quinte area. I replied, 'Welcome Home!'

He answered that he did not live in the area, but came
from Albuquerque, New Mexico. The family he was
researching was Diamond. Again, I replied, 'Welcome
Home!'

He answered, 'No, I'm from Albuquerque, New Mexico.'
We continued talking about genealogy and once again, after
giving me some more details, I again said, 'Welcome
Home!'

He finally looked at me and said, 'I'm obviously
missing your point.' I then told him that he was in the
exact location where his Diamond ancestors had landed in
1784, in the Bay of Quinte. He looked startled - mentioned
that any maps he had been able to find did not show the
Bay of Quinte.

The gentleman then visited churches, family
cemeteries, and land grants in our area. After doing this, he
returned to have afternoon tea at the Centre, where he
asked if we had any genealogical files on the Diamond
family. I handed him a published booklet entitled
'Diamonds Are Forever' - his whole family line!

The final whammy was the fact that he had only
stopped at the Centre to use the washrooms!"

I think **Kathleen Rees Klein of Rye, New York,** was *meant*
to "go home":

"I had always wanted to visit Cashel, County Tipperary, Ireland. It was home to my maternal grandfather, Joseph Gilbert, who came to America in the late 1880's. I had visited Cashel very briefly in 1983 on a whirlwind trip, but basically just got off the bus, took a picture, and proceeded on to the next stop.

In March of 1989, our church in Rye, New York held their annual St. Patrick's Party. My husband, Bill, and I purchased ten tickets at $10.00 each for the Grand Prize, a trip to Ireland with all expenses paid. A few days before the event, a couple who were good friends of ours tried to purchase chances, but to their dismay found they were completely sold out. 'Not to worry,' I said, 'Bill and I will sell you five of our ten chances, and keep five for ourselves.'

The night of the affair was clear and crisp. The highlight of the evening was the awarding of that free trip to Ireland by a representative of *Aer Lingus*. You guessed it! I was the winner! My jaw just dropped, as I was ushered up to the stage to speak. I do recall saying that I wanted to visit County Tipperary to find out more about my mother's family, the Gilberts. Little did I know the serendipitous and momentous discoveries that lay ahead of me on that journey!

After the drawing, the usher who had emceed the affair thought to himself, 'I wonder if I tried picking another ticket, maybe my own would come up this time?' For pure fun, he turned to the huge drum and mixed up the hundreds of tickets. He then proceeded to pick again.

Would you believe that *my* ticket came up *a second time*??!!

All the usher could say was, 'Someone must really want the Kleins to go to Ireland!'"

Sometimes a family historian will have quite an adventure, as did Doris P. Schultz of Alexandria, Virginia:

"My husband and I celebrated our fiftieth wedding anniversary in May, but delayed celebration until we could take a 'memory trip' on the Ohio River. My paternal grandparents lived on the banks at Gallipolis and from their front porch, as a child, I watched the paddlewheelers ply the river. Also, my earlier ancestors had arrived and lived at Marietta with the first settlers two centuries ago. The fall foliage cruise on the historic *Delta Queen*, with three stops, afforded a chance to walk the streets where my ancestors walked and to see Gallipolis again, albeit at night.

When we boarded the *Delta Queen*, the news and activity paper was in our room. The crew was listed. These *"Queens" (Mississippi and Delta)* always carry two pilots who alternate six-hour shifts for a month and are off a month. So the company has numerous qualified pilots. I couldn't believe my eyes when I read the names of the pilots assigned to our cruise - both with familiar names: Captain Shultz (my married name without our 'c') and Captain Powell (my maiden name and Gallipolis grandfather's)! Of course, I made it a point to meet and exchange family information, and a new distant cousin was found.

I asked Captain Powell when we would be passing Gallipolis and was disappointed to learn that it would be between 1:30 and 2:00 A.M., but I set my clock for 1:45 anyway. I lowered the shutter and leaned on the sill (I had asked for a room on the Ohio side so I could see Gallipolis). By 2:00 A.M., I thought I had missed our hometown, but leaned a little longer. At 2:12, I recognized the Silver Bridge north of town, the island that blocked the town lights, and the ferry ramp that Grandpa had led me down so many years ago. At 3:00 A.M., a car's headlights illuminated First Avenue where once my Grandfather's home stood. We rounded the bend below Mound Hill Cemetery where my parents rest with the other Powells, and all was still and dark. I slept well the rest of the night.

After breakfast, an announcement was made that we would be passing through the Gallipolis Locks, if anyone wanted to go on deck and watch. Had I been so anxious to see Gallipolis that I dreamed my sighting? 'No,' said Captain Powell. I had not dreamed it. We passed Gallipolis at the time I said, but around the bend the fog thickened, and we had to anchor for four hours - arriving late at the locks. My trip home was greatly extended. As Johnny Appleseed said, 'The Lord is good to me!'"

Elaine Hoover Bogino of Newburgh, New York, still wonders about her recent European trip:

"In early December, I felt an urge to visit Amsterdam and Ghent, Belgium, both considered as sources for my Van Siclen family. Since I travel alone, I looked for some group which would include more than an overnight in each of these places. None seemed to exist. But in January, I received a brochure, totally out of the blue, from a previously unknown (to me) company offering a cruise of the western coast of Europe, with an optional extension of two nights in Amsterdam and three in Ghent.

Before I left, I had been reading *Psychic Roots*, but I never gave a thought that the trip I was about to make might be a serendipitous experience. Although now that I think about it, even receiving an unsolicited brochure that gave an option almost of my design was a little strange.

A major goal was to photograph the three medieval houses in Ghent which were the residences of the Van der Sickelen family in the 13th - 15th centuries. In Lisbon and Amsterdam, our hotels were away from the center of town. What hope did I have that Ghent would be different! We were informed on the way to Ghent that our hotel was changed, and we were to spend three nights in a new hotel that had only been open for several weeks. It turned out to be in the center of historic Ghent, and the Sikkel houses were within one block. At the rear of one of the houses stood a tall, white, "Rapunzel-like" tower. Earlier on in Amsterdam, I had purchased at a flea market for about six dollars, a blue Stadteteller type plate with a tall, white tower for no reason, but I *had* to have it.

Why did I feel such a desire to visit these two places? Why did I get a brochure offering just what I wanted, albeit with a rather expensive cruise as the main item? And why was the hotel changed to one in my very own neighborhood? I must admit I felt very comfortable there. I don't know what my next steps will be, but I know the connection exists.

I feel it in my genes!"

Finding the family home itself can be quite a "trip!" George E. Flagg of Des Moines, Iowa, relates:

"I am a lawyer, and a couple came to see me about drawing up their wills. After a lengthy conversation, we determined that we were distant cousins. Fortunately, they had a great many records of the history of that branch of our family and shared them with me. They also told me where the family had immigrated from in Maine and even supplied me with a picture of the farmhouse.

On going to Maine some years ago, my brother and I determined to find the old homestead. We had been told that it was located along Highway 2, a few miles south of Bangor. We had driven up the interstate highway to a point twenty miles short of Bangor, when we decided we should take a side highway, cut over to the coast, and start looking along Highway 2 for the house. In discussing this plan with my brother, I said, 'Now, this picture is what the homestead place looks like. It is very similar to the house we just passed.'

I then did a double take, looked at the picture, looked at the house, and saw that *it was my ancestor's house!* In other words, we found the old house by accident - being on a highway where we normally would never have been. We stopped, knocked on the door, and were shown around by a lovely lady who practically was a twin of my mother!"

Jacqueline Baker Humphrey of Melbourne, Florida, contributes:

"A relative, Reverend Jim Baker, wrote a book that told that, from ca. 1870 to 1903, the old Baker family farm was on Shelby Road, leading to Medina, New York. In the 1960s, I resided near Niagara Falls, some 50 miles away.

One day I decided to traverse Shelby Road, which is many miles long, for the first time. As we were riding along, I suddenly told my husband, 'STOP HERE.' Overcoming my shyness, I approached the house and knocked. An elderly man named Smith answered the door. I stated that he might think I was crazy, but that I was trying to locate a former Baker farm on that long road. I was flabbergasted when he told me that I was at the correct house. Mr. Smith grew up on the adjoining farm, and his father bought it about 1903 when Charles Baker sold it.

I still get goose-bumps thinking about it!"

And John T. Humphrey of Washington, D. C., remembers:

"My interest in genealogy can be directly attributed to my paternal grandfather. You see, his mother was struck and killed by lightning when he was four years old, and his father deserted the family. For all intents and purposes, he was orphaned. This lack of family and a 'sense of his roots' undoubtedly instilled in him his intense desire to have at least some knowledge of his Welsh ancestry. Unfortunately, he had no idea of how to go about locating information on his family and really never pursued the matter.

When I started my search, at first I had no more luck than he did. But then a number of years ago, I was at the NGS Conference in Washington, D.C. and attended a session on Welsh ancestry given by now good friend John Rowlands. John noted that he and his wife, Sheila, conducted a course in Welsh family history at the University of Wales in Aberystwyth. It didn't take me long to decide to attend that course the following year.

I spent the first couple of days on that initial trip to Wales touring several places in North Wales where I knew the Welsh quarrymen who came to eastern Pennsylvania had their origins. On the second day of my visit, I traveled via a series of local buses to the towns of Bangor and Caernarfon, and, after visiting Dolbadarn Castle, home of the last Welsh Prince of Wales, I realized that I probably had enough time left to visit the parish cemetery at Llandegai, where I had reason to believe my recently found great-great-grandfather William Jones may have been buried.

The easiest way to that cemetery from Dolbadarn Castle was to take a fourth local bus across some back country roads through several small towns and villages. In one of these villages, Rhwilas, the bus driver drove up a long incline where he came to the end of the road at the edge of town. He then got out to talk with several of the neighbors. We were parked there for several minutes, which is why the location became fixed in my mind. Later, we arrived at Pehryn Castle and the Llandegai Church some distance from Rhwilas, where I searched for the gravestone of my Welsh ancestor with no success.

Two days after my visit to the Llandegai churchyard, I travelled on to Aberystwyth for the Welsh family history course. At dinner that evening, I sat next to Pete and Gwyneth Ruffell. It did not take long to find out that Gwyneth was born in Llandegai Parish and spent more of her childhood years there - which I found quite remarkable. You see, there were only twenty-seven participants in the course, and only three of the twenty-seven were from Wales, the remainder being Americans and English. Now when you realize that in Wales there are over 1,000 chapelries and parishes, the odds that someone was attending who lived in the parish where my family had its origins were fairly remote.

Pete and Gwyneth soon became friends, and it was with Gwyneth's help that I learned what I had found on my trip through north Wales by bus was not the grave of William Jones, but his place of birth. He was born within 100 feet of where the bus had stopped in Rhwilas. In fact, I later learned, the old farm at the edge of village had been for three generations the home of my ancestors!

John L. Scherer of Rexford, New York, is curator of Decorative Arts at the NY State Museum at Albany. He remembered:

"In 1972, I traveled to Corinth, New York to inspect some possible acquisitions for the New York State Museum at Albany, where I am curator of decorative arts. Coincidentally, my great-grandfather James T. Betts (1869 - 1944) had lived somewhere in Corinth in the 1890's, when my grandmother was born. When Mr. and Mrs. Thomas Palmitier answered the door at 2 Oak Street and led me to an upstairs flat, I mentioned the fact that my great-grandfather had lived in Corinth. When Mr. Palmitier asked for the name, I replied, 'James T. Betts.'

We were all stunned when we learned that this was *the very house* where he lived! It was an experience I will never forget. To this day, it is the only house in Corinth that I have ever been inside of."

Grant Michael Menzies of Oregon, and Klaus K. Stoehr of Hawthorn Woods, Illinois, both had similar moving experiences on trips to Germany. Grant's happened this way:

"While in the town of Kirchhain, south of Marburg, Germany, I was intent on getting into the old church there. Not only does it date from the lifetimes of my 16th century forebears in that town, but it also contained, according to various printed sources, the grave effigy of my 12x great-grandfather, Johann Lucan, a graduate of Marburg University who became Bürgermeister of Kirchhain and died in an epidemic in the 1560's. But when I got there, to my dismay the entire structure was being repaired, the bell-tower was swathed in scaffolding, and repairmen were going in and out the doors busily attending to their tasks. I knew that Johann Lucan's effigy had once been outside the edifice, but I found nothing in my search of the church grounds to verify this.

Fortunately just when things were looking bleak, a tall distinguished gentleman came toward me along a paved pathway from the church. I asked if it was possible to get inside, and, as luck would have it, this man was the Pfarrer himself. My enthusiasm was restored when he, on strength of my being an American descendant of the old patrician Lucan family, not only let me go inside the church, but escorted me to the door. But all was not yet wonderful, because though I was inside, cameras at the ready, I was dismayed to find most of the church's interior sunk in shadow, including a row of gravestones lining the opposite wall. I couldn't see anything, let alone a Lucan effigy, and it occurred to me that since being photographed years ago, it may have been broken purposely or accidentally.

The workmen, to whom I was totally oblivious, must have felt sorry for me, because suddenly some work lights came on directly above the row of memorial tablets. I practically vaulted the intervening pews, because there I saw my 12x great-grandfather's life-size figure gazing at me with a look about as surprised as mine must have been. I could have wept to touch that strange, ecstatic face, which unfortunately no photograph I took quite delineates accurately. My first thought was that the face was carved from a death mask, as Shakespeare's at Stratford was said to have been. I couldn't take my fingers off that face, those hands. I was aware that the church was very silent. I looked back and some of the workmen were watching me intently. One of them trained his beam on the effigy, making possible the photographs I took.

The air was alive with a sort of electricity. I loved my unknown ancestor at that moment, but I also felt a great outpouring of love for the pastor who happened to be walking toward me that morning, for the workmen whose presence would normally prohibit our entering the building but instead aided me in my quest. I was overcome by a sense of unseen benevolent guidance and protection, as some people are privileged to be once or twice in a lifetime, and this was not the only occasion either in Germany or elsewhere. And the abiding presence of my paternal grandmother, who gave me a blood tie to this carved gentleman in the cape and ruff, never left my side once during the whole two and a half weeks I roamed Hessen - in quiet moments atop castle ruins or in little country churches or watching the rushing Rhine, I spoke to her. I always said the same thing: 'Look at this, Grandma! I came here for *you*!'

I think Grandma probably understood very well - in fact, I have not the slightest doubt that she helped and helps me along the way."

Klaus K. Stoehr's travels brought forth this event:

"In the summer of 1993, while vacationing in Germany, we took a little detour to Fambach where my ancestor Christoph Rumpach had been born. Both he and his father, Kaspar Rumpach, had been pastors there. A kindly parishioner opened the old church for us and then went home to look for a booklet on the church's history. I walked around and, for some reason, came to stand in front of an illegible grave marker in the center floor of the church. I felt that I had reached something of importance and just stood there.

When a copy of the church chronology turned up, we saw Kaspar Rumpach's account of the horrors he experienced as a pastor during the Thirty Years War, and then a transcript of Christoph's 1706 gravestone - which was exactly where I had stood:

'Wanderer, don't look for golden crowns here
for Christ's servants have been crowned with thorns.
This is their award on earth. But look up above you!

Mr. Rumpach, the example of loyal teachers,
is adorned with heavenly bliss.
He carries the crown of righteousness.
Go! Believe what he taught, live and die like him,
as a Christian, and you will attain this crown too.'

Hank, I am very quiet about my religious beliefs, but I would testify that it was the Holy Spirit who had guided me there. I was overcome when I realized what a message it was, and how it had been communicated to the later generation."

The Reverend Leopold H. Hoppe of Kansas City, Missouri, contributed one of my favorite experiences:

"Timothy Harbaugh, my grandmother's maternal grandfather, was three-quarters Wyandot and Ojibway Indian, as well as of Pennsylvania Dutch ancestry. When my wife and I visited the site of his parents' John and Polly Harbaugh's residence on the banks of the Maumee River, I also visited the site of the Battle of Fallen Timbers. I had driven by the site on trips to Pennsylvania and New York to visit my daughters, but had never found it convenient to stop. When we finally got to this historic locale, I had the feeling that I had been in exactly the same place before - déjà vu. The landscape seemed strangely familiar to me even though I had never been in that place before.

I had a serendipitous experience there that shook me to the foundation of my being. I am a very matter-of-fact person, but on that day I heard 'voices' calling me by the name my grandmother called me as a boy - 'Lee' - but speaking to me in a language I could not understand. I will never forget the experience!

Perhaps there is something to what Stewart Holbrook calls 'an accumulated memory' in his book *The Yankee Exodus: An Account of Migration From New England*. And perhaps there is such a thing as a psychic inheritance, waiting to be claimed by persons removed for generations from the places where their ancestors lived, that allows them to instinctively recognize as familiar to themselves the sights and sounds that were once important to their forebears. Perhaps John and Polly Harbaugh's spirits had been patiently waiting for me, or some of their other lost children, to come to their last resting place to remember them.

I hope that they will never be forgotten again."

When taking part in a church service in Pennsylvania in a congregation where his ancestors had worshipped 146 ago, Tom Crane of Calumet City, Illinois, noted,

"It brought me great pleasure and honor to stand before God and the spirits of the past, and address that congregation. I felt that I had returned to witness the past and all those who had gone before us. Those of the past as well as the present must have been truly proud that we carried on with their religious convictions and traditions. We were spiritually united and, for that moment, time had no meaning. We were past, present, and future all at once. It was then that I began to grasp some idea of what eternity really meant."

AMEN, TOM!

10

DREAMS:
MIRRORS OF OUR SOULS

"A Dream is a Wish Your Heart Makes!"
Judging from the letters received for this sequel, I think the lyric of that lovely song from Disney's classic *Cinderella* can apply to family history research as well as to fairy-tale happy endings. Our unconscious is operating on all burners during our dream state to provide us with assistance in solving some of our thorniest genealogical puzzlers.

I love the story contributed by William L. Deyo of Fredericksburg, Virginia:

"Early on in my genealogical research, I obtained a blank 7-generation chart on which to record ancestors. I often used to have a dream in which I would be looking at that ancestor chart, completely filled out! But when I would wake up, I could not remember any of the names I saw.

After several years, I had found the names of all of my sixth generation ancestors except the wife of my third great-grandfather, Rodney Selden Jefferson Shelton. I desperately wanted to find her name. She was dead before the 1850 census and her daughter, Ellen Blanche Shelton, my great-great-grandmother, died during the Civil War when death records were not recorded in Stafford County, Virginia. I thought that if I could just find the death record of a known brother or sister of Ellen, it might give the mother's name; but I couldn't find a single one. I finally found the tombstone of Ellen's sister, Lousia [*sic*] (Shelton) Freeman, in the Fredericksburg City Cemetery, and she had died well after 1912. I sent for her death certificate and had great expectations that the blank for the name of the mother would be filled in. But I then received a notice from the Bureau of Vital Statistics that no record was on file for Lousia. That was my last hope, and I just had to go on to other things.

Shortly thereafter, I had another of my 'chart dreams.' I was determined to find the mother of Ellen Shelton, and in my dream I focused right on her space. When I awoke, I ran for a pen and paper to write down Ellen's mother's name. All I could remember was *'Pumphrey.'* That was not a familiar name in the area, and I did not put any faith in it. But the dream made me more determined than ever to find proof of my ancestor's name. I checked Aunt Lousia's obituary in the local paper. There was the problem! She was buried in Fredericksburg, but did not die there! She died at the home of a daughter in Portsmouth, Virginia.

I tried again for the death certificate with the corrected place of death. I received the certificate several weeks later, and the names of both parents were recorded. Her mother was 'Jane Humphries,' the name in Stafford originally being *'Humphrey'* - which in the late 19th century was still interchanged with 'Humphries.' The name in my dream, or at least the way I remembered it when I awoke, was *one letter off!*

That is enough to make me believe it was more than just a coincidence."

Ernest C. Gimblet of Houston, Texas, had a dream too:

"Throughout my life, I believe the experiences of serendipity and/or psychic events have occurred many times to my advantage. For the last ten years, my hobby has been family genealogy; and finding where my grandfather, John George Gimblet, was buried near Lawrence, Kansas became a major hunt. All the remaining relatives in the summer of 1989 had no memory of the cemetery in which he was interred. After a lengthy discussion with an older cousin, we decided to visit a likely cemetery the next day.

But during the night, my sleep was interrupted by what seemed to be a male voice speaking to me which said, 'The grave site you seek is located in the upper right hand corner of the cemetery - like a postage stamp on an envelope.' The following morning before the trip to the Flory Cemetery, I told my dream to my wife, Dorothy - just in case there was some substance to the instructions.

After arrving at the cemetery, which contained some three to four hundred headstones, I walked to the upper right hand corner directly to the tombstones of my grandfather and grandmother! As a youth of nine years, I possibly was at the grave site for my grandfather's funeral, but not my grandmother's; however, I have no memory of the event."

Another cemetery story came in from Dave Stutesman of Charlestown, Indiana:

"I recently saw your feature on *Unsolved Mysteries*, and I thought you would like to hear of my episode. In 1989, while doing some genealogical research, I made plans to visit a library in another county to do some digging on some ancestors who once resided there. I decided to go on a Saturday.

The Friday evening just prior to my trip, I had an unusual dream. I was in an old home that looked to be built in the 1800's. The house had high ceilings and flowery wallpaper. In the dream, an old woman in a bonnet and long calico dress grabbed me by the forearm and started pulling me. I yanked myself away and turned to run out the door. But then another woman, dressed much the same as the first, blocked my exit by standing in the doorway.

I woke up and just passed it off as a weird dream. The next day, I went to the library and found a list of burials in cemeteries of that county. On that roll I finally discovered new dates and data on my great-great-grandmother Mary Adeline Doolittle Robison (1836 - 1892) and her mother Elizabeth Rawlings Doolittle Bacon (1814 - 1906). I then decided to go to that cemetery and see if I could find their actual gravestones. I had never been there before and knew nothing of where the grave would be, but I stopped my car in the cemetery drive, got out, and walked immediately to the common headstone they both shared! It was in bad shape, the base having split and the top part having fallen over. The entire plot was covered with thick vines, but I cleared them off, leveled the base, and reassembled the stone as best I could.

I was never one to believe in communication from beyond, but after this, I know it had to have been my two grandmothers in my dream. No one in my family had ever known where they were buried. They wanted me to find their graves before the marker was totally destroyed and lost to time."

Jane Burrell of Lenexa, Kansas, shared this dream:

"For years, I had looked for my supposed 'Carey' family, only to discover last year that the correct spelling is 'Cary.' During sleep, on the night of this discovery, I became aware of people assembling in my big wall-to-wall closet directly in front of my bed. Once they had congregated, they emerged from the closet and stood at the foot of my bed.

Each was dressed in a costume style apparently worn during their lifetime. One of them was wearing a suit of armor! Instead of talking, they almost seemed to be chanting, telling each other and me their stories. When I awakened, there was no doubt in my mind that I had just visited with my Cary ancestors.

A short time later, I documented this lineage back to the 11th century."

Clarence Lemire of Escanaba, Michigan, wrote:

"I started my genealogy in January 1990 and collected small bits of family data, but didn't really progress much ... until one night I had a strange dream. I found myself walking in the snow, following some footprints. Even though the tracks went on, I grew disgusted because I didn't seem to be getting anywhere. I threw my hands up in frustration and sat down on a log off to the side of the trail. As my mind wandered, I found myself looking up at a woman's face in the sky. It was larger than normal, and she was smiling as she looked down on me. I heard her say, 'Don't give up - you're on the right track!' I asked her if she was a relative, and she said, 'Yes.' With that, her face started to fade away, and she was gone. As I stood up, I felt my tiredness leave me and new energy began to flow through me. I saw the tracks and began to follow them again.

My maternal grandmother Alma Duford died in 1937. I never knew her, as I was born in 1960. Besides being an expert photographer as well as a music teacher, she was always good at genealogy. From the pictures of her left behind, she looks *very* much like the woman who smiled at me in my dream. Over the past few years, I've come to love genealogy too (I also take lots of photos and have a real love for music of all kinds).

I wonder if she is my Guardian Angel?

Maybe!"

Grant Michael Menzies of Oregon related:

"I was thumbing through the latest issue of *Omni* this afternoon; and noticed the short article 'Ancestral PSI.' From the first sentence I knew that I could not be as mad as I thought, since here you were talking about 'psychic phenomena helping people trace family trees' - something I've been convinced of for several years now, but rarely talked about.

From the very first phase of tracing my late paternal grandmother's German ancestry I felt I was being 'helped,' either by her energies or those of forebears or a combination of both. She was a secretive woman, and I didn't really know much about her. I was fourteen when she died in 1978, and the strange thing is, I have only been discovering who she was since her death. I have had dreams, usually only once, that were like visits, in which I asked my grandmother many questions. Once I brought a letter which in reality I had found in a cabinet in her bedroom, written in old German script which at that time I could not read. In the dream, she told me it was from a cousin in Germany, and concerned an inheritance.

I had the letter translated by a German lady some time afterward, and this was exactly what it said!"

Peggy Posson Kindall of Hays, Kansas, had a genealogical dream that saved her life!

"In November of 1978, we took our girls on a trip to Denver. As usual, we got a late start; and, as usual, I was tired. Not as usual, somewhere along the darkened stretch of Highway 36 at night, I dozed off. Perhaps 'dozed off' is a little mild; in fact, I went into dream phase.

Now for some time I had searched for information about my great-grandfather's oldest sister, Wealtha Anna (Posson) Bentley. I knew her date and place of birth, that she was married in Wisconsin, and that she resided in or near St. Charles, Minnesota in early 1890 when her mother died. I also had been informed that she had three children. I have two photos of her that I know of: one is by herself when she was at least middle-aged; the other was when she was older, with three adults (perhaps her grown children?) in the photo with her.

When I fell into my dream phase that night in our station wagon, I saw her pictured with those three I mentioned. In my dream, the younger adults stayed in the distance; Wealtha, however, floated toward me, until it seemed she was standing right in front of me. I was thrilled beyond words - almost! 'Wealtha,' I cried, 'You came to see me! Do you know how long I have looked for you? I have so many questions to ask of you, so much I need to know!'

She smiled and said she would be glad to answer any questions I had, that I could ask her anything. I reached for a notebook, so I could write down the information she was going to give me, all the while feeling the thrill of discovery and the excitement of numerous questions going through my mind. We didn't get a very long visit, it seemed; in fact, I got absolutely no information at all. Her sweet, grandmotherly face faded, and she said she had to leave. I begged her, 'Please don't leave, I have waited so long to find you, to ask you all these questions. You said you would answer my questions!' She replied urgently, 'Not now; you must go back!! Go back!!' I began to cry; I didn't want her to leave, not so soon. I was so close to having my questions answered. My pleas were not unheard nor unheeded. But Wealtha's voice was insistent, very much so, 'You must go back!' Her image faded backward and got smaller, and I could only see her as she was, in the photo with her adult children, smiling. Crying openly, I called out, 'Come back, please come back!'

At this point in time, my crying had apparently awakened my husband! He had dozed off at the wheel and was heading for a ditch off the highway. Somehow, he managed to pull the vehicle back onto the westbound lane without overcorrecting, and the car was stabilized.

Was it a dream, a vision, or what? Did Wealtha really warn me? I don't know; I just don't know. I remember the dream, or vision, of Wealtha being so restful, so inviting. Have you had the experience of having a really relaxing, pleasant dream; and then were awakened by someone or something? It was like one of those times, when I could have easily ignored the interruption and gone back to sleep to pursue my dream and finish it.

But Wealtha ended this, not me!"

As mentioned earlier, I've certainly experienced the power of dreams too. One of the strangest things that ever happened to me along these lines happened a few years ago in Massachusetts after I spoke to the New England Historic Genealogical Society. At the conclusion of the seminar, genealogist Ann Lainhart drove me from Andover to Marblehead to visit my old friends Arlene and Steve Willard.

Their quaint house was located at the bottom of a hill at the foot of Marblehead's oldest cemetery. It had been in Arlene's family for generations. The Willards gave this Californian a taste of good New England hospitality and really rolled out the red carpet. Arlene cooked the tastiest lobster I've ever had, plucked by Steve moments before from the ocean. It was a clambake to be remembered.

After dinner, I certainly was "suffering from comfort." So we walked off our excellent meal by trudging up the hillside to examine the ancient stones in the cemetery. Some of the weathered markers went back into the 1600's, and the poignancy of their worn inscriptions made those Marblehead colonists almost come alive again.

That night - thanks to the seminar, the lobster(s), and the walk - I fell into bed, absolutely exhausted. Pulling my patchwork quilt over my head, I prepared to "settle down for a long winter's nap." But in the middle of the night, something very strange happened. It's hard to explain, but all I can tell you is, yes, I had a dream - but it was *much more* than a dream. It was as real as anything I've ever experienced - maybe more so.

I seemed to be in a whirlwind of images: colonial men with starched collars and stern looks, women wearing 17th-century garb holding primitive cooking utensils, Indians with painted faces and decked out in bright feathers - all swirling around me, speaking words I couldn't quite comprehend. As these images gradually grew in intensity, the entire bedroom seemed to whirl and pulse with an energy of its own. The house was alive with ghosts of the past! I felt like an intruder from another century who didn't belong there.

Downstairs in the kitchen, I saw my friend Arlene - or at least someone who looked to be Arlene - dressed in a 17th-century costume. She sat in an old rocking chair, smiling and laughing, as the colonial people whirled about her. The more she rocked, the more electricity seemed to crackle and pop around her. And then as the speed of the spinning bodies increased, they formed a vortex of energy - a funnel of souls that disappeared right "into" Arlene.

Gone, just like that! All that was left was my friend, who had incorporated each one of those ancient citizens of Marblehead into her very being.

When I awoke, I was dripping wet with perspiration. I poked my nose out from under my covers to see if it was safe to come out. I guess it was, but I was still terrified. It was all too real to be a dream. I couldn't sleep for the rest of the night.

The next morning, I went downstairs - trying to figure out how I would ever tell Arlene and Steve about my strange experience. Arlene, looking as normal as blueberry pie, was at the stove making coffee as I walked in. Trying to pull myself together and somehow get the words out, I fumbled around and finally said,

"Arlene, something happened last night ... "

She interrupted me, saying, "You've had *'the DREAM,'* haven't you?"

Chills ran down my spine. I gulped and said, "Yes! How did you know?"

She replied, "You're not alone. Other guests have had it too. It happens here."

I don't know *what* happened that night. I probably never will. I do know that I witnessed a demonstration of psychic energy of *some* kind that I will never forget. Again, all I can say is that it was not just a dream. I was a participant in some kind of ghost memory ... the graveyard, the old house, the colonists - everything seemed to be channeled into my friend.

For a time, there was no time.

I had a chance, for a moment, to observe eternity.

Joanne Wharfield Roberts of Miami, Florida, had a dream that has touched me deeply:

"One of the lines I am researching descends from Deacon Samuel Chapin of Springfield, Massachusetts. One early name that popped up in that line was that of Bethia Thurston, who married Samuel Chapin's grandson Seth in 1691. I found myself dreaming about Bethia, and she haunted my thoughts by day. I would be in that 'twilight zone' just before falling asleep, and her name would just repeat itself over and over in my brain. Finally, I said, out loud, 'OK Bethia - if you're trying to tell me something, I'll look into your family.'

The next day I wrote the New England Historic Genealogical Society in Boston to see if there was any published material. It turned out that there is a published genealogy, and the NEHGS sent me the relevant pages. To my surprise, there was information on the Chapin family, as a footnote, that I hadn't come across previously in all my research. It seems Bethia Thurston Chapin's sister-in-law, Mary, in 1682 married Joseph Adams, who became the grandfather of the second President of the United States, John Adams. Bethia and Seth Chapin's son, also a Seth, married Abigail Adams, the aunt of the second President, in 1713.

After I found this interesting material, Bethia never returned in my dreams again. Somehow I doubt that this is all she wants me to know, but I found it fascinating. I've made a promise to her and all the other women in my various lines, who all too often appear only as 'the wife of ...' that I will do everything I can to present them as the individuals they are. These courageous women will play as large a part in my writing of the family history as I can uncover!

To me, my ancestors are very real and much more than names on charts; I feel more a part of a family than ever before. In my mind's eye, I can see them all looking over some celestial balcony, cheering me on and hopefully guiding me. Since reading your book, the picture doesn't quite seem so fanciful anymore. I know they are all there: stern old Deacon Samuel Chapin and his contemporaries; Amos Chapin and Reuben Wharfield, the Revolutionary War veterans whose children met and married; Matthias Riffel and his descendant James Riffle, who fought in the Civil War when he was my son's present age (19) and took part in the siege of Atlanta; there are Bethia Chapin (who I just know is fun-loving), Dorcas, Tamor, several Marys, Catherine, Rocila, Mary Barbara and the other women who buried far too many babies and worked themselves to exhaustion (Tamor died in her mid-thirties, leaving behind six young children). They are Puritans, Roman Catholics, Lutherans, and Methodists - among others - and I plan to see to it that my descendants know and appreciate them and respect their memory.

I think you'll understand when I say that I believe they have somehow selected me for just that purpose.

I'll try not to let them down."

Joyce M. Tice has been blessed with a beautiful dream that we all can relate to:

"I have had a recurring dream all my life starting in my childhood and continuing to the present. I start out in my house which may be any one of the several I have lived in, or even, as in the earliest version, a junk room in my grandmother's house where I used to play. In every version, I find a door I never noticed before and go through to find another room full of either musty books, dusty antiques, curiosities of all sorts, or in some cases very opulent treasures, valuable metals and jewels, great riches. In that room are other doors and in those even more doors, and each door leads to more rooms full of interesting artifacts or valuable treasures. Always at the end, the last room opens up on a lush garden with all manner of trees, shrubs, flowers, birds.

I've always called it 'my discovery and new adventure dream,' but now that I have become so heavily involved in genealogy it is exactly like the dream. This is what the dream was always about: *I am living the dream!* Every discovery leads to more and there is no end. It goes on forever. I will spend the rest of my life following this path from room to room, exploring treasures waiting for me.

I have never had any interest in family. I am an only child, an only grandchild on my Tice side. I have no children, by choice. I am the least likely individual to become the chronicler of the ancestors and descendants of the settlers of Sullivan township, Tioga County, Pennsylvania. The project will take the rest of my life even though I have managed to create a framework of 19,000 people in less than two years. (I am an accounting system consultant and computers are my tool. I can make very good use of them in this new field.) Now I have to flesh out and bring these people and the communities that have existed over two hundred years back to life.

But the point is, they have their own life! The community is bringing itself back into existence through the project that my friend Joan Nash O'Dell and I are pulling together. It has its own life and energy, and it just flows toward me so I can put all the pieces together in the right place for others to see and benefit from.

We are immortalizing the people who preceded us.

Or possibly we are helping them to immortalize themselves!"

OH, I HOPE SO!

11
HUNCHES:
THESE FEELINGS WON'T LET GO

I like what Gary Zukav says in his marvelous book, *The Seat of the Soul*:

"Impulses, hunches, sudden insights and subtle insights have assisted us on our evolutionary path since the origin of our species. That we have not recognized the guidance that has come to us in this way is a consequence of seeing reality through only five senses. From the five-sensory point of view, there is no other place from which insights and hunches can come.

From the multisensory point of view, insights, intuitions, hunches, and inspirations are messages from the soul, or from advanced intelligences that assist the soul on its evolutionary journey. The multisensory personality, therefore, honors intuition in a way that the five-sensory personality does not. To the five-sensory personality, intuitions are curiosities. To the multisensory personality, they are promptings from, and links to, a perspective of greater comprehension and compassion than its own."

How true. The truly experienced and seasoned genealogist has learned over the years to trust his intuitive inner voice. As Joyce Sheckler Heiss of Jefferson City, Tennessee, noted:

"I can relate to many of the events in *Psychic Roots*. I have 'feel like' episodes about things. We have avoided accidents because 'I felt like' we should pull off the road for a few minutes or take a different plane or train. I usually don't talk about this except at home, but if I say 'I feel like ...' my husband listens because of past experiences.

Episodes like this related to my genealogical research are a multitude, so your book 'speaks' to me."

And Joyce M. Tice has an interesting perspective on this too:

"Thank you for writing *Psychic Roots*. My extraordinary diary story is perfectly ordinary in the context of your book. I am so pleased to see how common these experiences are. My friend Joan thinks my diary story (see p. 67) is the most extraordinary story she's ever heard. I told her your book has hundreds just like it.

I, too, am convinced that our ancestors want to be found. I am not a religious person. I am in fact an atheist, but there is a mental or spiritual energy which we do not understand yet which is operating on these projects. My accountant's nature wants to get everything catalogued and in its right place and documented. With an MBA in finance, I can apply statistical analysis tools to the data. I am also psychic and very intuitive in finding connections which later prove to be correct. Sometimes I go so far out on a limb I am almost ashamed and then I find that my guess, my hunch, was absolutely right."

Along these lines, Rollie L. Campbell of Ignacio, Colorado, recalled:

"I was having a long, fruitless afternoon of research at the Olympia, Washington Public Library. Being bored, I was idly scanning some titles on the book shelves when a book about Pennsylvania genealogical sources caught my eye (I have a Pennsylvania Dutch line on my mother's side). Being of a pessimistic frame of mind, I went right on down the aisle. I hadn't gotten three feet, when I felt compelled to go back to that book. Believe it or not, I still ignored the impulse! The next time it came, about two seconds later, I said to myself, 'All right! Just to show you that there won't be anything there for me, I'll look!'

Was there anything in that book? You'd better believe it! It led me to a source that even gave the latitude and longitude in Germany where my Strunck family had originally lived!"

One of my fellow Fellows in the American Society of Genealogists, Winston De Ville, had an intriguing hunch pay off:

"One of my favorite ancestors is Joachin de Ortega y Prieto, born in Spain in 1755, married well in colonial Louisiana, and became a representative from the southwest Louisiana area to the territorial legislature. I well recall that when I 'discovered' him (about 1960), something 'told' me that he had suffered grievous burns. I had absolutely no reason to have such an idea, but just 'knew' that. In early articles in *Louisiana Genealogical Register* and *La Voix des Prairies*, I alluded to the possibility that Don Joachin had been seriously injured by a gun-powder explosion.

So years and years passed, with occasional pertinent hints on the matter. Then recently (1992) - shazam! I found a letter while just flipping through some microfilm of *legajos* from Spain. This old 1779 document confirmed that de Ortega 'burned his hands and his face while drying some gunpowder in a boiler; he was holding his gun, moving the hammer, (and) a spark struck the powder; he had no time to get away ....'"

A hunch helped Vicki J. Hagen of Austin, Texas, engineer a moving family reunion:

"My father's parents divorced when he was one year old, and he was raised by his mother and grandmother. Later when grown, my dad would always check out the phone books in every city he would stay the night looking for his father's name. He never found anything even close.

I have always been interested in my family history - in fact you might say I am this generation's designated family historian. I always told my dad that I would find his father for him one day. I really began my research to make good my promise, but my dad just thought it wasn't going to be possible. I finally located a copy of my grandfather's birth certificate ... it hadn't been filed until WWII, when he was employed by the Civil Service. This was, of course, in 1941, and it was by this time, 1975. It had been filed by my grandfather's mother in Kansas City, Missouri.

I was excited, and showed it to my dad. He was happy that I even had found anything. We still didn't know if his father was still alive. The more I studied the birth certificate, the stronger my 'hunch' became until finally, I acted upon it. My great-grandmother had given a Kansas

City address at the time she registered the certificate, and I wondered if the address was still good. I felt so strongly about it, that I actually wrote my great-grandmother a letter, explaining who I was and that I was writing for any family information. Months went by, and I had almost convinced myself that my hunch had been wrong: a good try, but no results.

Then one day, when checking my mail, I noticed a letter from California addressed to me. I didn't know anyone in California! Taking the letter inside, I sat down and read it. It was from my dad's aunt - his father's sister. It seems my letter reached its destination in Kansas City and was received by my great-grandmother who was still living! After reading it, she had put the letter on her mantel. She didn't answer it. But when her daughter came from California for a visit, she discovered my letter on the mantle and told her mother she was going to answer it.

My 'hunch' had worked! She corresponded with me and my dad, came for a visit and helped to arrange for my dad to meet his father. He had remarried and was living in Oklahoma. My baby was under a year old at the time of the visit, and we took photos of four generations - my grandfather, my dad, myself, and my daughter. It was a great visit, and my grandfather came to Texas for a visit as well.

For myself, I can't describe the feelings I felt, knowing I had been able to give my dad something he had longed for all his life ... *his* dad! My grandfather has passed away now, but I feel very fortunate that they were able to spend some time together and get to know each other."

Bernice Ferous Weir of Huntington, New York, adds to this collection:

"Besides researching my Van Loan family of East Durham, New York, antique collecting is a big part of my life. One day I was in a little park where there was an outdoor show. Strolling through the aisles of the dealers, I came to a sudden dead-stop. My husband, George, asked me why I had stopped. I didn't answer him, but simply pointed to a booth and walked to it.

The dealer looked up as I asked him if he had any log or day books. He said he only dealt in military paper memorabilia. Something made me not want to leave, and I remained standing there looking at him. All of a sudden, he remembered something and remarked, 'Oh, I do have *one* log book. It's from East Durham, Greene County, New York.' I excitedly examined the old book and found many references to my family buying goods at the store. I love this piece of my history, when I know that my ancestors stood before that very book in their town.

I have had nudges all my life, clear thinking thoughts about unknown events. My eight kids are still amazed at my sixth sense. Of course ... I'm half Irish ... You should have guessed it!"

Peggy Posson Kindall of Hays, Kansas, remembers this story:

"While researching my Posson family, I had good luck in getting hold of members of three of the four main lines in the family, but little success in contacting descendants of Henry Posson. One day in 1981, I finally received information that led me to believe that, at long last, I had found one of Henry's progeny. I sat down at my typewriter, determined to write a letter to this descendant, Byron Posson. Ordinarily, I don't have any problem in writing letters, especially regarding genealogical pursuits. But this day was different, for what reason I would not discover until a few months later.

I began letter after letter, but something was very wrong. My letter just wouldn't 'write up' as I hoped it would. Instead, a little, insistent, nagging voice within me kept saying, 'Call, call ... CALL!' 'Ridiculous,' I told myself, 'It's the middle of the week. These people probably won't even be at home.' Besides, I always watched my long-distance phone calls and the timing of them. I continued to work at the typewriter, to no avail. After the first hour, my office wastebasket was overflowing with crumpled up papers, and I still didn't have my letter typed. All the while, the nagging little voice within insisted, 'CALL NOW!'

It wouldn't be silenced. I called information and asked for Byron Posson's number. I made the call, never mind the time of day or day of week. Byron was very nice, so excited to receive my call. He explained he would have missed it had I called another time, as they were just ready to leave for an extended trip. Before we ended our conversation, he suggested I call his older brother, Edward, in Eugene, Oregon, who had much information on the elusive Henry Posson branch. For some reason, I was able to easily type out a letter to Edward. Within days, a large manila envelope arrived, crammed with family data I had been seeking for years. In the weeks that followed, we exchanged much information that cleared up many muddled lines in the family.

Then one day, I received a letter from Byron Posson. With much regret, he informed me that his brother, Edward, had passed suddenly from this world - a victim of a car accident. I was so glad that I listened to that 'nagging little voice within' and that I telephoned Byron when I did. Otherwise, those several weeks in which Ed and I exchanged material might have been wasted, as I waited for Byron to return from his family holiday. So much would have been lost to me; and I am thankful that Ed probably enjoyed our exchange of information also in his last weeks before he passed away.

I can't explain why things happened the way they did; I only know that it was all for a good reason. And I still listen to intuition, expecially with regard to genealogical research."

Joan Search Hanson of Franklin, Pennsylvania, has hunches that manifest themselves in a physical manner:

"I thoroughly enjoyed your book. But I found no mention of 'tingling fingers.' My fingers tingle JUST as I am about to turn the page and find the long lost - JUST as I turn to the microfilm page. With censuses, this phenomenon is very helpful. If I miss the person, I go back because he IS there!"

Dr. David Faux of Hagersville, Ontario, Canada, once again reflects on this intriguing area:

"In the year 1967, long before I knew anything about my ancestry, I was working as a parking usher at Expo '67 in Montreal, Quebec. One spectacularly delightful sunny day, after working a day shift, I decided to do a bit of sightseeing on the way home. While driving my motorcycle west along the south shore of the St. Lawrence River, I felt my handlebars pull to the right. Always one to follow 'instincts' or 'hunches,' I took this as a sign that it would be interesting to take a side trip along this particular dirt road leading down to the river. Soon I reached a 'T' junction and was facing a broad grassy field with the huge ships plying the St. Lawrence Seaway in the background. However, all of this paled in interest value when I spotted a stone coffin-like box, shaded by a canopy. A large wooden cross stood as a sentinel guarding this monument, so otherwise alone in the open field.

The box's apparent antiquity stood in stark contrast to the modern ocean-going liners that seemed to be gliding along a sea of grass. The nearby plaque indicated that this was the burial site of Kateri Kekakwitha, the 'Lily of the Mohawks.' She died about 300 years ago, and is revered for her piety. As I stared at the grave, my mind began to have visions of life here, on this site, hundreds of years ago, and of events taking place over the mountains behind me, along an ancient river. I saw pastoral scenes of Native people going about their daily tasks. Then my mind turned back to the stone box. Shivers ran up my spine as I heard a voice saying something like (I don't remember the exact words), 'We are of the same blood.' This whole experience was profoundly distressing, and I put the motorcycle into gear and sped off - vowing to avoid this spot, and to not think about this again. To this day I have never gone back to this site.

While in graduate school, I took an interest in genealogy and soon turned my attention to the family of my grandmother. I was told by relatives that she was born on the Reserve (Six Nations - New Credit) near Brantford, Ontario where the Mohawk and other Loyalist Natives settled after the American Revolution. It did not slip my attention that Kateri was a Mohawk, but I did not dwell on the 'coincidence.' It also seemed odd that, of all places, I found my dream home (field stone farm house) on property adjoining the Six Nations - New Credit Reserve. I bought the home, and escalated my genealogical quest.

I quickly found that there was virtually no information on tracing Mohawk ancestors. It took many years, and many trips to the State of New York to eventually trace my

Mohawk ancestry back to the 1740s. Not bad really, but it seemed impossible to go any further.

Historical records indicated that the Mohawks were Christians from the 1600s, but were generally silent on where the baptismal registers, if existing, were located. Canadian record sources only mentioned the Church of England in connection with the Mohawks. The existing Church of England Records for Upstate New York were spotty, and included only the baptismal name of the children - without noting the parent's names.

Oh well. However, I had an unsettling feeling that said I should keep looking. Never one to give up, I checked every transcribed church record for the Mohawk Valley and surroundings. Low and behold, there were about a dozen Mohawk entries in the printed transcripts of the Schenectady Reformed Dutch Church, and a hundred or so in the Holland Society transcripts for the Albany Reformed Dutch Church. Both of these transcripts are well-respected, and I assumed that they must have included everything. They did give some additional details (e.g., marriage date of two ancestors), but I was still stuck in the mid 1700s. However, at least I could rest easy knowing that I had accessed all available records.

Over the next few months, however, I had another of those disturbing feelings, which in me translates into obsessive thinking which will not disappear until I perform the search necessary. Something (someone?) told me that I must continue with the quest, even though it seemed obvious that even if the transcribers had missed one entry, it would be somewhat unlikely that it would relate to my particular search. Little did I suspect the discovery that awaited.

Clearly the Schenectady transcripts seemed complete for the Dutch families, but in checking the original handwritten registers, written in Dutch, I found that the transcripts omitted hundreds of entries pertaining to Mohawk people. Oddly, the Albany records omit about half of the actual number of entries in the original records. Why would they selectively omit entries?

With this new data my family lines went back in one swoop to the mid 1600s. What is most haunting, however, is that my earliest documented ancestor, known as Crine Togouiroui 'The Great Mohawk,' was the uncle of Kateri!

To this day, I continue to wonder whether my unplanned trip to the grave of Kateri was just happenstance, and whether the eventual discovery of a blood connection is just coincidence."

WE ALL CONTINUE TO WONDER, DAVID.

12
HEAVENLY HELPERS

"There is no explaining the unexplainable, Lin Chou"
(Attributed to Confucius, ca. 500 B.C., after pondering strange ancestor-research stories he had heard while attending an "All-China Genealogical Jamboree" that year)

Rod Serling, move over!

You don't have a monopoly on "the spooky."

As the mail poured in from genealogists around the world, some letters contained experiences that truly defy explanation. And they came in so often that it was an unusual day when a real "Twilight-Zoner" *didn't* show up at my Post Office Box.

Let me share some of my favorites. Like the eerie occurrence that Betty Williamson Chan of Lynnwood, Washington, dared to send on:

"This incidence of serendipity took me almost thirty years to understand and really comprehend the whole story. Clarence Williamson, my father, didn't know his grandparents on either side. Three out of four of them had died before he was born. He was not interested in looking for his family history, but he took our family back to the Midwest to see his boyhood haunts in 1967.

On one leg of the journey, we traveled to St. Louis and went up in the Gateway Arch to look at the countryside for miles around. As I looked down at the foot of the Arch, I saw the Old County Courthouse far below. It gave us shivers down our spines when we saw it there, and my brother David and I suddenly wanted to see it.

The courthouse was an architectural gem, and had been turned into a museum of the Westward Movement, with historical exhibits and dioramas. When we entered one room on the tour, my ears started ringing. I heard screams of a man yelling: 'Do not cut off my leg! You cannot cut off my leg; I won't let you!' The smell of chloroform rose up around me and made me ill, and the room started to shimmer and lurch. I had to get out of there. I ran through the museum to the entrance and lost my lunch in the plantings outside the door. I started wondering if the experience was connected to me or my family. Still, you could not have paid me to go back into that room. I was still a little pale when my father came outside after the tour. 'Betty, you should have stuck around!' my father admonished. 'That was a Union Civil War Hospital - the Jefferson Barracks of St. Louis.'

I didn't find out what connection my experience and that hospital had to me and to my family's genealogy until 1994 when I sent for my great-grandfather Edward Thomas Williamson's military papers. In November and December of 1862, Edward Thomas Williamson of Indiana Company K was loaned to the Dubuque Battery. On 28 December 1862, the Dubuque Battery returned him to St. Louis with a bullet wound in his left thigh. At that time, Union doctors were paid bounties for cutting off legs with bullet wounds, because this practice saved lives in the unsanitary conditions of military hospitals in the Civil War era. My great-grandfather's point of pride was that he had not allowed the doctors at Jefferson Barracks Hospital to cut off his leg. They finally just took out the bullet. The doctors cleaned the wound as best they could and warned him that he was a 'walking dead man.' He was to walk with a limp the rest of his life.

So my great-grandfather Edward Thomas Williamson *was* yelling to defend his leg in the Jefferson Barracks Hospital in December 1862. And I heard him still when I entered that room of the Old County Court House Museum in August 1967. He really wanted to be found - and that was the rest of the story!"

Ernest Thode still can't forget an experience told to him:
"At a Palatines To America meeting in Columbus, Ohio in the 1980's, Clifford Neal Smith told about the time he was working on a Hessian soldier by a common name. At his home in Arizona, a Hessian soldier materialized on his veranda and spoke, telling him the name of the place he came from. Clifford looked in the lists, and there he was! Clifford does not have flights of fancy."

I spoke with Clifford Smith on the telephone 29 February 1996, and he verified that the aforementioned strange experience - word for word - was *true*. (This incident probably would come as no surprise to the more than 3300 readers recently polled by *PARADE* Magazine. Ninety-two percent of that number believed ghosts exist, and seventy-three percent said they actually had seen a ghost!)

Here, then, might be a good place for Barbara Freshwater to recount her story:

"Last year, my friend Pat and I went to Germany. While there, we found that different lines of our families had lived in the same small villages also. It really is hard to believe sometimes how we keep connecting, no matter what family line we are working on and no matter where we go.

We were in a church in the Black Forest. Pat's ancestors had been ministers there. Inside the church were reliefs with gothic inscriptions on them that we couldn't read. They looked like large headstones that had been lined up around the back and sides of the inside of the sanctuary.

Pat kept being drawn to one in particular and didn't know why. As she is an artist, Pat made a sketch of that one relief that had fascinated her. We had been at the church for several hours, and I said, 'Pat, we've got to go.' As we started to leave, she felt she had to take a picture of the relief. So we moved some chairs, and she took her photo.

We went out and walked down the road where I noticed a small museum. We went in, but found no one there to take our money to admit us. I heard loud voices upstairs, so I went to see if anyone there could give us an admission ticket. I saw the voices came from an old couple enjoying the museum rooms upstairs. As I looked around, I saw Pat's own family names on several displays, so I called her up to look around. We then found a room which had photos of the reliefs with their history written below them. Pat compared her sketch to the matching photo of that one relief, and was surprised to read that it was a monument to her own ancestor.

When we returned home from Germany and developed our photos, Pat called me and said, 'Come right over!' It turned out the photo of the relief showed a man, his wife, and a child - ghost impressions - in front of the relief!"

Some of my correspondents were open to all kinds of channels (literally!) in trying to find out more about their ancestors. Kathie K. Marynik of Granite Bay, California, told her story:

"In 1992, my second cousin Charlene was in town for a seminar, so we got together for lunch. As we both enjoy genealogy, the talk turned to our mutual line, the Crosley family. Charlene related how, earlier in the year, she had been searching, without success, for the headstone of Great-Aunt Clara Crosley who had died at the age of eighteen of tuberculosis.

It so happened that a map of the Inglewood Park Cemetery was on a table in Charlene's house when a neighbor of hers, Kim - who is a professional psychic - dropped in. When Kim asked about the map and Charlene told her about the search, Kim concentrated for a moment, and then indicated on the map the location of the elusive grave. She added the aside that Aunt Clara had a brother who died in Chicago. Not being a big believer in psychic phenomena and knowing of no Chicago connection to our Crosleys, Charlene shrugged off the information.

But then Kim began studying a wedding portrait of Charlene's grandparents, Fred Crosley and his third wife, Rebecca. Kim frowned as if in pain and then proceeded to relate unpleasant incidents that had occurred during this couple's marriage ... things like wife beating, and even an unsuccessful murder attempt when Fred had put ground glass in his wife's sandwich! Charlene was stunned. She had never heard of the sandwich story, nor had she told her psychic friend *anything* about her grandparents or that the marriage was unhappy and eventually ended in divorce. Charlene later shared the psychic's stories with her mother who confirmed them all!

As Charlene related these strange events to me, we shook our heads in amazement. This all must be just a series of weird coincidences, we thought. But the more I pondered all this, the more I wondered. And Great-Aunt Clara *d i d* have a brother named Arles whom we lost track of. The last record I had of him was in Arizona, and he was said to have died of tuberculosis somewhere back east.

As, of course, Chicago is 'back east' from Arizona, I decided to check out this Chicago lead - knowing that if I didn't I would be forever curious and bothered by it. After checking the index to Chicago death records, I found a reference to a man by the name of 'Arles Crossley' *(sic)* who had died there 1 August 1912 at the age of twenty-eight. The chills literally ran up and down my spine. It couldn't be true, I thought, but a name like 'Arles Crosley' is not a common one; and the age would fit! A request for a copy of the death certificate went out in the next mail, needless-to-say. Ten days later, I held in my hands a copy of the actual certificate. Arles Crosley, late of Chicago, had indeed been the son of Steve Crosley and Belle Smith ... my great-grandparents!

How did this happen? Arles had died in 1912, and his sister Clara in 1915. So many years had passed, but a psychic had casually picked up the information on Arles by looking at a copy of a cemetery map where his sister was interred. Maybe I should abandon the conventional research methods and simply take my genealogy files to a psychic for a reading!"

I've had my own share of weird events occur while investigating psychic phenomena too. *Psychic Roots* included one that happened on my first visit to the noted Southern California Society for Psychical Research. Well, here's another one. I'll preface it by saying (as so many other genealogists have said to me), "I've *never* told this to anyone else before, but here goes ..."

In my quest for knowledge about this whole area of "the unexplained," I've visited several mediums/psychics. Sylvia Browne, Jim Diehl, Freda Fell, Leslie Newman, James Van Praagh, and Suzy Morgan all were extremely accurate in their readings. Shama Smith was another. Shama was a lovely young woman who had spent much of her life studying in India and came with impeccable references. It was with eager anticipation that I made my first appointment with her

December 20, 1987 at her home in Los Angeles.

I remember her house was tastefully decorated with thick rugs and beautiful tapestries. A welcoming scent of sandalwood and incense floated through the rooms. Shama had portraits of gurus and spiritual leaders from different world religions placed around the comfortable den where my "reading" was to take place. She lit several candles on a coffee table in front of us and began the session with a heartfelt prayer that we might open our hearts and feel God's presence with us that special afternoon.

And then it happened. As she finished her prayer, I looked up. Shama's entire facial structure began to change in front of my eyes. Her cheeks inflated and deflated in and out, lines on her forehead appeared where no lines were before, and weight was added to her face where it had previously been thin. Where once sat a beautiful young twenty-year-old, a much older woman now appeared before me. I was witnessing a totally unexpected *physical* transformation.

And there was a spiritual metamorphosis occurring also. This "new" personage spoke from a wiser, gentler, more mature plane than Shama ever could have attained in her twenty-some years. She channeled information that day that was "right on," astounding me with her bulls-eye hits as to names, dates, and places during the reading. Then, as the session neared completion, she asked me to close my eyes in prayer. When I opened them up again, there was Shama once more - back to normal, looking like the lovely young lady who had answered the door when I arrived.

As much as I'll remember the meaningful spiritual material she brought forth that afternoon, it was her drastic change in appearance that still haunts me. I simply wasn't prepared for something like that to happen. Since then, I've done quite a bit of reading on the subject of channeled readings. I've discovered that a genuine change in appearance by the medium isn't all that unusual. Many documented cases of this have been reported by reliable witnesses.

Well, you can add mine too. I saw her change her physical appearance with my very own eyes.

Give me a Bible. I'll *swear* to it!

Others told their unusual stories along these lines. Jennifer J. Cummins of West Chester, Ohio, recalled:

"A few years before I began genealogy, I had a past life regression done on a whim. In one of my past lives, I said my name was Sarah, and that my husband was David. David died fairly young from a fall (I then confessed to having pushed him, though I said I hadn't meant for him to die).

In researching my mother's line, I was startled to discover that my great-great-great-grandparents were David and Sarah Canode. I have not been able to find much information on David because it appears that he too died fairly young and did not even make it into the 1840 census with Sarah and their children.

Maybe Sarah will help me again?!"

Gary Osborn of Okeechobee, Florida, recounted:

"For some time I have been compiling an Osborn Family History; tracing the descendants of James and Mary (White) Osborn, my immigrant ancestors. I had all but given up on the family of Alfred Osborn, my great-grandfather's brother. Alfred had died in 1894 at the age of thirty-nine. His wife had remarried, and they had apparently moved away. I had no idea where to look.

Two years ago while visiting my family near Erie, Pennsylvania, I heard an advertisement on the radio for Lily Dale, a spiritualist community in western New York about fifty miles away from where I was staying. I had heard of it before and had always been curious, so on the last day of my visit I decided to just go. It was a rainy, miserable day so I parked the car and, instead of looking around, went directly to the first house that I came to.

The sign outside said, 'Rev. Kitty Osborne, Medium.' To make a long story short, Kitty turned out to be the grandson of the Alfred Osborn I had been looking for! So, as a result of my visit to Lily Dale, many of my genealogical questions were answered, and that wasn't even my reason for going.

Or was it?"

Margaret A. Stevenson of Buffalo, New York, deserves Bert Lahr's "Cowardly Lion Courage Award" for sending on this wonderful story:

"I love your *Psychic Roots*. The experience I am going to relate to you I never have told my genealogy friends about, as it is so out in left field.

My mother had the faculty of 'inner knowing' as we called it. It gave me an understanding that we can be 'guided' often times if we are open and receptive. Praying about a problem is one way of being receptive, I believe, and we get answers to questions or problems from various sources, our own minds, an unexpected statement by someone, and numerous other ways.

When I married in 1974 Hugh D. Stevenson, I was aware that he and his first wife attended Spiritualist meetings on occasion and used the Ouija™ board also. After our marriage, we would use it as it did give some amazing answers. One such intriguing message came through the board on August 29, 1974, just prior to a trip we were going to take to England. It said, in part (all spellings as found)

MARGARET DONT GET OVERTIERD IN ENGLAND HUGH WILL GET ALONG OK. NOW HERE IS ONE YOU LOVE MARGAET MY GIRL I KNOW YOU WILL LOVE THAT TRIP TO ENGLAND WE HAD ANGESTORS THERE IN CHESTER JOHNSON. THEY HAVE BEEN WITH YOU WE COME BACK TO VISIT OUR DECENDENTS AND THEY HAVE VISITED YOU. THEY LIVED AT THE GATE IN THE NORTH WALL THE HOUSE IS STILL THERE GO TO THE SOUTH SIDE ALSO SEE THE NAMES ON THE DOORS BYE NOW HERE IS DAD. I AM PLEASED YOU ARE TAKING A NICE TRIP STOP NOW.

At that time, I knew nothing about my mother's Johnson lineage, other than her grandparents and great-grandparents were buried in Almond, New York. In 1974, the message was not taken seriously, per se. However, we did notice that a Johnson China Co. was advertised in Chester when we were there for a short stop. By 1976, a kind lady in Virginia helped supply me with my Johnson lineage back many generations, primarily through the Yale-Lloyd families which connected to the Johnsons.

Aug 29 - 74

APELIA FARE BERTTER UPON
READING THE BIBLE EACH DAY
HUGH BE CAREFUL ~~FILLS KNIFES~~
HE MUST NOT RUN Moreno
MARGARET DONT GET OVERTIERD
IN ENGLAND HUGH WILL GET
ALONG OK. NOW HERE IS ONE
YOU LOVE MARGARET MY GIRL
I KNOW YOU WILL LOVE THAT
TRIP TO ENGLAND WE HAD
ANGESTORS THERE IN CHESTER
JOHNSON. THEY HAVE BEEN WITH
YOU WE GOMEBACK TO VISIT OUR
DECENDENTS AND THEY HAVE
VISITED YOU, THEY LIVED AT
THE GATE IN THE NORTH WALL
THE HOUSE IS STILL THERE
GO TO THE SOUTH SIDE ALSO
SEE THE NAMES ON THE DOORS.
BYE
NOW HERE IS DAD. I AM PLEASED
YOU ARE TATING A NICE TRIP
STOP NOW.

The actual transcription of the Ouija™ board message

In 1979, I went to England again, this time with a group from the Connecticut Society of Genealogists. Chester was not on the original itinerary, but was included at the last minute when one man was unable to go, and the place of interest for him was deleted. I opted for a visit to Chester, and off we went. Thanks to work at the City Archives, I determined that Bishop George Lloyd, an ancestor via my Johnson family, was my Chester connection! On my tour, I saw a house on Watergate Street that did have a name plate on it, as the board mentioned. And the episcopal residence of my ancestor, Bishop George Lloyd, was on the site of King's school, which was indeed on the north wall - just as the message said!"

Donald C. Gaby of Miami, Florida, contributed this intriguing tale:

"I was always interested in my great-grandfather Richard Ashby for many reasons. As Richard was a man of some means, financial resources from his estate have helped me over the years - both with medical expenses and educational tuition. One might say I owed my health and higher education to Richard Ashby as much as to any other person.

For whatever reason, perhaps with a push from 'The Other Side,' when I settled in Miami in 1958 I almost immediately began to study Richard's real estate transactions insofar as they might be traced from the public records of Dade County. I now believe that Richard Ashby, still waiting on 'The Other Side' before his next incarnation, encouraged me in that effort. During the early 1960's, I met regularly for a seance with a trance medium, Ruth Gilbert, who led a group at a friend's home once each week.

Trained as a scientist, with a degree in Physics from Duke University, I was naturally skeptical at first. But I gradually became convinced after being asked to help set up the room for the evening seances during a period of several weeks while the owner of the house was away on vacation: I could find no evidence of fraud or trickery of any kind. It was the other attendees who wished to contact their departed relatives at these meetings, but imagine my surprise when someone came to *me* during the seance! That discarnate being introduced himself as Richard Ashby! I had spoken to no one about my great-grandfather, and was not thinking about him at the time.

Many years passed without further contact of which I was aware. Then in 1988, on many occasions, when I was having difficulty in obtaining cooperation from a librarian or other person - for example, seeking some document or information which the librarian said did not exist - Richard intervened to provide it. Eventually, books, records, and even a large glass plate photograph popped up unexpectedly to fill in some historical blanks. I might have a particular question, and the answer would come to me mysteriously (when this happened, the hairs on my right arm would stand erect, a sign that Richard was helping).

In October of 1988, Richard came to say that he was ready to leave and provided definite information of his intention in regard to his reincarnation. Specifically, he told me that he would make two attempts to be re-born to certain one of his own great-great grandchildren. He said he had been prevented from reaching his full potential in his last life for lack of formal education and the proper social background, and had carefully selected new parents who would satisfy those needs.

In order to have evidential proof of the communication and anticipated action, I printed some of this information on the back of a postcard dated 25 October 1988 and mailed it back to myself so it would bear the U.S. Post Office stamp and date. I put it away until 1990, when I happened to come across it again while preparing to move to a new home. By then, the great-great grandchild through whom Richard hoped to return was pregnant. She gave birth to a baby boy in November 1990. Only later did we learn she had had a miscarriage, and that this baby came from the second attempt!

Richard's last visit was in September 1990. It was a sad day for both me and my wife. Richard lingered on 'The Other Side' longer than most. In the end, he seemed pleased that someone had at last recognized his achievements, and he knew it would be done better with this second edition. Probably he could see that the squabble and litigation over his former property would take a very long time, and that the outcome was not worth waiting for."

My pal, Maralyn A. Wellauer of Milwaukee, Wisconsin, tried her hand at communicating with "the Other Side" also:

"When I was a junior or senior in high school, the writings of Edgar Cayce and Jeane Dixon sparked my interest in parapsychology. 'Automatic writing,' the production of written messages on paper, seemingly without the conscious thought of the living person, was one of the more intriguing methods recommended for developing one's psychic powers. It was appealing because it didn't sound too demanding. One was directed to spend a short time in a darkened room, in a meditative state, with a pencil and paper in hand. A spirit 'guide' would hopefully guide the loosely held pencil and impart a message.

A few years later, when I began delving into my family history, it occurred to me that contact with the psychic world could be quite helpful, so I tried my hand at contacting the spirit world. I recall feeling an expectation that some great revelation would result. So, during my lunch hour, instead of eating, I dimmed the lights in the office and picked up a sharp pencil. For a few minutes, there was no movement. Then, just as the books had predicted, the pencil began moving around the paper uncontrollably, as if drawing the coastline on a map.

For days, the only thing I produced were doodles around the edges of my paper, but I could feel my writing instrument was not under my control, so I wasn't discouraged. For a time, I didn't seem to be making any progress. Then all at once the writing became more controlled and deliberate. I could feel myself forming words. I made a mental note that I was forming the letters 'o' and 'a' backwards.

I felt 'contact' was finally made when my 'guide' finally addressed me by my first name. He introduced himself: 'Maralyn, I am Jacob Wellauer.' I was delighted! It was my grandfather's cousin. At last, a contact, and it was a relative! A major breakthrough in my family research was imminent, I thought.

Days passed as my 'guide' practiced his name, writing 'J. J. J. Jacob' and so on as if he were scribbling, and threw a word out here and there but nothing that really made much sense. I anxiously awaited his first meaningful message. Finally, it came. 'Maralyn, help your grandmother with the dishes.'

At first, I was deeply disappointed, but later was greatly amused. After all, I always did my grandmother's dishes. Why would he say such a thing? He should have known better, right? After days of just scribbles, I lost interest and stopped the sessions.

In retrospect, perhaps the joke was on me."

However, John Baldwin of Cleveland Heights, Ohio, adds a skeptical eye to all of this:

"You asked if I might have a contribution for your sequel - may I speak from the other side of the fence?

When I was in college, my aunt's life-long friend earned her living operating a tearoom and reading tea leaves. I think, by local standards, I can call her a 'reputable and distinguished practitioner.'

One evening I asked if she could help solve a genealogical problem - and then challenged her with the same Sweet puzzle for which fifty years later I seem to be seeking solutions, intuitively or otherwise. She assured the assembly of family and friends it could handily be done. Later that evening, forgetting the exact nature of my request, she asked how I went about research, and whether I might be able to help her with her own family! My cousin and I burst into rude hysterics, mortifying our mothers.

As it turned out, her 'talents' were inadequate, and those of a medium to whom she then turned on my behalf proved equally so. The third phase would have been a high-priced senior psychic, or whatever people called themselves in those days. With no urge to waste meagre school funds, and feeling rationality had triumphed, I declined. But maybe I should have invested - her fee was probably far less than my Sweet postage expenditures the last few years."

But then John goes on to write:

"Though I remain skeptical of mediums and the like, you will be amused by what befell me in the newest *Connecticut Nutmegger*: on page 386 was my article "Sarah (Benet) Fuller, a Conn. Pioneer to Ohio (wife of Howard Fuller)," and then on page 518 a query from Virginia "needs ancestry of Howard Fuller and Sarah Benet.""

I've already talked with the querist who'd seen the issue and has already been promised a copy of *Psychic Roots* for Christmas as a result. So I continue to indirectly support your sales."

Luella H. Brock of Churchville, Maryland, mulls over the continuity of these unusual happenings:

"And so the tantalizing coincidences float in and out of our research like wisps of smoke - or perhaps - ghosts of the past?"

And did those "ghosts of the past" help Ruth Merriman, who works at the Family History Library in Salt Lake City?

"I continue to work on the history of my husband's great-great-grandfather, Rees Merriman. One day, years ago in my novice days, a co-worker at the library acquainted me with a source I hadn't used before: the A.I.S. (Accelerated Index). 'What?' I said, 'Every Merriman in the country in 1850 will be in there?!' I couldn't believe it.

I was so anxious to check this new source for missing links that I wanted to spend the night at the library, but security wouldn't let me do it. So the next day, as I hurried down the freeway towards the library, all I could think about was finding that elusive Merriman family. Up ahead, a large truck carrying steel roadblocks hit a bump; one of the massive roadblocks, taller than my car, bounced off into my lane. The car ahead of me swerved to miss it, and there it was - staring me in the face! My initial reaction would have been to slam on the brakes and crank the wheel to one side, but a strange thing happened. My foot wouldn't move, and very quickly and smoothly, the steering wheel moved slightly to the left and then to the right; my car, at 60 m.p.h., eased around that steel barrier. My hands weren't touching the wheel! I glanced back in the rear view mirror with my heart pounding and saw the lady behind me do exactly what I would have done - her car spun out of control and rolled on its roof down the embankment.

After stopping and giving my account to the Highway Patrol, I hurried on to work. I pulled out the A.I.S. microfiche and found my people - in Monongalia Co., Virginia - now West Virginia - a state I never would have checked, not knowing at the time how the boundaries changed in that corner of the country. I feel like the Merriman family wanted to be found, and if I had died on the freeway that day, they would have remained lost. I truly believe someone else steered my car and allowed me to find them!"

I love the commonality of experiences shared by two researchers who wrote me recently. Ruby Coleman of North Platte, Nebraska, observed:

"I thoroughly enjoyed *PSYCHIC ROOTS*. Some of the stories confirmed that something is indeed happening in our genealogical research! Something perhaps that we do not necessarily control. People are becoming more and more aware of life after death experiences conveyed by those who have been brought back to life. These people are no longer referred to as 'crazies.' Therefore, I think your book was timely in speaking out about what I have always referred to as 'strange things' happening in my research.

While teaching a genealogy class at our local college, I met a young woman who had a sincere interest in tracing her genealogy. One day she stayed after class to visit with me. She seemed rather upset, and I anticipated something had happened in her research that was puzzling her. The conversation was amazing. She had traced her genealogy back several generations, well into another century, only to discover a familiar name. It was not a name handed down in her family or written in any family record which had survived. It was nothing she would have seen in a Family Bible, but yet very familiar.

The name of her ancestor, both given name and surname, was the name her brother had called his imaginary playmate as a child. I had no explanation except that strange things often happen when doing genealogy."

Linda Farroh Eder of Elgin, Illinois, can certainly identify with that story:

"While researching the history of their house, the Perenti's from Union, Illinois, were told that my grandfather, Claude Britton, could help them. Years ago, their house had been owned by Harley and Ellen Wayne, relatives of my grandmother, Esther Britton. One day, my grandfather and my mother visited the Perenti's while I went on to school. When I returned home from class, my very agitated mother greeted me at the door and asked if the name 'Thanke' (pronounced 'Tanke') meant anything to me. I replied, 'no' - and then my mother told me this story:

Apparently during the conversation that afternoon, the Perenti's mentioned the name of Harley Wayne's mother, 'Thanke.' My mother said she was astounded! 'Thanke' had been my imaginary playmate when I was a child. Until the Perenti's mentioned the name 'Thanke,' no one in the current generations had ever heard the name except in connection with my invisible playmate!"

Even the technical tools we use in genealogy can give us a little nudge once in a while too. Donna J. Porter of Denver, Colorado, reported:

"A friend of ours, who didn't have a computer, brought over a floppy disk over to see if my husband would print out his family group sheets. It contained data on just his own family, not his wife's as she hadn't started doing her lines yet. My husband agreed to print them out for him and began the next day to do so. He didn't use any of our genealogy programs to print nor did he use the program on PAF in our computer containing my niece's father's families and her husband's families.

Even though none of these programs were used to print our friend's family data, each time he printed the index the surname 'Nay' kept printing out. My husband tried and tried to get the computer to print without that 'Nay' surname being included, but to no avail. In frustration, he finally told our friends he was sorry, and they would have to use the printout with that 'Nay' surname included.

When I went over to our friends' house to return the materials, Norma, Dick's wife, answered the door, and I explained what had happened. As she looked over the printout, she exclaimed, 'Where did you get my great-grandfather's name? I didn't have any of my families on Dick's disk.' I told her that the Nay families were my nieces' families, and that I would check with my niece for more information. It turned out that these two women are related!

But how did the Nay families print out when my husband didn't use the PAF program to print out the index for our friends?"

Miss Lou Duprey of Danville, Illinois, had a weird thing happen:

"I was in the courthouse in Terre Haute, Indiana about thirty-five years ago. The clerk took me to the attic where I had only one light bulb (with no shade) and a long string to turn it on and off. That attic was scary! I was searching through an old box of Chamberlain records when the light went out. I jiggled, pulled the string a few times, and the light finally came on. But as I continued to search, the bulb kept going out.

I was beginning to get a little irritated. I said aloud, 'OK! I promise that if I find something I think you don't want revealed, I will never show it!' The light then stayed on, and I worked about three hours there. I found an extremely embarrassing notation about my ancestor in that time span, but since I have promised, I can't tell you what it said.

No! Not even thirty-five years later."

And sometimes the documents themselves give us unexplained assistance in our searches. Donna Potter Phillips of Spokane, Washington, remembered:

"Back in 1975, I was a 'greenbean' genealogist, the lowliest of beginners into the hobby. All I had going for me was an overabundance of enthusiasm. My friend and I took a basic beginners class, and we began talking to relatives and filling out our charts, and right away we decided that we *had* to go to Salt Lake. In retrospect, our time might have been better spent honing our local and mail-using skills, but Salt Lake was 'mecca,' and it was calling us.

So on a bright spring morning, we loaded our suitcases into the car and drove the 700 miles from Spokane to Salt Lake in one long wonderful day. I recall getting in to Salt Lake about dusk, and parking 'nose-in' around Temple Square (how many recall *that?*). We stayed with a cousin of Pat's up by the University of Utah, and figured we had it made.

On my chart, I'd listed my great-grandmother's name, 'Magdalena REGNER.' Mom was full of family stories, and I knew that Magdalena had come in 1866 as a teenager to join a married sister. She soon married Henry JOSEPH, who had come from the same village of Alzey in Germany. The family story said that they didn't know each other in the old country, which I'd always suspected.

Looking in the card catalog - and in 1975 it *was* a multi-drawered, full-of-little-cards, card catalog - no computers yet - I found one lonely card for the surname REGNER. I was so excited. With help every step of the way from the sweet staff of the library, the card led me to a film. With the film firmly in hand, I was shown how to load the thing onto the machine, and then I was left on my own. You can't imagine my surprise when the record on the film was written in German! I was so 'greenbean' that I hadn't yet discovered the truth of things like that.

The record on the film was handwritten, and looked like a little 9" x 4" pocket diary of some fifty pages. I could discern the date of 1909 on the first page, and a big fancy 'R' with what looked like 'Regner.' But the handwriting was dense, and IN GERMAN, and I quickly dropped to discouragement. But something kept my hand rolling that film along, and I felt really frustrated knowing that all that information was unobtainable but right before my eyes.

Then all of a sudden, there it was! In letters 2" high, *much larger than for any other listing in the whole diary*, and clear as a bell, was an entry I could read! While I was delighted and excited again, I didn't feel it was anything other than a writer's enthusiasm that this one entry was so big. And, like a silly girl, I took the fact that I could read it way too matter-of-factly. Beginners!

'Magdalena Regner, born February 14, 1850 in Alzey, daughter of Peter Regner and Clara Flick.' I couldn't really read much around that entry, but I didn't care - and I certainly didn't know enough to know I should care and should look! And here's a confession: I didn't know enough to make even one photocopy of the information. I just scribbled it down, in pencil no less, rewound the film and put it away and considered myself only a very lucky girl. Even my friend took the event matter-of-factly.

The real 'miracle' occurred some dozen years later. Realizing that I had never looked at that film again, I made myself a note to look at it on my next trip to Salt Lake. (By this time I was teaching genealogy and going regularly to Salt Lake. And readers of this story will rightly chastise me, asking why did I wait so long to document that find?) This time I looked up 'Regner' on the Library Computer Catalog and got the film number, but the box wasn't in the drawer. The attendant explained that they'd have to get one from the vault - this was a film that was hardly ever used. So I waited two more days.

Finally the film came, and I routinely put it on the machine. I knew I still could not read German, but I felt fairly confident that I could pick out information because I had been donating my time to the German Extraction Program and so had a bit more experience than before. So I rolled the film slowly along, looking for that 2" entry. And I rolled, and rolled, and ROLLED, clear to the end of that handwritten record, and was stunned to not find the entry. Of course, I hadn't been looking too hard, because I knew that 2" entry would be easy to spot.

There was *no* larger-than-the-rest entry in the entire record. It was a handwritten, personal chronology and diary of the Regner family, penned in 1909 by a self-proclaimed family historian. All the handwriting was uniform, none larger than the rest. What had happened?

Well, upon careful study, I did find the entry for Magdalena, but I really did have to hunt for it. I have since copied the whole darn thing, and now have it at home for my personal study. I occasionally drag out the precious box and look at it again and wonder what really happened that day back in 1975.

I think I have the answer. I think some higher power intervened and made sure that I would find the right entry. I was a beginner, and I know I never would have been able then to find the correct entry in the midst of all that German writing. I needed extra help right that moment, and I got it! I shall always be in awe of the memory of that experience, and thankful that it happened to me."

And I love the similar experience that happened to Catherine A. Cissna of Jackson, California:

"In my early days as an amateur genealogist, I did what most of us do - began to collect all of the basic family information that was readily available. Since I planned to trace my husband's family as well as my own, it was necessary to query his parents and relatives also. My husband's paternal grandparents were Walter Edwin Cissna and Nettie Mae Turner. I was disappointed when my in-laws couldn't provide the name (maiden or otherwise) of Nettie Mae's mother. All I knew of Nettie Mae's family was that her father was John Wesley Turner, and she had a sister, Ella.

In November of 1978, my mother-in-law gave me a box of old photos, one of which was a family grouping taken ca. 1892. In the photograph were Nettie Mae, her mother, father, and sister, Ella. On the reverse of the photograph, in Nettie Mae's handwriting, was a listing of names of those in the picture. Strangely she had written, 'J. W. Turner; M. E. Phillips; Ella M. Turner; Nettie M. Turner,' with each name on a separate line as though making a list. Excitedly, I read and re-read the name 'M. E. Phillips.' I now had the name of Nettie Mae's mother! Subsequent research revealed that 'Maggie' Turner had been buried in Pomona, California in 1893, and shared a plot in a cemetery there with J. W. Turner and with her nine-year-old daughter, Maude.

About six months later, during a phone conversation with another genealogist friend, I remarked how lucky I had been in filling in that crucial piece of information from the name labeling on an old photograph. I remarked again about the odd way that Nettie Mae had used her mother's maiden name - but that I was grateful that she had. Just as I was saying this, I turned the photo over to look at it again. To my utter astonishment, the names no longer appeared in the manner I had previously seen them. This time it read, 'J. W. Turner; *Mrs. M. E. Turner;* Ella M. Turner; Nettie M. Turner.'

I established through Maude Turner's birth record in Iowa that her mother Maggie's maiden name was indeed 'Phillips,' which none of the family had known or remembered. I have no explanation for this strange experience. I do know that every time I read the names on the back of the photo, I consistently read 'M. E. Phillips,'

J. W. Turner
Mrs. M. E. Turner
Ella M. Turner
Nettie M. Turner

© G. Lecher 301 West Water St. Milwaukee

The inscription on the back of the same picture

The front of the picture of the John Wesley Turner family

rather than 'Mrs. M E. Turner' - that is, until the day of the conversation with my friend. Or maybe it appeared to me as 'M. E. Phillips' just long enough for me to establish and prove Maggie's identity for my records."

Catherine goes on to reflect:

"The Turner and Phillips lines have been particularly difficult ones to research. And on several occasions, I have had strange things happen which have helped me get beyond certain stumbling blocks. There is no rational explanation for any of these occurrences, other than to say I must be psychically attuned to this family, or that I'm being guided by one of them.

On another occasion, I had three large cartons of genealogical books and periodicals on my living-room floor, which had just arrived as a gift to our local genealogical group from one of the state libraries. On this particular evening when I was preparing dinner - and dinner was truly the only thing on my mind - I was suddenly interrupted by a nearly, but not quite audible voice that urged me to go open the carton of books and start going through the Indiana periodicals. It was not at all like the inner urgings that make you want to dig and explore. This really seemed to come from somewhere *outside* myself. I resisted the urge at first, intent on getting dinner ready. But this odd feeling wouldn't let go. It was as if unseen hands had a hold of my shoulders and were gently shaking me and saying, 'Go look ... *now!'*

So while I had a few minutes until dinner time, I went into the living-room and to the cartons on the floor. The first carton I opened had Indiana quarterlies on top, and I lifted them out. There were quite a number of them. I flipped through the top one and noticed that it had marriages from one of the counties in Indiana. Nothing really caught my eye that would tie in with any of our families as I flipped through the second one in the stack and then the third. I somehow had a sense that I was looking for 'Turner,' although we had many family connections in Indiana.

I had been at a point with the Turner research where I didn't know what I was going to do next. One source had indicated that John Wesley Turner was born in Ohio in

1850. I knew that his father was also a John Turner, and the family believed that his wife was Margaret Crawford, but there was no proof of that. I had obtained a listing of all John Turner entries from the 1850 Ohio census index, of which there were more than fifty. One by one I had been checking the various counties and censuses, but before completing the 'needle in a haystack' search, I came across another source which said that John Turner was born in Indiana. Instead of narrowing in on my objective, the field was becoming broader.

As I opened either the third or fourth issue in the stack of Indiana quarterlies, it fell open to the section of Grant County marriages. I scanned the alphabetical listing of grooms' names, and finally came to the name TURNER. And before I could even read the given name I had wondered if it would be 'John' - and it was! As my eye continued across the page to the next column which contained the bride's name, I was hoping against all hope that it would say ... Margaret Crawford. YES! ... it did say 'Margaret Crawford, married on 10 September 1843! It was fortunate that we had no close neighbors, for they surely would have heard the whoop and holler I let out.

I have no explanation for this experience either. I don't know whether I was more excited over discovering the proof of the marriage, the date and county - or over the way the discovery had come about. However these events might be explained, it is only in connection with the TURNER family research that I have experienced them with personal genealogy.

Sometimes an inner voice like that nudges us along. Other times, it can be an almost physical prod. Witness the experience of Diann L. Wells of Phelan, California:

"In the 1970's, I was doing research at the Genealogical Library in Salt Lake City, Utah. I was looking for the marriage record of my great-grandparents, Peter Beauvais and Rachel Smith. After finding Peter's name in the groom index on one film, I jotted down the page number, and located another film that had the actual marriage records.

Excitedly, I put the film on the reader and turned to the page. The marriage record wasn't there. I looked a few pages ahead and a few pages back. I couldn't find it. I decided that I had made an error somewhere, so I went back to the index. There was no mistake, I had written the numbers correctly for the page and microfilm. I put the film back on the reader, turned to the page again, and still couldn't find it.

Then, I decided the index must be wrong and maybe the numbers of the page had been inverted. I tried every combination of that number, searching each page carefully. I couldn't find the record. I was so disappointed. I couldn't think of another thing to do except read that whole roll of film. But my time was limited, so that idea was dismissed. I leaned my head against the reader, and began rewinding the film. Suddenly, I felt a light touch on my shoulder, as if someone had gently laid their hand on me. I turned to see who was there - there was no one. I turned to the right of me and asked the person at the reader if he was trying to get my attention. He looked at me like I was weird, and said, 'No.' I looked to the left of me, but that person didn't look up. I then turned and glanced at my reader screen.

There it was - my great-grandparents' marriage - right in the middle of the page in front of me! I couldn't believe it! I looked at the page number, and it wasn't anywhere close to the pages I had searched!"

GOOSEBUMPS, ANYONE?

13

NO BUDDY QUITE SO TRUE

Back in the early days of television, when Tennessee Ernie Ford wasn't singing about how loading "Sixteen Tons" made him "owe his soul to the Company Store," he often would mine the depths of his considerable talent and give moving renditions of modern spirituals. One was a special favorite of mine:

"If I Can Help Somebody As I Pass Along ...
Then My Living Shall Not Be In Vain"

I've learned that that lovely sentiment certainly holds true when applied to the genealogical community. We may start out climbing the family tree individually, but, more often than not, our successes really result from teamwork and networking with other family historians. Genealogy seems to be a textbook example of the "Buddy System" at work. If we can't solve one of our own thorny research problems, often a colleague will come along and help us - without even being asked to!

And how the new contributions mirrored this! Lydia Streeter of Hutchinson, Kansas, communicated:

"One of my friend's ancestors and my ancestors lived in the same area of Connecticut, Massachusetts, New York, and Michigan. As far as we know, they did not migrate at the same time, but did live in the same areas approximately at the same time.

One day she was looking at some newspapers on microfilm when I happened in the library. I asked her, 'What are you looking at, Arlene?' She said, '*The Hudson Gazette*.' I then asked her at which years she was looking. She responded, '1860 - 1865.' My great-grandparents lived near Hudson in Hillsdale County in the late 1850's when my grandfather was born (1857) and appeared on the 1860 census. My great-grandmother had died sometime between 1860 and December 1866 when my great-grandfather married the second time in Knox County, Illinois. I had never been able to find when nor where she died. Never thinking there was a ghost of a chance that she would find it, I said, 'If you find the death notice of my great-grandmother, let me know.'

That night, she called me and said, 'I found it!' I couldn't believe it! I said, 'You didn't.' She said, 'Yes, I did: it says she died in Hudson on Friday, the 30th ult. of consumption, ___ ___, wife of Chester Fuller, aged 30 years. It was in the January 7, 1865 issue.'

Whenever I think about it, I still can hardly believe she found it. I would still be looking!"

Linda Stufflebean remembered:

"I was working on my husband's Whitmer family and traced John Whitmer's son Valentine back to Rockingham County, Virginia. I was talking on the telephone with my friend Nancy Maxwell about my genealogical problem, remarking how difficult the search was as Rockingham was a 'burned county.'

Nancy said she recently had received some information from a penpal interested in one of her German families who had lived in Rockingham at about the same time. She went to look in her records and came back to the phone. Nancy told me that a volume of church baptisms existed for the Friedens Union Church there from the 1780's, and that this correspondent had sent her a photocopy of a page that included the baptism of one of Nancy's people. The lady had circled the relevant baptism, which was near the bottom of the page.

But Nancy was astounded as she read on: the very last item on that one page was the baptism in December of 1786 of Valentine Whitmer, son of John and Catherine!"

My friend and cohort Joy Reisinger of Sparta, Wisconsin, had welcome assistance from a family member:

"In 1976, my sister Linda, my daughter Barbara, and I went to Quebec to research. We had been there earlier in

1973, and this time I wanted to go to the Protonotary's office in Joliette to read duplicate parish registers to solve a tough problem. Two generations in a row of my mother's Hetu line were difficult to connect because the marriages weren't recorded in the published répertoires.

Barb was 20 and bored, and I kept telling her to take the car and go sight-seeing. But, she stayed in the musty, dusty basement and found *every single act* that I needed - none of which were included in the index to the register. She would come to me with a register (each year is in a separate register with an index chronologically under each letter) and ask if what she found was what I was looking for. What is amazing is that the records were all in French: Barb had had five years of high school Spanish, but didn't know a word of French!

She became so excited about the finds that when she went back to college, she enrolled in a French course and had a near-minor in that language."

Anne Rebstock Cummings Neale of Berkeley Heights, New Jersey, wrote:

"I have had some amazing experiences doing genealogical research for the past sixteen years - some eerie, some uncanny, and some just unbelievable! When I first started climbing the family tree, I went to a library in nearby Plainfield, New Jersey to see if they had any information on Pennsylvania. I was directed to a massive collection of books that filled aisle after aisle. I was so overwhelmed with the quantity of material that I didn't even know where to begin.

Suddenly, a lady appeared who seemed to be researching also. I asked her where the Pennsylvania section of books were, and she said, 'Let me help you.' She took me to the aisles with the Pennsylvania collections. 'Let's see,' she said. 'Give me a name of one of your ancestors you are researching who lived in Pennsylvania.' I had been looking for several who resided there, so I just picked one out of the air and replied, 'How about Henry Goepfert?' The lady looked at the row after row of books on Pennsylvania and, from the many, many volumes, picked one at random and said, 'Let's see if we can find him here?' She rummaged through the chosen book, and then said, 'Here he is!' And there he was! I was totally in awe.

I've been back to that library in Plainfield many times and eventually checked out all - and I mean all - the Pennsylvania books in their collections, looking for more on Henry Goepfert; and the book the lady picked out of all those books was *the* only one that had the name of Henry Goepfert in it ... *the only one!*
How do you account for that?"

Sometimes our "Genealogical Helper" (that's generic, not the Everton's magazine) doesn't even have to be human! Ask my friend Peytie Moncure of Clifton, Virginia:

"I have been working on a set of genealogies that the Peyton Society is preparing to publish. Right now, everything is on about 10,000 family group sheets. The other day I picked up a loose leaf binder to file away a family of only three generations, the oldest being Ransford Peyton, an unusual name. As I stood up, my dog knocked another book down and open to another Ransford Peyton!

She wasn't psychic, she had a biscuit hidden on top. But why on *that* book? Anyway, a letter went off to both parties suggesting joint research."

One never knows just who will be a caretaker of someone else's family memorabilia and help unearth long-buried treasures. Mrs. Frances Underwood of Great Missenden, Bucks, England, reports:

"I am researching my grandmother's line in Maidstone, Kent, England, and I undertook reciprocal research with a member of the Kent Family History Society who has ancestors in my neighborhood. He did a great deal of research for me in Maidstone, taking me back several generations. One of the finds was the marriage of my great-grandparents.

Some time later he was searching through some documents in his spare room to find some stamps for his grandson who had just taken up stamp collecting. The spare room was full of papers and bits and pieces which his wife had brought home from the antique shop where she worked. Much of the shop's stock came from house clearance sales. Whilst he was searching, he came across an old certificate, which on opening, he found to be my grandparents' original marriage certificate!"

Don H. Berkebile of Mercersburg, Pennsylvania, adds a twist:

"When I left my hometown of Johnstown, Pennsylvania in 1955, I left many of my belongings in the home of my parents, where they remained until my mother sold her house several years ago. I then cleaned out my old closet and found a small bundle of papers of perhaps 20 early documents - obviously part of someone's personal papers. But I didn't remember where I got them or who gave them to me.

I looked through them, found dates ranging from the 1790's to the 1830's, and then, on one, found a familiar surname. This surname was the name of my close friend Richard - and I then recalled that it was he who had given me the papers in the first place. My fuzzy memory suggested that he had simply given me some of his own family papers in which he had no interest. I had heard that his daughter was interested in genealogy, so I contacted her about the find. 'Yes, they are my ancestors!' she told me excitedly, and happily took the treasure-trove with her.

But the surprising part of the story is that my assumption that these were papers handed down through Richard's family was incorrect. Back in the early 1950's, Richard was helping another mutual friend clean out his attic, filled with junk left by a previous occupant of the house. They had started a large fire in the backyard to burn the trash. Among the items headed for the fire were the contents of two large trunks filled with someone's old family papers. Richard, being a thoughtful fellow and knowing of my interest in old documents, grabbed a handful of the papers to show to me, but consigned the balance of the documents to the flames. I never got around to looking at them and just put them in that closet in the home of my parents. While Richard's daughter was delighted to receive the papers, she will have to wonder for the rest of her life just what was in that immense wealth of family history that her father unknowingly burned years ago."

Deborah M. S. Brown of Laurel, Maryland, recalled:

"Some seventeen years ago, I first began doing research

on my family. My grandmother told me that my grandfather's family had lived in an old house in Hardy County, West Virginia, and that there was a family cemetery on the property. I contacted the present owners of the old house, a British couple who lived in Washington, D. C. and only used the house on weekends. They invited us down to take a look at the property.

When we walked inside, my grandmother noticed a picture on the wall and said, 'That's John's grandparents!' The picture of my grandfather's grandparents was still hanging on the wall! The same thing happened again and again to other pictures in the home. After we had been there awhile, the owners brought out a metal box, stuffed to overflowing with old papers. 'When we moved into this house twenty years ago,' our hosts said, 'we found this old box of papers. We tried to give them back to the seller, who was one of *your* relatives, but he just said to burn them because nobody would want them. But we kept them instead, feeling that *someday* someone from your family would come back for them. Why don't you take them now?'

I was thrilled to say the least, but it was nothing compared to what I found when I went home and went through the box. For what this wonderful, history-loving British couple had handed me was my family's history for almost two hundred consecutive years. From the earliest tax receipt showing my earliest known ancestor Henry Miar paying his taxes for the year 1755 to cancelled checks my grandfather's uncle had written in the 1930's. There were receipts, wills, deeds, and many letters from family members. It was truly a goldmine.

I feel sure that 'someone' had whispered in my ear to go back 'home' and get those treasures."

If someone isn't helping you, *you* can always help someone. Witness Jennifer J. Cummins' story:

"A couple of months ago, I sorted fourteen years of accumulated miscellaneous genealogical data. I came across a will for a George Arnold that someone had sent me twelve years earlier but that didn't apply to my own research. After I got to bed that night, I couldn't sleep, so I got up and opened my *Genealogical Helper* magazine. On the very page the magazine opened up to was a query for information on a George Arnold of Fairfield, Ohio.

My will was from Fairfield County, not the city of Fairfield (which are a few hours apart). I sent a copy of the will to the person who had placed the query. It turned out to be the will of her ancestor! I had no memory of having that will until my cleaning spree earlier that day."

Rollie L. Campbell of Ignacio, Colorado, reflects on all this mutually beneficial interaction:

"I would like to comment about a facet of research that wasn't covered in your book, but that has been proven to me countless times. This is that when you help someone else, the favor is always repaid in full measure - maybe not by the recipient, but from somewhere a bonanza falls into your eager hands! I find that one of the greatest joys of doing my family history is having the opportunity to help others!"

Miss Lou Duprey echoes this:

"For some reason, I save clippings on several subjects. My son calls me 'The Mad Clipper.' Sometimes, I make copies and send them to friends. Seems they are always welcome, and they send their thanks. I try never to pass up a chance to do something nice for someone - anyone! It brings many moments of pure delight - I call some of these moments 'serendipity.'

Maybe that's why I want to share what I collect. I've said many times that I get just as excited about finding something for someone else as I do for myself. Seems like I'm always in an excited state of anticipation - just waiting for another unexplainable, awesome thing to happen. I EXPECT IT TO HAPPEN! I'd rather 'win one' of these experiences than win the lottery.

Being a genealogical researcher gives a whole new meaning to ...

'I will go where He leads me.'"

HOW TRUE. LEAD ON!

14
PRODS & NUDGES

Yes, if there is a common thread to most of the experiences contributed to *Psychic Roots* and this book, it would be that many genealogists strongly feel they are being "led" or "nudged along" in their searches. Some guiding force, some benevolent power, some *something* was helping them attain successful results as they climbed the family tree.

And many family historians went on to personalize that *something* into a *someone* - very often, a deceased ancestor or relative. My friend Sharon DeBartolo Carmack of Simla, Colorado, observes:

"I, too, have always had a fascination with the paranormal. I have always believed in guardian angels, and that they are usually our ancestors. I like to think that the only grandmother I ever knew is my daughter's guardian angel. My grandmother died almost a year to the day my daughter was born, and when my daughter was born, she bore an uncanny resemblance to my grandmother. My grandmother used to tell me I was her favorite grandchild because I looked like HER mother."

Marilynn Munn Strand of Lakewood, Colorado, writes:

"Are these long gone ancestors hovering around us? You bet! Sometimes their presence is almost palpable. And do we favor one more than another?
I believe it!"

Glenna W. Jamieson of Langley, British Columbia, reflects:

"I sometimes feel as if I am being helped by the spirits of my ancestors, particularly my women ancestors. As the years have gone by, many eerie experiences have led me to believe that maybe I was *not* alone in the solitude of an old cemetery or in other places I research."

Suzanne W. Guinn of Westphalia, Kansas, in regard to her search for her ancestor, Caleb Trask, recently wrote:

"It's been weird, but I have felt driven to find where he was buried. It's almost like a sign that someday I will find where he was born and who his parents were. When I stood at his grave, I almost felt like he was encouraging me to keep looking - and that someday I would find the rest of the story!"

Jennifer J. Cummins of West Chester, Ohio, notes:

"This past year I have been doing some research for a friend in New York. I enjoy working on 'city people' for a change rather than my country ancestors, but I am always encouraging this friend to do research too. He finally went to the Municipal Archives and was looking at a microfilm of marriage records for one of the boroughs of New York City.

He was unsuccessful in finding the record he sought, but, as he rewound the film, he stopped. There was the marriage record of his great-grandmother's brother which gave the town in Germany they were from, parents' names, etc. I found this especially interesting, because this ancestor, Eugene Zeitler, had always been the helper in the family - the sole supporter of his mother and siblings by the time he was fourteen, and later taking care of his mother and his sister and her children.

Four generations later, he was still helping!"

Patricia Stover Fair recalls:

"When I was born, we lived in Williamsport, Pennsylvania, just down the alley from my paternal grandmother, Sara Stover. Her maiden aunt, Mary 'Emma' Harris, lived in the apartment above the garage behind Grandma's house. We soon moved from Pennsylvania to New York, but once a year made the trip back to visit Grandma and Emma. Emma died when I was only five years old, but in the short time I knew her, she left a lasting impression. I had always thought she was fascinating, but didn't really know what made me feel that way. For whatever reason, I never forgot her.

In 1982, I became seriously involved in finding my ancestors and returned to Williamsport, where my grandmother was still living. I was interviewing her about the family history when she suddenly mentioned that Aunt Emma had also been interested in genealogy too. I asked what happened to Aunt Emma's things when she died, and Grandma replied that she just threw out all her papers, thinking they were worthless.

My heart sank. But then Grandma pulled out an old envelope which had been carefully opened at every glue seam. There, on what had been the inside of the envelope, was our family tree, handwritten by Aunt Emma. It started with my 4th great-grandfather Peter Harris, and then continued down through the generations to Emma and my grandmother, and then Grandma's three sons. And there, at the very end, was *me* - the first child born in my generation on our branch.

I couldn't believe my eyes. Emma must have known that I would be the one to carry on the family research. And using Aunt Emma's wonderful envelope as a starting point ... I have!

I'm going to start talking more to my ancestors. I just hope they want to help me to find them."

My friend, Dr. David Faux of Hagersville, Ontario, Canada, adds yet another "gem":

"I am becoming more and more receptive to the notions put forward in your first book, and there is much that is coming back to mind. Fortunately, I can verify my recollections with entries in a diary that I have kept since 1985.

Two reasons fuelled my trip to England in 1987. First, I wanted to find a photograph or painting of my great-great-grandfather Charles Faux in his military uniform. The story of this discovery was profiled in print *(Psychic Roots)* and on television *(Unsolved Mysteries)*. The second reason was to locate evidence to fill in an annoying gap in the Faux family tree.

Robert Faux of Norfolk County, England, was married in Banham in 1746, and buried in nearby Eccles in 1814. An Isaac Faux and his wife Ann lived in Banham during the eighteenth century, and were of an age to be possible parents of Robert - but there was nothing but circumstantial evidence to link them. It was interesting to note that in the church registers the name of both Robert and Isaac was sometimes spelled as 'Forkes' - a reflection of the way it is pronounced in that part of the world, and a clue that would be of particular help later.

A researcher in England had previously determined that Robert was not baptised in Banham. She did, however, establish Isaac's parentage back to 1641. It became a virtual obsession to confirm or disconfirm the suspected connection between Robert Faux (Forkes) and Isaac Faux (Forkes). In preparation for the trip, I wrote to the rector of the church in Eccles, and arranged to view the baptismal registers, housed a few miles from Eccles in the church at Kenninghall.

After basking in the glow of the discovery of the painting of Sgt. Charles Faux, I felt that perhaps I had used up my supply of good fortune. Still, it was a gorgeous day, and a drive through the Norfolk countryside would be a reward itself. As per the plan, I met the clerk of the Kenninghall Church at her home, and drove her up hill and down dale to reach our destination of Kenninghall. After opening the main door to the Medieval stone church with a large skeleton key, she ushered me in to wait at a table while she opened an ancient chest full of dusty old books. Much to my relief (I had come a long way to be told something like, 'Oops, I forgot, the one you want was destroyed in a flood') she located the Eccles register.

While I searched its pages with an eager anticipation born of potential discovery, the clerk rummaged through the chest to find materials for another client who had arrived on his own. In the process she discovered a small grey wrinkled book which she brought to me, with the suggestion that if time permitted, I might leaf through it. She had guessed that I might like to see something that had been in that chest for well over 200 years. I recall a flash of irritation, since this 'intrusion' disturbed my intense concentration on the Eccles book, but I quickly recognized that it was a rather kind gesture on her part.

Disappointment - there were no baptismal entries with the Faux surname in the Eccles register. All this way from Canada, what a let down. Oh well, it was worth a try. Now it was decision time. Leave or stay. Feeling downcast often brings with it a desire to escape, to go elsewhere. There was still time for a leisurely drive on a delightful summer day. I recall putting on my glasses in preparation for leaving, since my myopia requires corrective lenses for driving. However, the clerk interpreted this action as indicative of some difficulty in reading the faded ink of the little book I was about to hand back to her. She apparently had concluded that I was far-sighted and needed the glasses to read. She then pointed to a huge oak table which was feeling the full effect of a large cone of sunlight streaming in through a stained glass window. Not wanting to offend, I complied.

Seated in a sturdy oak chair, the sun radiated on the back of my neck and helped calm jangled nerves. It also cast its multicolored sanctified light on the small parchment item held in my hand. The symbolism did not elude me, it really did feel like I was basking in Heavenly light, and my flagging enthusiasm was in turn given a boost. The cover of the book indicated that it contained entries for early baptisms in Kenninghall, the very church that now surrounded me. The book, when perched on its spine, took the shape of a V, then seemed to anxiously pop open, lying flat at a place of its own choosing. Within an instant, a name jumped out, emerging into the light of day for probably the first time in 250 years - 'Robert, son of Isaac ()orkes and his wife Anne.' The first letter of the surname looked like an 'H,' but 'Horkes' didn't make much sense. Looking through other entries a similar letter came into view - '()rances.' Clearly it was 'Frances,' and so the surname in question was 'Forkes.' BINGO! And I was ready to up and leave? I recall thinking at the time that there was something just a little mysterious about this find, especially when juxtaposed with 'The Picture' discovery.

Back then, I gave tentative voice to the possibility that perhaps unseen forces, wishing to have their existence validated, guided the willing hands of their descendant. Did the spirit of Isaac want me to know that he was in fact my ancestor? Today, almost ten years later, I am much more inclined to be receptive to the idea, and am no longer reticent to share details like those above out of fear that it will compromise my reputation as a scientist.

Once again, Hank, I must thank you for prompting me to think more deeply about things I had brushed aside as mere coincidence."

June A. Vaughan of Humble, Texas, commented:

"Your book, *Psychic Roots*, is about a subject I have definitely believed in the last twelve years because I have experienced it myself, although I have been unwilling to discuss it with most people.

I started my family tree twenty years ago. My maternal grandmother helped me tremendously in the early years with her remembrances, etc. She passed away in 1982, but I believe she - or someone - has been pushing me to continue climbing the family tree and learn the intricacies of research since her death. While reading your book, I made notes under your various book categories to see how many areas I fit into. The main category would have to be 'being led' as I have been led through the last twelve years and actually feel 'watched over' in all aspects of life.

You mentioned the playfulness and hilarity of situations ... I have had so many funny and protective situations they are too numerous to mention. This 'Guardian' felt very close during the first nine to ten years after my grandmother died ... almost as if she was looking over my left shoulder. The last two to three years I still feel her, but very far in the distance. I am now in my early forties; and in looking back, it almost seems as though she was there to keep me on the genealogy track during years when most people might have other interests to occupy their time. Now that she has gotten me totally obsessed with genealogy and sure that I will stick with it, she is now fading from my senses.

She has made me feel this is what I am supposed to do in life."

And Diane J. Graziano of Pittsford, New York, even relates how her grandmothers seem to communicate with her directly:

"Serendipity and intuition are my friends in research. But, most amazing, are three mental messages I have received, superimposed over my own thoughts, from my three grandmothers - dead long before my birth!

The grammar and choice of words were distinct from my own usage. They made their identities known, and I have concluded that they are highly pleased to have a descendant trying to reconstruct their lives. These ancestors, I believe, are at the root of my experiences of serendipity and intuition."

Mary Deyerle Hodge of Fulton, Maryland, reveals:

"I am obsessed by the lives of my Deyerle ancestors, particularly Mary Henderson Deyerle. When I found her gravesite, my heart flopped around in my chest like a fish thrown on a bank! I cannot explain why I am drawn to this woman. I am appalled that she probably led a hard life without any help from the rest of her Deyerle family, and that - as evidenced by her old tombstone - her descendants didn't even know the correct spelling of her family name. No living person in my branch of the family ever heard of her children, let alone knew what became of them.

I have made it my goal to somehow search out every speck of information I can find on her and tell her story!"

Jean Laws of Olympia, Washington, also has a particular affinity for a certain ancestor:

"In my thirty-plus years of doing genealogical research for myself and others, I have had numerous experiences as described in your book. The most outstanding and persistent were the happenings surrounding my search for my great-grandmother Nancy Day Fletcher, who died in California at the young age of twenty-eight. I think I can safely say that after twenty-five years in her pursuit, she found me!

I have a large portrait of Nancy done by her artist husband that gazes down at me from a wall in my home. After examining sources found serendipitously and following unexplainable urges that made me recheck certain census records I had examined previously, I finally discovered much about her in records from several states. I have since been in touch with descendants of her several brothers and sisters, none of whom had known what had happened to her since she was the only family member who 'came west.'

She needed to be found. As her portrait looks down on me, she looks very satisfied."

Carol MacKay had a picture "lead" her also:

"I was most impressed by serendipity when I was working on my own family research. My mother had told me that my Grandfather Simonsen, a Dane, was interviewed by a Danish newspaper, either the *Aalborg Amtstidende* or *Aalborg Stiftstidende,* in the 1950's about his impressions of Canada. I hadn't actively tried to find it because I was, at the time, unable to get the newspapers on microfilm, and I did not have an approximate date. My Mother passed away in 1992, and shortly after, I had a compulsion to find this particular article. I knew from my mother that it was published after 1953 and before 1961, the year Grandfather died. I had a span of eight years to search, in two newspapers.

I ordered up the microfilm from the Edmonton Public Library, who amazingly, were able to locate the papers. I chose to order the *Amtstidende* for the first three months of 1955. As I read through the newspapers, I was disheartened because it was so difficult for me to concentrate on finding the article: I couldn't read Danish as well as I would have liked, and many of the pages were poorly and improperly microfilmed. I then wrote to the Danes Worldwide Archives in Aalborg who had copies of the *Amtstidende* and told them what I was trying to find. They searched the next three months for me, but didn't find anything. They said they would search again for me if I could provide them with a more approximate date. I gave up on it at that point ... for a few months.

I remember sitting at my computer desk one Sunday, looking up at the row of photographs that line the wall above. I found myself staring at the photograph of my Grandfather Simonsen, sitting on the running board of a Model T Ford. The compulsion to find that article came back again, stronger than ever. I typed out another letter to the Archives and, for some unexplainable reason, wrote that I had narrowed down the date to December 1954! One month later, I received the article in the mail from Danes Worldwide Archives. The article had indeed appeared on the 21st of December, 1954. I don't know why I chose to concentrate on the one paper over the other, or why I told them, so matter-of-factly, that the article was published in December of 1954, when I really had no idea.

I do know that this article is one of my most prized discoveries. It made my grandfather come alive again and gave me new insights into his character. It now is in a frame above my computer, as a reminder to follow that little voice that is often called intuition or sixth sense!"

Pastor Alfred Hans Kuby of Edenkoben, Germany, can identify with many of his ancestors on a day-to-day basis:

"In 1946, I began to study theology, not completely sure whether this was really my profession and calling - as it turned out later that it was. At that time I knew that two of my paternal great-great-grandfathers were Protestant theologians (Wilhelm Kuby, 1804-1874, and Konrad Schmitt, 1796-1882), and I also knew about a few Lutheran pastors named (von) Scheven among my mother's ancestors. But as I gradually traced my diverse lines back in time through genealogy, I learned that over *eighty* of my direct ancestors had been Protestant ministers! I've given up counting their exact number, but I know all their names and am conscious of my rich heritage."

If an ancestor doesn't seem to be forthcoming with assistance, some family historians have had to take more drastic action. Just as noted in *Psychic Roots* with other genealogists, Carla Dixon-Wolcoff of Prescott, Arizona, gave her forebears a good talking-to:

"While visiting my mother in California in 1986, I was given an old Bible with the name of Eliza McDaniel on the cover; a tintype of a small boy; and a black and white copy of a cameo picture of a young man with 'faded' eyes. My mother told me that the Bible had belonged to her grandmother Eliza Wilkins McDaniel. She did not know who the pictures were of.

On the way back to my home in Alaska, I dropped off the Bible at a book bindery in Seattle and went home. The two pictures of the young man haunted me, as the eyes resembled my grandmother Lennie McDaniel; so I decided to have them enlarged. A week later, I picked up the pictures, placing them on the front seat of the car as I drove towards the library to do more research. Out of frustration, I spoke to the picture of the young man and said, 'If you are my grandfather Eli Luther McDaniel, then tell me where you are, and let me find you today!'

That day's research went as it had before, without finding any more McDaniels. All of a sudden, an idea popped into my mind: maybe Eli and Eliza Wilkins had been childhood friends. So I began to look for Eliza on the 1870 Census of Wayne County, Illinois, and there she was at aged 19. A few houses away was an Elijah McDonald aged 18, son of Eli McDonald and Susan (later the name was changed from McDonald to McDaniel).

A few weeks later, I received a note from the book binder in Seattle telling me that I would receive the Bible in a few weeks. But he wanted to send me the bookmark that had fallen out of it. I looked at the bookmark and realized, to my surprise, that it really was my great-grandparents Elijah Luther McDaniel and Eliza Wilkins' original marriage certificate, dated 25 December 1873."

And Lee Nichols of Topeka, Kansas, remembers:

"I could never discover just why my ancestors Thomas Reed Lakey and his wife Millie Spring had come to Beloit, Mitchell County, Kansas. By studying the groups that arrived about the same time, I learned that most had arrived from Williamson County, Illinois. True to form, both Lakeys and Springs were found there. But *why* the move?

In the genealogy classes I was teaching, I often talked about group migration. I used, as an example, the Aaron Bell family who arrived with a group from Williamson County after losing family in an Indian raid. After much frustration about not finding the 'whys' of the migration in regard to my own family, one evening I sat looking, for what seemed to be the millionth time, at an old newspaper article that mentioned my Lakey-Spring family. But this time I didn't say to myself, 'Why did Thomas R. Lakey come to Mitchell County?' I said instead, 'Why did YOU come to Mitchell County?'

And for the first time a sentence popped out in the article that said, 'Mrs. Bell's brother, Robert Spring, ran to warn the neighbors that Indians were coming.' Spring? There was my connection! Robert and Nancy Spring Bell were brother and sister to great-grandmother Lakey. It wasn't the Lakey movement, it was the Spring movement. Further research eventually documented this."

But it isn't always just our ancestors who influence our searches. Sometimes a genealogist feels led or nudged by a contemporary. Ruby Coleman remembers:

"A few years ago, I received a letter from a person who needed cemetery information on an ancestor who died in my county. Her letter revealed that the ancestor was buried in a small, country cemetery in the southern part of the county. She didn't have the name of the cemetery, just a general location.

The cemeteries have been canvassed and are in two, large bound books in the genealogy section of the local library. A local genealogist recently had canvassed some of the county cemeteries more thoroughly and placed them in a notebook-type book alongside the other two books. I dreaded going to the library that morning because I knew, without a cemetery name, I would have to search page by page through the unindexed volumes to find her ancestor.

The genealogy section in our library is upstairs. Going up the stairs, I was almost at the landing when I realized that somebody was sitting at a table researching. I had been walking up the stairs very quietly. The lady at the table never turned and, in fact, had her back turned to me as I approached the genealogy section. She seemed very intent on her research. However, I recognized from the back of her head that she was the one who had written the third book of cemetery records.

Just as I entered the genealogy section she spoke. Never lifting her head or turning around she said, 'The information you want is in that book.' She pointed at the book she had written. All the time she never moved in position from her research at the table. I was startled, but decided not to say anything to her. I pulled the book off the shelf and immediately found the people I was looking for

... in the small, country cemetery in the southern part of the county.

I proceeded, with the book in hand, to sit down at the table. The lady lifted her head, looked at me in surprise. She greeted me and said she didn't hear me come in. I am sure to this day she does not know that she spoke to me or that she guided me to that book."

Miss Lou Duprey contributed this experience:

"One day in 1964, my husband and I were searching for a cemetery we were not even sure existed. We had about given up the hunt when a boy about ten years of age rode by on his bicycle. I called to him and asked if he knew about a cemetery nearby. He said, 'Sure - I'll show you!'

Show us he did. He led us through a thick stand of tall trees that would have been a maze to us. After plowing through this jungle of foliage, there was a cemetery all right - and there was my whole Prater family! I asked the little boy to stay with us or we would never find our way out. He sat on the grass while I copied furiously. He seemed quite content. When we were ready to go, he led us out, got on his bike, and just rode away. He wouldn't take anything for his trouble except a candy bar and some potato chips.

My little angel?"

There appear to be a myriad of ways we are led. That excellent genealogist, Esther Littleford Woodworth-Barnes of Clemson, South Carolina, noticed:

"My genealogical books have been, to a large extent, a compulsion to finish the work of others. It seemed a shame that material had been gathered, but not made available to other family historians.

I seem to be led from one to another. In 1958 and 1964, Edwin Neff asked my first husband, E. Huling Woodworth, to be the prime researcher for the Alden family of the Five Generation Project of the Mayflower Society. On Mr. Neff's second visit, Huling would not talk about it, knowing that he had only months to live. Consequently, Mr. Neff asked me, the co-compiler of Huling's large collection of Aldens - over 80,000 (and a like number of other Mayflower passengers) - to be the prime researcher. Thirty years later,

I am *still* working as prime researcher. Little did I know what a chore it would be to find primary references for the many undocumented statements.

Ray Greene Huling began his genealogical work about 1878, put it aside when he started a family, and died in 1914 without publishing. My great grandfather and great aunt also did work on the family. The pressure was there to do something with what little material they had collected. Here again primary sources had to be found. The projected 250 page book turned into one of 700 pages, and *The Huling Genealogy* won the Jacobus Award.

I've done work on the Littleford family and my Knox County, Indiana ancestors too. Another family waiting to be heard is my Spooners. They have a fascinating story, which I expect to publish next year. I feel that I am being kept alive to do this book. My genealogical pursuits give me a purpose in this life, having been widowed a second time twenty-two years ago."

I've noticed that when a genealogical colleague dies, very often, long-unsolved problems suddenly find their solutions. When a Palatine co-researcher recently passed away, within days of his demise the German background of the prominent Irish-Palatine/American Methodist Philip Embury was finally discovered. This was followed by another near-miraculous find in Dutch records: more long-buried emigration materials on the Palatines, something that my late co-worker and I had been looking for for thirty years!

Janice B. Heller of Chula Vista, California, has had similar experiences:

"There were some indications of psychic abilities in my father's family, and I really believe they communicate with us from 'the other side.' If they didn't, I would have a lot more work to do on my family history.

Often, when someone in the family dies, I get new clues for research, or some unknown relative contacts me. I have walked into a library and randomly selected a book which opened to my family's data; been in a German archive when someone researching my family walked in; my letter has arrived in a German office at the moment my cousin did; and I have found my way from the train station to the street where my grandfather was born in a town I'd never seen before.

My genealogy started with a paranormal experience when I was hanging up pictures of my mother's family. It seemed that Grandmother was 'telling me' to 'find Francis!' Also, among the things I was hearing, were the words 'German-American Club.' When I eventually found 'Francis,' she was not the male cousin for whom I was searching, but his aunt - someone I'd known as 'Francine' - and she was in Grandmother's Irish-English family. Francine had married a German man, and they had recently travelled from California to Bavaria with a German-American Club. This cousin's birth name was 'Frances,' and she had almost died in an accident about the time Grandmother 'told me' about her.

Now if I could just learn how to turn on this 'intuition' when needed, maybe I could complete my family history!"

Kay Waters Sakaris of Pasadena, Texas, has had one of the most moving experiences I've ever heard of:

"My co-author, Carolyn Owens Hervey and I are in the process of writing our book, *The Long-handled Spoon - An American Family Saga*. It is the story of two families - one white, one black - who are connected by slavery. My great-great-grandfather was Willie Nichols of North Carolina, who moved to Arkansas and brought with him his twenty-eight year old slave, Calvin Nichols, an ancestor of Carolyn's.

When we met in 1986, little did we know how deeply entwined our relationship would become. Two literary agents to whom we have submitted our manuscript commented about the 'mystical' quality of our story, and that it seems to be almost a preordained connection. We agree: it *had* to be predestination that brought us together - our childhoods almost parallel in the events that prepared each of us to pursue family research. We each had a grandparent who carefully nurtured an interest in the family's past, and each of us began our search at a fairly early age.

We are somehow connected - either on the same 'wave length' or by some other phenomena. We can finish each other's sentences. Some months ago, I went to bed early one

Kay Waters Sakaris & Carolyn Owens Hervey

evening and awoke at 2:30 A.M. - wide awake - came in and started writing, having no idea where the stuff was coming from. The next day when Carolyn and I talked, she mentioned having quit working at 2:30 A.M. because she was 'stumped' and couldn't get out what she was trying to say. When I told her I had started work at that exact time and what my subject matter was, she was flabbergasted - I had written what she was having trouble with and finished her chapter!

Carolyn has an older brother whom she had not seen for ten years, and one day she received a telephone call from him. He was at the airport in Little Rock and told her he HAD to see her asap. She told him she would see him at their mother's house that weekend, but he said that wasn't soon enough and came right over to her house. He proceeded to tell her all about our work together - the grant we received, the kind of records we have searched for, all about me (down to a physical description), and that we have not found all the records we need. He told her things that only she and I had discussed about my great-great-grandfather, Willie Nichols. He told her that he was murdered, and that the man who did it got away with it and with the money from his estate. He had been having dreams. They started about four years ago when she and I were in the midst of our research for the book. He has continued to have them - it seems like he knows what we are doing or going to do before we do it.

Somehow, we are all connected in this thing - we know we are connected by blood, but this seems like something larger than that."

I AGREE, KAY. IT'S SOMETHING THAT TOUCHES US ALL!

15
REFLECTIONS

The many uncanny experiences contributed by my colleagues have enthralled me. But their thoughtful comments about those events are what linger even more in my memory. I continue to be humbled and inspired by the wisdom and insight of my fellow family historians.

Several contributors addressed the mysteries behind the serendipities. Irene Burton of Wakefield, West Yorkshire, England, observed:

"There cannot possibly be another subject so prone to coincidences, serendipity - call it what you will - as genealogy!

Do the souls of our ancestors, I wonder, ever watch our efforts at digging and delving into their lives and times, and perhaps feel we need a hand sometimes?"

Patricia Law Hatcher of Dallas, Texas, has strong opinions about the subject. She wrote in Desmond W. Allen's *PGA Newsletter* (now the *Hist. & Gen. Mag. of Arkansas*):

"I suggest that genealogists who sit on their you-know-whats and wait for serendipities find fewer than those who continue to pursue good research practices. Why? In order to *find* something, you have to recognize it when you see it - and that requires some basic (yes, sometimes boring) research. I don't believe that research is sufficient; sometimes we need serendipities. I also don't believe that serendipity comes without research."

John Titford of Hallfieldgate, Derbyshire, England, wrote an excellent article in the *Journal of the Lincolnshire Family History Society* which contains his musings on this fascinating matter:

"It wouldn't do to get too philosophical about coincidences, would it? It might or might not help to split the word into 'co' and 'incidence' - that is, two things that happen together, or are brought together, in a way which you find uncanny or unusual. The interpretation you offer of a coincidence will probably reveal your general frame of mind, since the world has been separated from time immemorial between those who believe that all human experience can ultimately be explained in very rational terms - scientific terms, if you like - and those who prefer some metaphysical or psychic explanation. This is the distinction between a classical and a romantic view of the world, between behaviourist and gestalt theories of psychology - and even between main-stream and holistic medicine. No I *am* getting philosophical - sorry! For me, family history coincidences often do give me an eerie sensation - as if long-since-departed ancestors are wanting to be found and to have new life breathed into them. Much of the time a psychic explanation - 'sixth sense' - is simply more believable, more simple than a boring and convoluted 'rational' one.

Not all coincidences are really coincidences, if you see what I mean. I don't know about you, but the longer I carry on as a family historian, the more coincidences I find. It's almost as if your research and your reading create thousands of little loose tags in your brain which are simply waiting for a coincidence to latch on to them. So one day I'll come across a very rare surname or a very obscure place name - names I have never encountered before, as far as I know. Then, blow me - within a week or two I hear of someone discussing the same name in a record office, or come across it in a printed or manuscript book, without even looking for it. Coincidence? Yes, except that your brain has stored an interesting name, so chances of your 'noticing' this same name again are dramatically increased. Perception is selective, after all - our eyes and our brain reject infinitely more information than they actually register - as you can prove very easily next time you scan an unindexed parish register for just the one surname you require.

Never far away from coincidence is our old friend 'serendipity' - the process whereby you stumble across something interesting while you're really looking for something else. You turn a page en route to the one you are really seeking, and there is a nugget of information which you never suspected existed, and that an index might not have helped you locate. Serendipity can be the family historian's greatest friend, and it's always worth giving yourself just enough time and space to allow the God of Serendipity to work for you. How many times have we gone straight to a single household in a census return to find our Bloggs family, copied out the information and then reeled the dreaded microfilm back to the beginning and put it in its box? What a mistake! What other gems might have been lurking in the street or the area where the Bloggses lived? Microfilm, microfiche and computer searching via CD ROM and the rest make serendipity more difficult - but if you take your time, it can still work for you."

But sometimes it isn't all that easy. Don H. Berkebile cautions:

"I note how many of your contributors believe that our ancestors want to be revealed, and somehow manage to guide us. Yet I am forced to agree with another of your contributors, Helen Leary, who comments on pg. 191 (of *Psychic Roots*) about a 'flit-about ancestor, the kind who seems determined to keep his identity a secret...'

All too many of my ancestors fall in this group, and seem to do all possible to prevent me from ever discovering their identities. I know I am not unique in having this problem, for one can find the many thousands of ads in the *Genealogical Helper* of folks who are similarly afflicted. Also, with my own lines, numerous distant cousins have worked on my same problems, and yet these stubborn ancestors continue to defy the efforts of all of us."

And my long-time Palatine-research compatriot, Dr. Arta Johnson of Columbus, Ohio, avers:

"*Psychic Roots* contains a lot of serendipity. Any researcher can vouch for serendipity: all of us who comb out the old records come across items we did not expect to find and certainly weren't looking for, but filled in a hole for somebody.

Do I feel any special kinship with my old ancestor, Jacob Renner, any sense ever that he is 'with me?' No. I am aggravated at the old cuss, that I cannot find where he was between selling out in Hassloch, Germany in 1847 and marrying in Belleville, Illinois in 1853. No. I have felt far more empathy with long-dead people I have found in various church records, no relationship at all, but have rejoiced at their happy moments, snickered at the snide remarks made by the Pastor, and nearly cried over the pathetic incidents. Am I possibly receptive to influences I am not aware of?

I do not deny the existence of psychic phenomena. I know they exist. There is ESP in my family, me included, but it has never played a part in my genealogical research that I can point to and say *this* is unexplainable.

For those rooted in a purely scientific background who find this whole area difficult to accept, I like what Birdie Monk Holsclaw of Longmont, Colorado, had to say:

"I'm afraid I haven't had the kind of experiences you're asking for. I do believe that others have them, as I've heard many examples, and I also believe that there are rational explanations for such experiences (even though science may not have discovered all the explanations yet). I don't know why *I* don't have these experiences; perhaps it's because I approach my research with such a methodical outlook. I take this approach to everything in life, so that's not surprising.

I was discussing your project with my sister, who has no interest in genealogy. But she does have an interest in me, and once she visited a local genealogical group to hear me present my talk 'Beginning at a Black Oak: Reconstructing Your Ancestor's Neighborhood with Tract Maps.' In the discussion with my sister, I said that I just wouldn't have any intuitive experiences to send you.

She challenged that statement, reminding me of my 'black oak' research experience; and I replied that I *didn't* use intuition in that research - that I developed a hypothesis, and then took a step-by-step approach to proving my hypothesis. Then my sister said: 'Birdie, hypothesis is just a safe word for intuition.'

So, Hank, *if* my sister is right, that's as close as I can get!"

Several letters led me to the realization that to *really* be an excellent genealogist one must have not only a keen mind, but a sensitive nature. Tom Crane of Calumet City, Illinois, observed:

"Now that your book has entered in upon the scene, I somehow think that there will be some legitimacy attached to what I have been trying to say all along. I now have in my possession a source that I can refer to that lends support to my theory that there is indeed something beyond our mortal comprehension at work whenever we seek to explore the lives of those that have already passed into the great beyond.

I think that whatever it is that divides us from those who ignore the obvious is nothing more than a matter of sensitivity. A person either has that sensitivity or not. It is more or less up to the individual to recognize that sensitivity and to make use of it. No amount of explanation will satisfy those who suffer from of lack of comprehension in that regard, and I guess one can say that is what makes each of us rather unique."

Norman K. Crowder of Nepean, Ontario, adds a twist to this talk about sensitivity:

"My wife and I and many friends have had numerous lucky breaks, and they all illustrate Helen Hinchliff's point in *Psychic Roots* that feeling as well as thinking about one's ancestors usually results in a more successful search. That may well explain why all my serendipitous experiences have occurred only when looking for people in my own family lines. I have done a lot of research for others, often with very good results, but never with any of these fantastic breakthroughs."

Have you ever pondered, "Why *me*?" when contemplating your addiction to genealogy? My old friend Dr. William ("Bart") Saxbe of Oberlin, Ohio, echoes this common thought held by so many of us:

"I am delighted with *Psychic Roots* and am on my third reading. I can imagine that the book might provoke apprehension in some of the pillars of the discipline, those concerned with our reputation among academic historians.

('Bad enough we have so many amateur genealogists with
no commitment to accuracy: now Jones wants us to be
spiritualists too!')

Not me: I think it's good to look at these things. Even if
a lot of our experiences defy explanation, they call out for
attention. Have you considered the question of *why*
genealogy should be so compelling a study for some people
while it leaves others completely cold. What is the
psychology of the genealogist, the source of his/her
enthusiasm?"

Miss Lou Duprey also touches on Bart's question:

"Your book calmed a lot of fears because only one person
in each family seems to be the designated (by Whom, I
wonder?) genealogist. It's good to know the young folk are
stepping in .. with a lot more awareness than we find in the
old-timers.

Perhaps the 'work' is a prerequisite to all of us one day
working together, crossing the D-dimension, and thinking
nothing of it.

I like Carl Jung's definition of synchronicity. I could
add that synchronicity makes you more aware, and in being
more aware, you see much more synchronicity."

Pamlea M. Langston of Rock Island, Illinois, contributes:

"I have just read your book *Psychic Roots* with great
interest, and it confirms my belief that while primary and
documented evidence is of paramount importance in the
study of genealogy, intuition also plays a great part. I have
been involved with the research on my own and my
husband's family for over ten years and several times with
no real evidence, I have felt instinctively that a certain
person belonged to a certain family or that conversely
material sent to me by correspondents, which they claimed
to be true, was in fact false. Most of the time I have
subsequently been proved to be correct.

I often wonder why I feel compelled to spend most of my
time now that I am retired working on my own family
history and helping others with theirs. There seems to be
something driving me to find all my ancestors as far back as
I can go and to know who they were and to reunite not only
my own family but those of others.

Who knows what the reason may be?"

My fellow Fellow, Myrtle Stevens Hyde of Ogden, Utah, reflects:

"Your presentation gives us much to think about. How fascinating. And how special that so many people shared such personal experiences. Your poem at the end particularly touched a warm chord. Yes, someday we will know.

One idea that came forcefully to my mind as I finished reading (and wished there were more), is the overall picture that the accounts portray without saying anything about it - the astounding (incredible, extraordinary, and other related superlatives) evidence of GENERAL guidance. Why do you do Palatines, and I do the Aldous family, and Bob Anderson the Great Migration, and someone else does Mor, and another person searches for McDonalds, and my sister is totally immersed in a project of reconstructing from wills the early families of a little parish in England?

We don't become dedicated to a project and then find out that someone else has also spent years doing the same thing. We may do things related to what someone else is doing, and then when we find each other learn that our work overlaps and adds to what the other has done, but we don't do the *same* things! As I pondered this idea this morning, I remembered that people starting genealogical research have asked me how they should decide which families to seek. My answer, 'I can't tell you. Start, and you will know.'

And we do!

A scripture came to mind, Acts 17:26: '[God] hath made of one blood all nations of men for to dwell on all the face of the earth, and hath determined the times before appointed, and the bounds of their habitation.' I feel that the bounds of our research regarding the men on all the face of the earth are also appointed by a higher power than we understand. Someday we truly will know, and we will rejoice."

The whole research process and the very nature of "discovery" continues to bring forth comments from our colleagues. Dr. William B. Saxbe writes:

"In regard to the process of discovery, have you ever had the feeling, following a genealogical breakthrough, that in retrospect the solution was obvious, if not inevitable? We all have, right? Well in line with the ancient observation that there is nothing new under the sun, this feeling has been elegantly recorded and reported by a famous late great. I have the pleasure to pass along to you, for your reflection, enjoyment, and use, the following literary tidbit:

' ... *so easie it seemed*
Once found, which yet unfound most would have thought
Impossible ...'

I ran across these lines in an article about Orville Wright. They come from Milton's *Paradise Lost*, Book VI, lines 499-501."

Lester J. Hartrick of Buffalo Grove, Illinois, reflects:

"I have come to believe that some of us are blessed (cursed?), to varying degrees, with mental propensities that have been acquired neither through experience or training. These we have inherited from our ancestors and by studying these people, we can begin to better understand both who we are and why we are as we are. The German philosopher Emmanuel Kant wrote of this phenomena in 1781. In the preface to his book, *The Critique of Pure Reason*, Kant says, 'Human reason, in one sphere of its cognition, is called upon to consider questions, which it cannot decline, as they are presented by its own nature, but which it cannot answer, as they transcend every faculty of the mind.' He further describes having knowledge of an object prior to being presented with that object, as knowledge gained *a priori*.

I do believe that the mind is, to some extent, genetically programmed. The extent of this programming appears to be an accident of nature. The programmed information appears to be a function of who our ancestors were. Of what practical use is such theoretical knowledge? In my own case, it has provided a platform upon which I could understand my own feelings and what their origins might have been. As a member of the Illinois Army National Guard, I served several short tours of duty in Germany. As such, we were required to learn the basics of the German language. I found this easy for me and attributed the fact to German being an easy language to learn. I even 'made up' words in German, if I didn't know them, and surprisingly found they were correct.

On one of my tours, I was quartered in a hotel on a small lake. After a good German breakfast, I looked out my window and with the euphoria of the good meal thought to myself, (in German), 'Ich liebe Deutschland!' (I love Germany!). I had the strangest feeling of being at home and belonging there.

You can imagine how I felt some years later when I discovered that my Hartrick family originally came from this very area of Germany. All of these things fell into place. My ease of learning the German language, the feeling of being 'at home' in Germany as well as being able to use words in that language that I had never heard. These were all due to my genetic programming. I had learned about myself: the who and the why of a couple of my mind's facets. I do believe there's a case for our intuition being genetically shaped. I also am willing to consider that some of the people that I've met who are also of Irish Palatine descent have become friends not only by virtue of our having similar interests, but by a 'sixth sense' that attracts us.

This brings me to the most valuable end result of the study of our genealogy: the meeting of new and beloved friends! Friends that are older than we know and can only speculate on the true roots of our friendship. Other friendships that are based on mutual interests and support in the pursuit of these interests, are equally precious."

In another letter, Lester expands on this and notes:

"Recently I saw one of those nature programs on television. This covered the migration pattern of the Monarch butterfly. Starting from the central highlands of Mexico, they fly north to northern Wisconsin and Upper Michigan. Having been raised in the U.P., I can attest to their being there; they were quite common in the summertime. They then migrate south again to Mexico.

The thing that is unique about this is the fact that the Monarch's life is so short it takes eight generations of these butterflies to make the complete circuit! The only way that the 'flight plan' could be given to succeeding generations is through inheriting the experiences and memories of their ancestors.

I believe that Jung was right when he said that, 'We inherit the wisdom of the experiences of our ancestors ...."

Lester's remarks dovetail with some of the thoughts brought forth in LaVonne Harper Stiffler's magnificent work *Synchronicity & Reunion: The Genetic Connection of Adoptees & Birthparents*. Dr. Stiffler notes that psychiatrist Arnold Buchheimer challenged the prevailing assumption that memory is exclusively a function of the brain. Based on empirical observations in therapy, as well as other research done by psychobiologists, neurophysiologists, and psychologists in the late 1960s and early 1970s that linked cellular learning with long-term learning, he proposed that memory storage exists throughout the body. That memory storage is protein related. His thinking is that RNA is the memory storage facilitator in cellular protein, and that RNA stores, accumulates, and transmits memory.

Dr. Stiffler goes on to say that, in her study of adoptee/birthparent reunions, this factor may explain how a mother and child retain memories of each other. "In their search for both wholeness and a self," she says, "they are internally preoccupied, conscious of being part of a larger whole, and open to synchronicity." Many of the case studies she presents do indeed reflect a high incidence of synchronistic events suggesting a continuation of the prenatal bond, and a psychic connection of the ruptured family system that transcends time and space.

It's such an intriguing subject. Edwin C. Dunn of Albuquerque, New Mexico, reflects:

"I agree with the comment that 'chance favors only the prepared mind.' If one has not spent time and work researching, then an encounter with a fact will never be recognized as significant, and if a person has not reached a certain state of spiritual awareness, then no matter how welcome, or unlikely, the so-called chance discovery, the source of help, other than 'luck,' will never be suspected or recognized.

During twenty-five years of searching for elusive ancestors, I can state that I have had many instances when I have made 'lucky' discoveries that had nothing at all to do with a logical research plan. When I go to the Family History Library in Salt Lake City, I take along a plan of research, but I always allow plenty of time just to browse amongst the stacks with no real purpose in mind - always profitable.

Yes, I believe there are forces, spirits, consciousness (call it what you like) in another dimension who take an active interest in what we do here. This belief developed, not from my genealogical research experiences, but from other experiences in life. Why would our 'dear departed ancestors' care about our pursuit of family history? If they do, I can't believe it is based on any desire on their part to 'set the record straight' or to ensure that they be 'remembered' in the published records of this three dimensional universe. That would seem to me to be a rather self-centered point of view incompatible with a joyful spiritual existence. But I do think they are very much interested in helping us grow spiritually during our sojourn in this earthly classroom.

There is a hunger by people in today's chaotic and fast-changing world for roots or ties to something stable. Ties to family are one way to fill this need. Hence, we have an explosion in recent years in interest in genealogy (as well as religious and spiritually related matters).

Why mightn't we be receiving spiritual help in this area of endeavor?"

This acknowledgment and acceptance of spirituality in genealogy brought forth many letters. Cynthia Marie Bernadette Drayer of Portland, Oregon, stated:

"A lot is written today about the mechanics of genealogy: where to find information, how to preserve it and organize it, and finally how to prepare it for publication. But there is another aspect to genealogical research, the spiritual side, which can be just as important, if not more so, because it is the answer to 'why?' Why do genealogical research?

I am constantly surprised by the way some genealogical information is made available to me. I would randomly pick up a book and thumb through it. As I read with unbelieving eyes, there was my grandfather, his father and mother, brothers and sisters, aunts and uncles, with a description of their settlement in Ohio. This would happen many times, books I would pass on a shelf would almost fall out, or it was as if a small voice in the back of my head would whisper, 'look at this book, pull it down now.' And sure enough, there was a birth or marriage or death of an ancestor I was searching for.

I began to realize it was not 'luck,' but a spirituality to genealogy. It is a special guidance by our ancestors to help us find our past, for only by knowing our past can we understand our future."

Speaking of knowing our past, Suzy Morgan of La Jolla, California, passed on a fascinating excerpt from Kryon's *Don't Think Like A Human, Book II* that certainly gives us something to think about:

"You are your own ancestors, and many of you participated in all of the history that you now read about ... leaving messages for yourselves. It is with great irony that you dig them up now ... exposing your own words and your own actions!"

And Jeff Carr of Hambleton, West Virginia, gives us all inspiration:

"I have always been aware of my intuitive/psychic tendencies (something of a maternal family trait), and I was fortunate enough to have grown up in a family that surrounded me with family history: reunions, funerals, and stories, stories, stories. As I look back, I can now see that my genealogical inspirations and activities have been an immense training ground for me: intellectually, creatively, and spiritually.

Slowly I learned to be more open; through my early twenties, I began to use that openness to explore my spirituality. This became a 'self-feeding' cycle, that is, my deepened spirituality created more genealogical sensitivity, and my intuitively-guided genealogical work (and success) deepened my spiritual awe and wonderment. The past four or five years have been incredible! My genealogical finds have far surpassed what I can account for with my own ability; I truly feel that God has blessed me - that somehow, I'm just a conduit.

I don't know how to say this without sounding pompous or arrogant, but now *nearly all* of my genealogical endeavors have the serendipitous, synchronistic, psychic quality to them! I feel very uncomfortable saying that, because a very strong sense of humility accompanies those genealogical gifts. About the only time I *don't* feel 'inspired' is when I'm doing really tedious work (such as general-survey census work); even then, I know that it is preparation for the inspiration.

Hank, in all honesty, the further and more this phenomenon grows in me, the less I feel like a genealogist. This summer it occurred to me that I'm becoming more of a clerk - a 'clerk to my inspiration and revelation.' While the 'Other Side' seems responsible for guiding and directing me, the bulk of *my* responsibility and work is to see that I remain open, and to carry-out my 'clerk' duties. The former entails emptying myself of prejudices, pre-conceptions, inaccurate details, and allowing myself just to 'receive' and be 'nudged'; this in itself really takes a good bit of effort. The latter entails 'busting my butt' to find evidence and documentation to support/negate a given hypothesis.

My research companions have noticed that I am so 'lucky' they repeatedly share their 'I'm stuck' problems with me, hoping that at some point I'll stumble across their line(s). While all of the researchers that I know of have experienced the occasional serendipitous or intuitive break-through, I'm the only one I've heard of that seems to experience the near-constant 'rush' of guidance and inspiration. Hank, am I alone? Has anyone else responded with such a report? Is that what you're describing in yourself?

I sincerely believe - no, I *know* - that God has used genealogical work as a conduit and tool for me to grow and be fulfilled."

Tom Crane continues to hold forth on this intriguing area in his thought-provoking book, *Green Is The Valley, Blue Are The Hills*:

"If one were to assume that I had merely been engaged in a hobby or a pastime that was genealogical in nature, that part of my life would have quickly ended as I struggled to maintain a livelihood. To make that assumption is to miss the point of all that I have been trying to say. The word 'genealogy' distorts the perspective of my story because it is defined in very limited terms. It evokes an image of dusty shelves, old books and family charts.

I will now seek to escape from that image by telling you that my journey through the past resulted in the restoration of a faith that was oftentimes overlooked or even forgotten. Yes, I did use genealogical resources in order to place myself on the path of discovery, but what I found along that path helped to rekindle a faith that had flickered with a very low flame. Success in any venture builds self-confidence. I not only experienced success, I was placed in situations and I met people, both past and present, that gave me cause to believe that life is not as haphazard as one would normally think. Life follows a definite plan, and, if you can reach out from within yourself, you will gain a greater appreciation of that plan."

Judith Meier poignantly writes of her feelings:

"The longer I am employed at the Historical Society, the more spiritual my work with past souls has become. I think that we who are immersed in the past develop a sixth sense to pick up clues, make connections, become open to providential leading. As I said in the introduction to my last book,

'Having spent so many years reading about the day-to-day, week-to-week activities of our nineteenth century forebears, I have developed the deepest respect for contemporary researchers looking for their ancestors, for they are really looking for themselves. Aren't we all the sum total of all our ancestors? These were flesh and blood people who felt joy, suffered hardships, nurtured hope, and dreamed dreams. They are precious memories and faithful inspirations - so great a cloud of witnesses.'"

Judith goes on to say:

"Finally, let me share with you a story told by Clarissa Pinkola Estés, Ph.D., in her remarkable book, *Women Who Run with the Wolves: Myths and Stories of the Wild Woman Archetype* (©1992 C. P. Estés, Ballatine Books, New York), as she tells her original literary story, *La Loba*. As I read Dr. Estés's story, *La Loba*, its relevance to my life and my 'genealogical calling' truly resonated:

'There is an old woman who lives in a hidden place that everyone knows but few have ever seen. As in the fairy tales of Eastern Europe, she seems to wait for lost or wandering people and seekers to come to her place.

She is circumspect, often hairy, always fat, and especially wishes to evade most company. She is both a crower and a cackler, generally having more animal sounds than human ones.

They say she lives among the rotten granite slopes in Tarahumara Indian Territory. They say she is buried outside Phoenix near a well. She is said to have been seen traveling south to Monte Alban in a burnt-out car with the back window shot out. She is said to stand by the highway near El Paso, or ride shotgun with truckers to Morelia, Mexico, or that she has been sighted walking to market above Oaxaca with strangely formed boughs of firewood on her back. She is called by many names: La Huesera, Bone Woman; La Trapera, The Gatherer; and La Loba, Wolf Woman.

The sole work of La Loba is the collecting of bones. She is known to collect and preserve especially that which is in danger of being lost to the world. Her cave is filled with the bones of all manner of desert creatures: the deer, the rattlesnake, the crow. But her speciality is said to be wolves.

She creeps and crawls and sifts through the montanas, mountains, and arroyos, dry riverbeds, looking for wolf bones, and when she has assembled an entire skeleton, when the last bone is in place and the beautiful white sculpture of the creature is laid out before her, she sits by the fire and thinks about what song she will sing.

And when she is sure, she stands over the criatura, raises her arms over it, and sings out. That is when the rib bones and leg bones of the wolf begin to flesh out and the creature becomes more furred. La Loba sings some more, and more of the creature comes into being; its tail curls upward, shaggy and strong.

And La Loba sings more, and the wolf creature begins to breathe.

And still La Loba sings so deeply that the floor of the desert shakes, and as she sings, the wolf opens its eyes, leaps up, and runs away down the canyon.

Somewhere in its running, whether by the speed of its running, or by splashing its way into a river, or by way of a ray of sunlight or moonlight hitting it right in the side, the wolf is suddenly transformed into a laughing woman who runs free toward the horizon (pp. 27-28).'

Yes, I said to myself as I read this passage: this is just what I do; I put the bones together; put sinew and flesh and fur on the creatures; and breath life into them again!"

This beautiful and appropriate passage certainly hit home to me too. Its very arrival in my mailbox was even synchronistic: I received Judith's letter and read the above section from *Women Who Run With The Wolves*; then, the *very next* letter I opened that morning was from my friend Dee Lillegard - who cited the *very same* passage as being relevant to this book!

I THINK IT WAS *MEANT* TO BE INCLUDED, DON'T YOU?

16
GRASS ROOTS WISDOM

Well, there you have it: *More Psychic Roots* from the "grass roots." Hopefully, this sequel has indeed provided a "safe place" for genealogists to share some of their unusual and uncanny experiences.

Some may say that all these stories - and there are nearly 300 of them in this volume alone - have a sameness to them, a repetitive quality. But I decided early on not to worry about "too much of a good thing." I *want* to show that these events are *not* isolated incidents. They occur often - especially to those open to the reality of their existence. I think now, with both books, that we finally have amassed a considerable body of evidence to show that serendipitous events and unexplainable experiences really are quite normal in genealogy. They're "part of the territory" - something to be enjoyed, celebrated and shared!

And while we're talking about sharing, allow me to share just a few other thoughts that rang true and came through loud and clear as I compared notes with my colleagues:

First of all, the consensus is unanimous: the research process seems to work best when we lighten up a bit. Genealogy is a celebration - not a funeral! After all, it's God's way of letting us play Sherlock Holmes. We should relish the tidbits of information that amuse us. Let's savor the crazy names we sometimes uncover in our research: people like "Solomon Gommorah" and "*Another* Smith." Why, my favorite discovery in all my years of work on the 18th century Palatines was when I learned that Johannes Dings married Anna Maria Dongs!

And this can carry over into life! There's a certain wackiness to our existence that's reassuring. Who wants to be trapped in a dull and somber world? My Universe *does* have a sense of humor. Someone once said, "What this world needs is more propeller beanies!" I certainly agree. And I'll never forget what Stan Laurel once told me:

"You can lead a horse to water, but a pencil must be lead."

How true!

I've lived my life by it!

Other comments hit home. Some colleagues emphasized how important it was to be flexible in our attitude and outlook - to give elbow room for the unexpected to surprise us. It's been said that a coincidence is God's way of performing a miracle anonymously. I love that! But I'm afraid that sometimes we have a tendency to overplan and to overthink the research process. We don't leave space for synchronicities to pop up and point us in new directions. To counter this, I've found that, once in a while, it's a good idea to visit the library *without* an agenda. It keeps us open and primed for the serendipitous discovery. We're *ready* to be amazed!

BRING ON THE MIRACLES!

I've also come to believe that one of the worst things a genealogist can do is to get to the destination before making the journey. It never works when we start climbing the family tree by saying, "I will now set out to discover that I am a descendant of Charlemagne." That kind of battle plan only encourages flimsy research and faulty conclusions. No, it's better to see where the path will lead. Usually the results are far more exciting than whatever we've imagined.

And I feel strongly that anything that *humanizes* our ancestors can only be a positive. We should never be afraid of what we might find in the old records. For example, some of the Palatine families had long-held family traditions of noble ancestry that then were shot down by German documentation. So what? I've always said it took much more courage to come to America *without* the "silver spoon." Then, too, some Palatine immigrants were derogatorily called "dreamers" in some of the old records I've found. But, you see, I think that's an *endorsement!* America was settled by dreamers! Our immigrant ancestors had some special spark within them that enabled them to gamble their lives on the unknown and "take the risk."

To be sure, it's always exciting to place a distinguished person with historical significance on our family group sheet. By all means, we should revere our *Mayflower* ancestor, but don't forget to honor the horsethief also! They too have their story. I'm intrigued that one of my colonial forebears was asked to depart his Vermont town two different times; that one of my Dibble ancestors divorced his poor wife on grounds she was a witch; and that my 17th-century Crippen immigrant was accused of being a panderer of his wife "in lightnes and laciviousenes [*sic*]." What a guy! I love the fact that my '49er great-grandfather, Isaac Hillman, ran a "Temperance House" in San Francisco where no liquor was ever served, but that the recipe book for his patent medicine, "Hillman's Cure-All," requires opium and ten gallons of pure-grain alcohol to brew it.

Lord knows, I'm sure not perfect. Why should my ancestors be any different?

Some other views from my associates also made a lot of sense. Several contributors said that genealogy seems to work best when there is a *balance* to our life. We all tend to eat, breathe and sleep family history to the extreme sometimes. But we shouldn't make it the "be all" and "end all" of our existence. It's best, we've learned, to have other interests too!

In keeping with this, I'm reminded of my friend Robert Charles ("Bob") Anderson, who's engineering that massive Great Migration Project for the New England Historic Genealogical Society. Besides immersing himself in the lives and times of all those elusive 17th-century colonists, Bob manages to make time to indulge himself in his passion for baseball - seeing as many games each year as he can. He's even a contributor to the *Baseball Encyclopedia*, using his genealogical skills to help ferret out biographical information on obscure 19th-century players. We all can use a breather from genealogy every so often. Take a lesson from Bob Anderson and see a baseball game once in a while.

Lately, I've been trying to practice what I'm preaching here. The past year as I worked each night hovering over my home-microfilm-reader and barely coming up for air, a little voice kept telling me, "HANK - GET A LIFE!" So, to help keep a balance and attain some harmony between genealogy and "the real world," I went back into the recording studio again, after nearly thirty years absence. I cut three albums of ballads I never got around to recording when I was singing on RCA back in the Stone Age. They've just been released on Epitomé Records. I must say that, aside from climbing the family tree, it's the most fun I've had in ages. And I think my genealogical work is all the better for my musical sidetrip. The balance is back!

Another thing: my colleagues reenforced my own belief that - to make genealogy *really* work - it's necessary to have an emotional relationship with our ancestors. I'll say again what Helen Hinchliff said in her foreword to *Psychic Roots* ...

"Feeling about one's ancestors, as well as thinking about them, usually results in a more successful search."

She's so right. Our ancestors were not just names and dates. They were people who cared and dared, laughed and cried - just like us! We can have great success as family historians if we try and walk in our ancestor's shoes. If we can figure out what made them tick - immerse ourselves in their communities and time-frames - they *will* reveal themselves to us. I really believe that our ancestors *want* to be found! Genealogists have been blessed with great power: we can bring the dead back to life - if we do it *right*!

And I'm convinced that one way to do it right is to follow our intuition and see if the facts back up our hunches. Each intuitive nudge and every synchronistic event is an invitation to look inward. And when we trust that inner voice, we're getting in touch with our higher selves - the *real* **us**, if you will. The more we are in tune with our soulful core, the more centered, balanced, and successful we *have* to become. It just works that way, pure and simple.

There's a great line in that Broadway classic song "What I Did For Love" from *A Chorus Line*:

"The Gift Was Ours To Borrow ... "

That's exactly the way it is with our intuition. We can use it, or not use it. It's up to us!

Finally, I've grown to believe that we're not human beings with a spiritual side. We are spiritual beings who happen to be in human form this time 'round. I like to think that we're all "Holy Thoughts in the Mind of God" - in "school" right now, here on Earth. And genealogy is a terrific classroom - a golden opportunity to learn, interact, and grow with kindred spirits on a common path. From a metaphysical point of view, we all are climbing the family tree for a reason. It's what we do. More than that, it's what we're *supposed* to do. It's our soul's task.

As Gary Zukav so beautifully put it in *The Seat of the Soul*:

"What does it feel like to remember your soul's task?

When the deepest part of you becomes engaged in what you are doing, when your activities and actions become gratifying and purposeful, when what you do serves both yourself and others, when you do not tire within but seek the sweet satisfaction of your life and your work, you are doing what you are *meant* to be doing. The personality that is engaged in the work of its soul is buoyant. It is not burdened with negativity. It does not fear. It experiences purposefulness and meaning. It delights in its work and in others. It is fulfilled and fulfilling.

Take your hands off the steering wheel. Be able to say to the Universe, 'Thy will be done.' The final reaching for authentic power is releasing your own to a higher form of wisdom."

I'd like to close by giving you a gift that I gave myself not too long ago. At first glance it may not seem relevant to genealogy at all. But I think it is:

Years ago when I was starting out in the entertainment business, I had a chance to spend some time with a great man ... a great soul. His name was Nat Cole, known to the world as "Nat King Cole." And he *was* a "King!" When you met him, you couldn't help but be struck by the power of his goodness.

Nat used to tell the story of how one day in his offices at Capitol Records on Vine Street in Hollywood, a disheveled man with a long beard, wearing a flowing white robe wandered in through the door. He smiled, gave Nat the manuscript of a song he had written, and left. Everyone sort of laughed at the stranger's weird appearance, but Nat picked up the sheet music and read the lyrics and hummed the beautiful melody.

He was so struck by the song that he persuaded the brass at Capitol to let him record it, and it became one of his biggest hits of all time.

The song was by Eden Ahbez and was called "Nature Boy."

Have you ever heard something, but never really heard it? That happened to me recently, when I pulled out some of Nat's old albums to soothe me after a particularly hectic day. Nat died years ago, much too soon, but there he was again - singing softly in that warm, mellow voice of his, bathed in a blanket of beautiful strings.

And I finally *really heard* what he was singing. After 30 years, it finally registered what he was saying:

> *"The Greatest Thing - You'll Ever Learn*
> *Is Just ...*
> *To Love*
> *... And Be Loved ... In Return."*

You see what I mean ...
That *is* about genealogy.
Genealogical research is *our* gift of love to our ancestors ...
to our descendants ...
and to ourselves.

May "St. Serendipity," who seems to be the "patron saint" of family historians and genealogists, smooth your path as you climb the family tree
... and may you always have the happiness of pursuit!

EPILOGUE:
MEMORIES
HAUNT THE CORNERS OF MY MIND

The two careers I've had over the years - show-business and genealogy - have something very much in common: *fascinating people!* Both professions are filled with some of the most interesting, fun, and vibrant individuals God ever put on this planet.

We are not only the product of our experiences, we are the product of our relationships too. If you'll allow me a brief digression on these final pages (and while I've got a captive audience - I've been dying to tell some of these stories for years!), let me share this collage of "people memories" with you. They're from both eras - and they still make me smile:

I suppose I've always been a "people person." I grew up in a family filled with go-getters and individualists. Most of my relatives seemed to march to their own drummer, and I hope it rubbed off. For example, I had two maiden cousins, Helen and Alice Burton, who were special favorites of mine. They were interested in *everything!* Besides genealogy, one of their many hobbies was seashell collecting, of all things. Believe it or not, they used to give slide lectures on that seemingly dry subject to the prisoners in San Quentin. At first, the convicts almost had to be dragged to their talks. But once the Burtons started their presentations, they made the seashells seem so fascinating that it was "standing room only" in Cell-Block B.

You never knew what to expect from those two. Once, they were arrested in a Near Eastern country for sneaking into a Mosque with a camera. They told the police that they meant no harm, but that they didn't want to miss anything. And one of their last escapades took place when they were in their 80s and became shipwrecked in the Antarctic. Helen and Alice were marooned on the ice for about five days. But not to worry: they ended up with a bunch of new penguin slides to show the convicts on their next trip to the slammer.

Helen and Alice Burton were a hard act to follow.

As I was growing up in Northern California, my parents always had a houseful of intriguing guests around. At one time, my Dad was speaker chairman of our local San Leandro Town Meeting. One of my parents' jobs was to host the featured speakers to a home-cooked dinner prior to their talk. One night, when I was about eight years old, the special guest at dinner was a heavy-set, rather plain woman who had very short, salt-and-pepper colored hair. I remember she kept encouraging me to play the piano for her and was very interested in what books I was reading (*Treasure Island*, I think I said). I liked her! She was very kind, didn't talk down to me, smelled really good, and, as I recall, had the most *comfortable* lap.

Years later, I asked my parents who the nice lady was who had made such an impression on me as a youngster? My Dad said, "Oh, that was Gertrude Stein. We liked her too."

I suppose that's when I first learned that ...

"*A lap ... is a lap ... is a lap!*"

(And no, she didn't offer me any "brownies").

That was just the beginning. Since that time, I guess you could say it's been a long and somewhat wacky road. As I mentioned in *Psychic Roots*, I started out in the entertainment business, first as a singer/songwriter, at the age of sixteen. My singing partner, Dean Kay, and I sure paid our "dues." In the beginning, we played every engagement we could get. Sock hops, USO shows, seedy clubs, college proms, what-have-you. We even had the audacity to sing "Jailhouse Rock" while performing a New Year's Day show for prisoners at Santa Rita Prison Farm. Talk about chutzpah! (It was a point of pride to Dean and me that we were among the youngest members of the San Francisco branch of the American Guild of Variety Artists whose total membership at that time seemed to consist entirely of strippers, female impersonators, and *us*!"). We would spend nine months a year at our respective colleges

(Stanford and San Jose State) getting an education - and then take our summer vacations in Hollywood, making the rounds trying to land a recording contract.

How we hustled! I remember as a young songwriter driving all the way up to Harrah's Club in Lake Tahoe with our co-writer/friend, Larry Ray. We wanted to pitch a song we had written especially for the nightclub act of the legendary "Last of the Red Hot Mammas," Sophie Tucker. When we finally arrived at her hotel, we called her room.

A male voice gruffly answered the phone and said, "Hello."

I replied, "Good afternoon, sir. I'd like to speak to Miss Tucker please."

The voice answered curtly, "This *is* Miss Tucker!"

WHOOPS!

The cliché about Hollywood being populated only by "the sleeze element" certainly didn't hold true from our reference point. We seemed to only run into nice people who wanted to help us. Publishers and record producers had an open-door policy, encouraging our musical talents to blossom. Singer Bobby Darin (of "Mack The Knife" fame) was especially kind, going over some of our early songs with us and suggesting ways to make them better. (Some ten years later, this good advice paid off: my partner, Dean Kay, wrote the song "That's Life" for Frank Sinatra, and I was lucky enough to get Mel Tormé to record my tune "Midnight Swinger.") And finally, after five years of pounding the pavement, RCA offered us a recording contract, and we were off and running.

A few weeks later, we were signed to appear as co-stars of the five-day-a-week *Tennessee Ernie Ford Show* on ABC-TV. What a training ground: we learned, while America watched! It was a thrill to work with all the wonderful guests Ernie had on that program. Talk about *people memories*! To bring just a few of the many back to mind, there were:

Minnie Pearl - such a kind, warm, and funny woman, a leader of Nashville society (Mrs. Henry Cannon) who, in reality, was just the opposite of her image and would *never* wear a price-tag on her hat when off-stage ...

Bob Hope - "Mr. Cool" and all professional, a man who needed an audience's laughter like anyone else needs oxygen ...

"Peapickin," with Tennessee Ernie
Ford & Dean Kay

Rehearsing with Minnie Pearl
(sans costume) & Dean Kay

With Anita Gordon, Dean Kay, Ernie Ford & Bob Hope

Western character actor Andy Devine - who made us laugh when he told Dean and me in his gravelly voice that we should enlist in the submarine branch of the US Navy, because, if we were torpedoed, we'd die quickly with very little pain ...

Movie tough-guys George Raft and Peter Lorré - again, contrary to image - both truly "*gentle*"-men ... pussycats! ...

Country singer Patsy Cline, so natural and unaffected - who pulled her wig back to show us the scalp scars she had received from a bad auto accident, ironically not knowing she would be dead in a plane crash within a few weeks ...

Richard Nixon - always running for office even when he wasn't; shaking every audience member's hand, trying *so* hard to be just one of the gang (but blowing it by calling Ernie by the wrong nickname: "You Old "*Bean*picker" instead of "*Pea*picker") ...

And Robert Kennedy - frailer and shorter than I thought he'd be, surrounded by Secret Service Men who followed him even into the bathroom!

But my fondest memory of the *Tennessee Ernie Ford Show* was Ernest Jennings Ford. What you saw - was what you got! He was a down-home, fun-loving, *very* talented, good guy, somehow thrust into the limelight with no place to hide.

It was easy to be caught up in the excitement around him, but it was kind of sad to see. When you ate with him in a restaurant, Ernie often would have to sit in the back booth, facing the wall. Otherwise, his meals would be a series of constant interruptions by well-meaning strangers eager to get his autograph and socialize with him. And you almost took your life in your hands when you drove in a car with him. People would pull alongside, recognize him, and in their excitement, start to swerve into his lane of traffic. All privacy went out the window with his success. But Ernie was always was so patient with his fans, and pretty much accepted the whole thing as "part of the territory."

Ernie Ford's "Sixteen Tons" remains the fastest selling record in Capitol Records history. But it was his hymn albums that were the biggest and most consistent sellers over the years. Dean and I were honored to appear with him on his *I Love To Tell The Story* album and backed Ernie up on his moving rendition of "How Great Thou Art." His true nature and sincerity really came through on those old classic spirituals.

Ernie had a great social conscience, but was so disappointed when some of his fans from the Bible Belt didn't follow suit. I remember when he sang a duet with black singer Diahann Carroll. As they took a bow together, Ernie nonchalantly draped his arm around her shoulder. The vitriolic racist "hate mail" he received for that innocent and natural gesture of affection wounded him deeply.

In his later years, he lived in Portola Valley in the hills behind my old alma mater, Stanford University. In his semi-retirement, Ernie often would drop in at the neighborhood garden and hardware store, wearing his old jeans and Pendleton shirt. He'd casually take out his pipe, and then proceed to work behind the counter all day, showing surprised customers where to find seeds, manure, and the latest tools. He remained just "one of the guys" to the end.

Just before his death, Dean and I got a chance to visit with him again, when the Nashville Network celebrated his 50th anniversary in show business with a TV special. It was a wonderful experience, because we had a chance to sort of "close the circle." When the three of us posed for a picture together, he winked and smiled, saying, "Well, here we are again after all these years ... the famous team of 'Art, Bart, and Fargo!'"

I was proud to be a member of his team, and I miss Tennessee Ernie Ford very much!

While I'm still nattering on about the Ford Show era, let me tell you about an incident that led to one of the happiest "people memories" of my life. One day on the program, Ernie asked the cast, "Of all the great people in history, who would you like to spend an hour with, if you had the chance?" Dean said, "Abraham Lincoln." Singer Dick Noel reflected and answered, "Leonardo DaVinci." Announcer Jim Lange thought and replied "Beethoven." And I said, very seriously, ... "Stan Laurel." I'd been a lifelong fan of Oliver Hardy's skinny partner and considered him the funniest man ever to grace the silver screen.

Well, guess what? I was the only person on the show who got his wish! (DaVinci, Lincoln, and Beethoven were unavailable). Stan heard about my response, and we started a correspondence that lasted several years. In his many letters, he generously gave me performance tips and commiserated about the feast or famine aspects of show business when I was "between pictures" (which was often!). And then one day in late 1964, out of the blue, I received a phone call:

"Hello, lad," said a soft, unmistakable English voice. "Come on over, let's have a visit!"

What an afternoon we spent. He lived in a smallish Santa Monica apartment, filled with a lifetime's worth of memorabilia. Stan was much more outgoing and gregarious than his timid character on screen. His eyes twinkled with good humor, and he had the most marvelous belly-laugh - so contagious, you couldn't help but join in. He was the *real* director of the Laurel and Hardy films. They were largely formed from his inspiration and comic genius. I had a ball picking his brain for answers to questions I'd wondered about for years. Stan enthralled me with stories about how he and Charlie Chaplin came to America on a cattle boat together as members of an English Music Hall troupe. And he let me in on some of the technical secrets that helped their film gags come off so well.

I WAS IN HEAVEN!

One thing that struck me was his genuine modesty. Stan was absolutely amazed at how many people around the world seemed to love him. He showed me his new color television set, sent as a gift anonymously with a note attached from "just a fan who wants to say thanks for all the laughter you've given us."

And the stories he told! He related how one time after they retired from films, he and Oliver Hardy were making a tour of Europe and docked at Cobh, Ireland. He said there were hundreds of boats blowing whistles, and mobs of people screaming on the docks. Laurel and Hardy thought, at first, all the commotion was for someone else on board the ship - royalty, maybe. They just couldn't understand what all the ruckus was about. But then, Stan said, something happened that they never forgot:

Stan Laurel (1890–1965)

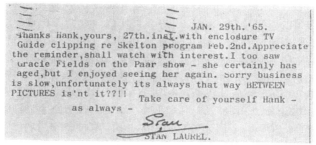

A typical note from Stan

All the church bells in that little Irish town started to ring out the Laurel and Hardy movie theme, the "Cuckoo Song," as the crowd below sang along and cheered. He looked at Hardy, Ollie looked back at him - and they both cried.

That wonderful afternoon went on and on. I thought I might tire him out (he already had suffered two strokes previously and had a bad heart condition). But Stan insisted I stay and talk some more. Finally, it was time to leave. As we said our farewells, he said cryptically to me, "Well, Hank, the next time you see me - I'll have 'me hat on." I really didn't know what he meant, but I smiled and said goodbye.

Ten weeks later, Stan Laurel was dead.

A few months after his passing, I was watching an old Laurel and Hardy short subject at home on television. In one scene, he and Oliver were preparing to be hanged for some offense relating to their glorious ineptitude. But they were both concerned that they wouldn't be able to recognize one another and be buddies when they finally got to heaven.

And then, in the movie, Stan said something that sent chills up my spine. He consoled his friend by telling him, "Don't worry, Ollie, you'll know me up there ... when you see me, *"I'll have 'me hat on!"*

In 1963, Dean got his "Greetings from the President of the United States letter," was drafted, and we left the Ford Show. But since I'd been doing comic sketches as well as singing on each program, my managers and agents thought I should give acting a try. So I then began what turned out to be a twenty-year career playing inept bumblers and innocents in films and television. I hate to say it, but maybe this was type-casting ... the bumbler part, at least. To wit:

My very first day on the Desilu lot shooting my initial episode of *My Three Sons* certainly had a less-than-auspicious start. When I arrived, I had to dodge a speeding golf-cart careening in front of the soundstage, driven maniacally by Lucille Ball. The world's most famous redhead owned the lot - and she knew it! Lucy had her hair in rollers, a cigarette dangling from her mouth, and was cackling loudly and ordering everyone to get the blankety-blank out of her way.

Welcome to Hollywood!

On *My Three Sons*, with Don Grady, William Frawley & Gale Gilmore

On *The Patty Duke Show*, with Patty Duke

At that moment, up walked my representative from the William Morris Agency with movie star Robert Young in tow.

My agent said, "Hank, I'd like you to meet Robert ..."

Before he could speak another word, I enthusiastically interrupted him saying, " Oh, I'd know Mr. *Taylor* anywhere!"

GOOD, HANK ... VERY SMOOTH!

But again, it was the *people* who stood out! What a bunch of characters (in the *best* sense of the word) to work with. On *My Three Sons* I had a recurring role, playing one of the high school friends of Don Grady, who played "Robbie" on the show (of course, I was 23 playing a 16 year old, but I managed to fool 'em!). The star was Fred MacMurray, a reserved, quiet man who had the greatest contract in TV history. It guaranteed that he only had to work about two months a year filming his role for the entire season's shows. Then what he had shot was inserted into every episode. The rest of the cast filmed the show all year round. So when the time came for me to do most of my scenes with Mr. MacMurray, he was long gone. The dialogue I supposedly did with him was filmed with the script girl saying Mr. M's lines back to me.

William Frawley ("Fred Mertz" on *I Love Lucy*) first played the old uncle on the program, and then was followed by veteran thespian William Demarest in a similar role. Both men were gruff and curmudgeonly and pretty much played themselves. And (how can I say this delicately?), no starlet's "backside" was safe from a playful pinch if Bill Frawley was around. At 80, he seemed to have the libido of a 20 year old!

Those shows in the '60s and '70s seem just a blur now. But grinding them out at a fast clip was the best education a novice actor could get. They sure weren't great art, but they paid the bills: *Petticoat Junction, Mr. Novak, No Time For Sergeants, Love American-Style, Mod Squad, The Patty Duke Show, Emergency, Love Boat, The Jeffersons, Family Affair, Mork & Mindy* ... on and on. They still come back to haunt me on Cable TV and make me feel old when I see them. And I must confess it's very spooky to watch a scene from long ago and realize that everyone in it - but me - is now *dead*!

All the commercials I did were fun too, and some even won awards. Singing and dancing for MacDonald's in their big musical extravaganzas. Having twenty voluptuous blonde starlets chase me down the beach yelling, "What's that aftershave you're wearing?" in my Hai Karate ads. Standing on my head because I was a bored apprentice repairman with nothing to do in Maytag Appliance spots. And having a parrot fly right out of a pirate movie, land on my shoulder, and bite my nose (he *wasn't* supposed to do that!) to show that Panasonic TV's were super-lifelike in their commercials.

GREAT ART, INDEED!

I especially enjoyed working with the older character actors. They were living reminders of the "old" Hollywood, and most could still act anyone else off the screen. What a treat it was to share a scene with class acts like Edgar Buchanan, Elsa Lanchester, Dean Jagger, Lee J. Cobb, Hermione Gingold, Joe E. Brown, Arthur O'Connell, and Spring Byington. And the younger batch of supporting players were equally fun and taught me a lot. Wally Cox, Richard Deacon, Herschel Bernardi, McLean Stevenson, Vince Gardenia, Terry-Thomas, Jim Backus - all great, but, sadly, all gone now.

It was never dull. I remember working several times with the great character actor Walter Brennan. And he *was* a character! Walter's politics have been described as being "a little to the right of Hitler." His specialty was to wait until the other actors were being made-up, bleary-eyed and out of it at 6 A.M., and then pouncing on them to discuss politics. You couldn't win. All you could do was nod and listen - there was no escape because you were imprisoned in the make-up chair! Oh well, I had literature from the John Birch Society to take home after work.

But I also recall the *kindness* of Walter Brennan. The three-time Oscar winner spent one entire afternoon coaching this green-behind-the-ears, fledgling actor in camera techniques. He didn't have to do that. He patiently demonstrated, for instance, how (by looking with my right eye into his left eye) more of my face could be seen by the audience in our scenes together. His only goal was to make *me* look good. I've never forgotten his generosity, and I was able to use his tricks of the trade on-camera for years.

Oh, and he did the *best* Walter Brennan impression I've ever seen!

In *The Family Band*, with (among others) Buddy Ebsen, Walter Brennan, John Davidson, Lesley Ann Warren & Goldie Hawn

In *Blackbeard's Ghost*, with Dean Jones & Richard Deacon

In *The Cat from Outer Space*, with McLean Stevenson

You always hear about temperament and ego when it comes to big stars. Phooey! Not in my experience. I know it sounds saccharine, but - truly - I've found that the bigger they are, the nicer they are! Twenty years of fond "people memories" prove it!

There was the time I was to film a TV show with Henry Fonda. I didn't know what to expect, working with a living legend of that magnitude. I'm afraid I arrived on the set with trepidation, trembling in my boots a bit. Fortunately, his make-up man was a friend of mine and had told him that I was coming. When I arrived for make-up, Mr. Fonda sat in an adjoining chair and put me at ease by saying, "Hi, Hank! I'm a 'Hank' too ... just call me that, and we'll get along fine."

And I did ... and we did!

Some "people memories" of those days remain only as fleeting impressions of images and moments past, but I still treasure them. To share a few:

Sitting next to a stonefaced little man at Stan Laurel's funeral and realizing only later that it was Buster Keaton ...

Eating at an Italian restaurant in Hollywood next to Frank Sinatra's table and feeling nervous every time his bodyguard readjusted his shoulder holster ...

Not knowing what to say when silent screen comic Harold Lloyd pulled off a glove to show me how a movie-explosion-gone-wrong years ago had blown off some of his fingers ...

Having a chance to spend time alone laughing with Jack Benny, when he and I both showed up an hour too early for an industry banquet ...

Confidently telling dancer/director Gene Kelly at a movie audition, "Of course I can dance!" and then promptly demonstrating that I had two left feet and was certainly *no* Gene Kelly ...

Being at a Beverly Hills fund-raiser filled with "fat-cats" who'd seen it all, but noting how all eyes turned when a surprisingly tiny Mae West sashayed in, flanked by two beefy muscle-men ...

Trying to conduct business with one of my agents who had a big sign over her desk that read, *"Remember - It was an <u>actor</u> who killed Lincoln"* ...

Remembering the class Fred Astaire showed at an ASCAP meeting, when he gently chastised the photographers who were blocking his view of the songwriters - to whom he felt he owed so much ...

Sitting in with George Burns on a casting call that soon became a gag-writing session, and marveling that Gracie's husband could toss off a multitude of comedy lines so easily, with just the flick of his cigar ...

Being awed just being in the presence of Lillian Gish, who had been part of movie history from its very beginnings, from D. W. Griffith on ...

Driving to work at the studios through Beverly Hills and seeing Cary Grant pick up his daughter from grade school in a car-pool like any normal parent would; and chuckling as Jimmy Stewart wrestled with two huge Irish setters on leashes who evidentally thought they would try and walk *him* around the neighborhood ...

Delaying regular Wednesday-night invitation-only movie preview screenings at 20th Century Fox Studios until "the one ... the only" Groucho showed up: beret on head - cigar in hand - blonde on arm ...

Hearing firsthand about Tin Pan Alley and the formative years of American popular music from my songwriting idol Ira Gershwin, and longing to be a part of that bygone magical era ...

Trying to deliver my lines straightfaced while working with Robin Williams, but "losing it" and breaking up at his non-stop comic antics anyway ...

Not recognizing the stunning Natalie Wood in my dentist's office, and, knowing she looked familiar and that I'd seen her someplace before, asking if she had once worked as an extra on *My Three Sons* ...

Watching Vincent Price, who had to be the sweetest man in the world offscreen, rub his hands together in utter glee when I told him how he had scared the bejabbers out of me in movies as a child ...

Dumbfounded at my first sight of Elvis Presley on the set at MGM, so contrary to my preconceived image: in a high-backed director's chair, nattily dressed, smoking a stylish cheroot, and reading *The Wall Street Journal* ...

Playing Ringo Starr's twin brother in an NBC-TV musical version of "*Prince & The Pauper*," under layers of make-up so skillfully done that we would often switch places at lunchtime - with me going to the commissary as "Ringo," fooling everyone, and seeing what it was like to be a Beatle ...

Fond memories all!

But the people I've met from my years in genealogy are *just as special* to me. Genealogy seems to attract the interested and the interesting. Who'd have thought that individuals initially met by simply answering a query in a genealogical periodical would eventually turn out to be life-long buddies - kindred spirits on a common path. Here are some of my colleagues - sadly, all gone now - whom I'll never forget:

The very first family historian with whom I ever came in contact was Van Buren Lamb, Jr. of Summit, New York. His special area of expertise was the colonial Dibble family, from which we were both descended. On a trip to the east with my parents in 1957, I had a chance to visit his rustic home. It was located in Schoharie County, the lovely upstate New York region where my Dibbles had settled after moving there from Cornwall, Connecticut in the 1790's. Mr. Lamb's old house was a ramshackled, sprawling affair, crammed to the rafters with genealogical books, periodicals, and charts. A smell of musty and decaying papers permeated everything. I loved it! He had chronicled his beloved Dibbles on a series of index cards - and ended up with so many of these yellowed notes that they literally were popping out of their file drawers. The disarray was very attractive to my budding pack-rat mentality.

But my fondest memory of that initial encounter with a *real* genealogist was Van Buren Lamb's absolute delight in *sharing* his largesse with me. He didn't have to do that - I was just a skinny pipsqueak of a teenage kid, who asked too many questions and wanted all my answers "yesterday." But in person, and later via years of correspondence, he patiently took the time to instruct me on how to climb the family tree the *right* way. To weigh family traditions carefully and not accept them as Gospel truth. To try and base each of my family connectives on documented sources contemporary with the event. To realize that genealogy is ever-changing and to stay abreast of new articles and books that might change previously held concepts of family structures. To double-check everything I found in print to see if the original sources verified what was on the printed page. And to oh-so-carefully weigh the preponderance of available evidence when a needed source crucial to a connective was no longer extant.

Truly, Mr. Lamb was *a giver* - perhaps the most common character trait I've found among those individuals who are really *great* genealogists. He felt it was his happy obligation to pass on his accumulated knowledge and experience to others. I guess you could say that Van Buren Lamb taught me that genealogy is really "a calling." He was living proof of the old chestnut which says that "God's gift to us is our talents. What we do with those talents is our gift to God." By heeding "the call" of genealogy, we have an invaluable opportunity to give back what has been given to us. And that's exactly what Van Buren Lamb did!

June Barekman of Chicago was another early genealogical influence. We both shared a common German surname in our ancestry: "Bergmann," which ended up "Barekman" in June's case, and was changed to "Barkman" and then was anglicized to "Hillman" in my family. Many's the time at Stanford I would sneak down to the dormitory hall phone booth and have lengthy genealogical conversations lasting far into the night with June back in Illinois. My roommates must have thought that I had a girlfriend in Chicago - and, although there was a 25 year difference in our ages, I guess I kind of did. Because June Barekman was a true friend to every family historian she ever met. She seemed to know everybody, and everyone appeared to know her. I sometimes think she joined every patriotic and genealogical organization known to man, and then happily served as an officer in each group. Outgoing, interested, empathetic ... she was a catalyst, a matchmaker, putting people together for their mutual benefit.

But, to me, the great lesson that she taught was *attitude.* June Barekman was genealogy's "cheerleader!" Negativity was simply not in her vocabulary. It was she who taught me that "pessimists make lousy genealogists." Her life was a testament to her positive outlook. The glass was always half full, not half empty, and she believed that elusive ancestor *could* be found if only you dug a little deeper.

FGS FORUM, editor, Sandra Luebking, remembered June as a "person of breadth and depth, who loved other people at all levels. She always asked you who you were and where you were from - and ever after remembered your name." And her compatriot Loretto ("Lou") Szucs observed that "many who were never privileged to know her will benefit from her many works and good influence for years to come."

June Barekman touched me, and touched us all.

Genealogy certainly can be a humbling pastime. Lord knows, I'll never have the pure brain-power of some of my fellow Fellows of the American Society of Genealogists. Many are in a league unto themselves in that regard.

My late colleague John P. Dern was like that. His little grey cells, as Hercule Poirot called them, continually worked overtime. I've always felt that, to John, the questions raised in genealogy were perhaps more important than the answers found. Sometimes when dealing with Dern, it was as if you were on the hot seat in the interrogation room of the police station, so many questions were asked. And I always said that you really didn't have to completely read John's excellent books, such as *Pioneers of Old Monocacy*, *The Albany Protocol*, or his study of the *Rauenzahner Family*. All you needed to do was look at his footnotes, which were like books unto themselves, and that could keep you busy for a decade or two. Each footnote could have been a springboard for an entirely new volume. John's lesson to all genealogists was that *good scholarship* and *meticulous documentation* were absolutely paramount in setting down a family history correctly. In preparing all my Palatine volumes, John and I continually bounced ideas and theories of origin and connection back and forth, and my books certainly were the better from his considerable input and feedback.

And there were so many other people who have passed on whom I'll never forget:

With Van Buren Lamb, Jr.

With John Dern

With June Barekman

Rabbi Malcolm Stern, whose integrity and ability to rise above the fray helped settle many a conflict between warring factions in genealogical organizations and brought them all together to serve a higher purpose ...

John Insley Coddington, along with Donald Jacobus one of the creators of "scientific American genealogy," whose knowledge and mastery of the subject had no equal (one of my most nerve-racking moments was trying to give a speech on genealogy with John Coddington sitting directly in front of me in the first row - as if *I* could have told him anything he didn't already know) ...

Kenn Stryker-Rodda - another kind man, another "giver" - always ready to be your rooting section and urge you on to be better than you ever thought you could possibly be ...

Effingham P. Humphrey, Jr., like a character out of a Dickens novel, very bright, very funny, and very good at helping others laugh too as we all climbed the family tree together ...

Norman C. Wittwer, Jr., the quintessential local historian, whose many friends had an ongoing campaign to make him write down all the valuable information on New Jersey Germans he carried around in his head ...

Rosabelle Leetham, a sweet little old lady from Arizona, so supportive of my Palatine research that she mailed me part of her pension check every month to help with the enormous expenses of my ongoing overseas investigations; she closed each and every letter with, "I send my love to all!" ...

Unforgettable - *every* one.

But now, I want to tell you more about the most special person I've ever met in genealogy ...

Carla Mittelstaedt-Kubaseck.

I've already briefy mentioned how my sending Carla on her first search for Palatines in their ancestral German homes was my introduction to what some have called "The Twilight Zone of Genealogy." Well, finding Carla was also my initial exposure to what I would call "The Heaven-Sent Factor" in family history research: doors open, and people pop up in your life who are true "God-sends."

All right, I'll say it ...

ANGELS!

All you can think, in retrospect, is "what in heaven's name would I have done if I had never met this person?"

In heaven's name indeed!

I had tried for several years prior to meeting Carla to find *someone* to literally go village-to-village for me overseas looking for those thousands of Palatine emigrants. I inquired of such German-research icons as Dr. Fritz Braun of the Heimatstelle Pfalz and Friedrich Krebs of the Speyer Archive. They both said they would look for ten or twenty families for me, but that trying to document thousands was absolutely out of the question. I even requested help from the eminent Baron Karl Friedrich von Frank in Austria. The Baron answered that he too would only search for a few emigrants. He added that, if I wanted more information, his secretary would respond in time. (A friend later visited Baron von Frank in his castle in Austria, and reported that the good Baron was his own secretary.)

Finally, my friend Kathryn Schwartz Callaghan of Rhinebeck, New York, told me about a little German lady whom she and her fellow-searcher Peytie Moncure had used in gathering data on their Sagendorf family. Her name, she said, was Carla Mittelstaedt-Kubaseck.

(GESUNDHEIT! - That's *some* name, I thought!)

I presented Carla with my ideas for these massive European searches - my *dreams*, really - and she immediately wrote back, "*I* can do that!"

And she did! For nearly twenty years, this dear woman went village-to-village for me in Germany in areas where I had theorized these future American colonists might be found. And she hit genealogical paydirt wherever she went. I knew I had found the right person when one day she wrote me a half-page letter apologizing for leaving an umlaut off of a vowel in one of her reports!

She was "on the road" for me two or three weeks *every* month, rain or shine, in all kinds of weather. I have many postcards from her that said, "The weather is terrible, I can't see through the fog and ice, it's going to snow ... but I found an emigrant today!"

Carla's lesson to us all was her *dedication! Her* experiences on these sojourns would have made a marvelous book. She had to deal with pastors who didn't even know where their churchbooks were, as no one had asked to see them in years. Some pastors had the attitude, "why do you want to study these poor people? They were only peasants and never amounted to anything."

Carla even ran into clergymen who refused to show her the old churchbooks because, "after all, she was a woman - and what do they know anyway?" Chauvinism reared its ugly head! That's when Carla went into what I call her "fullback mode." She did an end run around that kind of pastor and went straight to his bishop or other superior. Woe betide the clergyman who tried to pull that on Carla! She had the drive of a Doberman! It usually resulted in a severe repremand for the pastor, and Carla *always* ended up seeing every old register that they had tried to withhold from her. You never mess with "The World's Greatest Digging Lady!"

Sometimes her stories were sad and poignant. In one little German village, the pastor sat Carla down and informed her that, in May 1945, it was so terrible in that region that the old churchbooks had to be burned as fuel to heat the parsonage! And sometimes the registers were destroyed in the necessary bombings by allied troops that took place in southern Germany in World War II.

One time, Carla wrote ahead to a library, explaining she would like permission to examine the 18th-century Oaths of Allegiance that the repository held. She received her permit and drove 800 miles from her home near Munich to the archive. But upon her arrival, she found a sign on the door that said, "Closed for painting." Carla was dumbfounded and disappointed, having traveled so many miles for naught. She angrily pounded on the door, until the archivist timidly opened it a crack and looked outside to see what all the commotion was about. Sticking her nose through the small opening, Carla informed him in no uncertain terms, "I wrote you. You sent me the permit. I drove 800 miles to get here ... I *will* see the files in the archive!"

The poor civil servant was so intimidated by her unwavering determination that he not only invited her in for a private visit to search their files ... he also brought her tea and cookies to enjoy while she searched!

Eventually, all those Palatine families became family to Carla - just as they had become family to me. Every "find" of a 1709 emigrant became an unimaginable thrill. Her letters would say things like, "Ring the bell: Today I have found Nicolaus Bellinger!" At first, her reports arrived airmail from Germany. But then, as more discoveries were made, even airmail became too slow. She became so enthused she couldn't wait; so Carla started calling me on the transatlantic telephone with news of the new finds.

Unfortunately, Carla had *no* sense of time. She'd telephone at all hours, exclaiming, "Ring the bell! Ring the bell! We've found Michael Freymäuer!" Eventually, she even got what sounded like a big cowbell by her phone to dramatize her "Ring the bell!" discoveries. And I would be groggily awakened at 3 A.M. by this big "KA-DUNG, KA-DUNG" sound, with Carla laughing uproariously and excitingly telling me her good news!

I have so many memories of Carla. She too was a "giver." I noted in *Psychic Roots* how she just happened to run across my colleague Annette Kunselman Burgert's long-sought-for ancestor, Bartolomaeus Kuntzelmann, in the Wendolsheim churchbook. She then presented Annette with this marvelous discovery, as casually as can be, on a day that turned out to be Annette's birthday.

And Carla was brave too. What a life she had led. She barely survived the war with all its horrors, and, as a refugee, had to raise her daughter, Barbara, as a single mother in the aftermath. The terror of those days never left her. I remember taking her to Disneyland on one of her visits to California and getting on the old "Rocket To The Moon" ride. The loud noises and vibrations, designed for fun, absolutely terrified her - they reminded her of all she had to go through in the bombings. They had to quickly stop the ride to let her off.

Carla Mittelstaedt-Kubaseck

Carla hard at work, chasing Palatines

But oh - she was *fun*. Carla loved to eat. When we travelled together, after a nice meal she would keep insisting she couldn't eat another bite - but then always had room for the goopiest of desserts. She was always worried about "her line" (meaning "her figure"): "I have to watch my line," she would say. Carla also had an appreciation of the opposite sex. When an especially good-looking gentleman would walk by, she would whisper, "Ah-hah, a handsome cavalier!"

And my goodness, she was a *terrible* driver. Her specialty was driving slow in the fast lane of the German autobahns. I'll never forget how all the burly truck drivers whizzed around her, shaking their fists and swearing blue-blazes at her tiny VW poking along. She would then turn around, look at my wife Bonnie riding nervously in the back seat, and then inquire with a wink, "Still alive???"

Carla wasn't afraid to show her true feelings. On a visit to America in 1976 during the bicentennial, I took her to services at Hollywood Methodist Church. The minister had put out for display a large-sized copy of the Declaration of Independence. He encouraged the entire congregation to sign their names to the document as a gesture of recommittal to its principles. We all went up to the altar one-by-one to do this. Some of the churchgoers kind of kidded around and didn't take it all too seriously. But not Carla. She walked straight up to the Declaration and signed her name boldly in big letters, right under John Hancock.

When I went back to my seat in the sanctuary, Carla didn't follow me - and I couldn't find her. I was worried, so I got up and started looking all over the church for my friend. I finally discovered her behind a pillar, weeping uncontrollably. I said, "Carla, what's wrong?" And she replied that she was so *honored* to be asked to sign that old document, so moved to be included. She said she couldn't believe a group of Americans would allow a *German* - from the country they had just fought in the war - to sign their own Declaration. I gave her a big hug and told her we were all one family now and always had been - the human family.

So many memories.

But in January of 1994, at the young age of 81 and against her daughter Barbara's wishes, Carla drove in the ice and snow to Heilbronn to do some research in the archives and church office there. While she was crossing the street, a speeding car approached so quickly that Carla had to jump out of its way - but she wasn't fast enough. She suffered major contusions and fractures, and, unfortunately, her poor old weak heart just wasn't strong enough to recover. After a few months of being in a wheelchair and then bedridden, Carla Mittelstaedt-Kubaseck died on Easter Sunday in the arms of her daughter, Barbara.

Barbara later wrote me:

"I told her so many times to slow down and take it easy - but she worked like a young person. The month before she died, she was even taking a computer course from her wheelchair. Sometimes I was an admirer of her research work, but also I was annoyed with it. I can't understand her lifestyle - that genealogy was her only interest. She looked at the world differently.

But she really was a very good researcher. Admiration and recognition from the Palatine genealogical community made her very happy. The books about the Palatine emigration that she wrote with you, Hank, were her happiest work - her biggest contribution, she felt."

I feel such a loss now that Carla's gone. But she went with her boots on - at the age of 81, hit by a car as she was heading to an archive to look for Palatine emigrants! What a way to go! I'm certain it was what she would have wanted.

I used to call her "the world's greatest digging lady" - and she was. But, if you think about it, Carla Mittelstaedt-Kubaseck really isn't gone at all. She's with everyone who's reading this book, everyone who loves genealogy. She was one of the many who led the way and illuminated our path in helping us find our ancestors.

So please - whenever you pick up one of my books - remember, it's *Carla's* book too. Her special spirit is on each and every page.

In loving memory of my special friend, now for one last time -

LET'S "RING THE BELL" ... FOR *CARLA!*

BIBLIOGRAPHY
(& SOME MORE GOOD BOOKS TO CURL UP WITH ON A RAINY NIGHT)

Brinkley, Dannion, with Perry, Paul. *Saved by the Light.* (New York: Villard Books, 1994).

Cayce, Hugh Lynn, and Cayce, Edgar. *God's Other Door and the Continuity of Life.* (Virginia Beach, Virginia: A.R.E. Press, 1958).

A Course in Miracles. (Tiburon, California: Foundation for Inner Peace, 1975).

Combs, A., & Holland, M. *Synchronicity: Science, Myth, and the Trickster.* (New York: Paragon House, 1990).

Duncan, Lois, and Roll, Ph.D., William. *Psychic Connections: A Journal into the Mysterious World of PSI.* (New York: Delacorte Press, 1995).

Estés, Ph.D., Clarissa Pinkola. *Women Who Run With the Wolves: Myths and Stories of the Wild Woman Archetype* (New York: Ballatine Books, 1992).

Ford, Arthur, & Bro, Margueritte Harmon. *The Autobiography of Arthur Ford: Nothing So Strange.* (New York: Paperback Library, 1971).

Hardy, A., Harvie, R., & Koestler, A. *The Challenge of Chance.* (New York: Random House, 1974).

Kurtz, Paul, ed. *A Skeptic's Handbook of Parapsychology.* (Buffalo, New York: Prometheus Books, 1985).

MacLaine, Shirley. *Going Within: A Guide for Inner Transformation.* (New York: Bantam Books, 1989).

Mitchell, Edgar, ed. *Psychic Exploration.* (New York: G. P. Putnam's Sons, 1974).

Moody, M.D., Raymond, with Perry, Paul. *Reunions: Visionary Encounters with Departed Loved Ones.* (New York: Ivy Books, 1993).

Morse, M.D., Melvin, with Paul Perry. *Transformed by the Light: The Powerful Effect of Near-Death Experiences on People's Lives.* (New York: Villard Books, 1992).

Peck, M. Scott. *The Road Less Traveled.* (New York: Bantam Books, 1978).

Progoff, Ira. *Jung, Synchronicity, and Human Destiny.* (New York: Julian Press, 1973).

Roberts, R. M. *Serendipity: Accidental Discoveries in Science.* (New York: John Wiley and Sons, 1989).

Rogo, D. Scott. *Miracles: A Parascientific Inquiry into Wondrous Phenomena.* (New York: The Dial Press, 1982).

Stiffler, LaVonne Harper. *Synchronicity & Reunion: The Genetic Connection of Adoptees & Birthparents.* (Hobe Sound, Florida: FEA Publishing, 1992).

Weaver, Warren. *Lady Luck: The Theory of Probability.* (New York: Anchor Books, 1963).

Whitfield, Barbara Harris. *Spiritual Awakenings: Insights of the Near-Death Experience and Other Doorways to our Soul.* (Deerfield Beach, Florida: Heath Communications, Inc., 1995).

Zukav, Gary. *The Dancing Wu Li Masters.* (New York: Quill, 1979).

Zukav, Gary. *The Seat of the Soul.* (New York: Fireside Books, 1990)

INDEX OF NAMES

CPSIA information can be obtained at www.ICGtesting.com
Printed in the USA
LVOW070848290212

270678LV00004BA/6/P

9 780806 315249